Language and Social Justice in Practice

D0071378

From bilingual education and racial epithets to gendered pronouns and immigration discourses, language is a central concern in contemporary conversations and controversies surrounding social inequality. Developed as a collaborative effort by members of the American Anthropological Association's Language and Social Justice Task Force, this innovative volume synthesizes scholarly insights on the relationship between patterns of communication and the creation of more just societies. Using case studies by leading and emergent scholars and practitioners written especially for undergraduate audiences, the book is ideal for introductory courses on social justice in linguistics and anthropology.

Netta Avineri is Associate Professor of Teaching English to Speakers of Other Languages/Teaching Foreign Language (TESOL/TFL) at the Middlebury Institute of International Studies at Monterey.

Laura R. Graham is Professor of Anthropology at the University of Iowa. She served as Chair of the American Anthropological Association's Committee on Human Rights and is founding Chair of the Association's Committee on Language and Social Justice.

Eric J. Johnson is Associate Professor of Bilingual/ESL Education at Washington State University Tri-Cities.

Robin Conley Riner is Associate Professor of Anthropology at Marshall University.

Jonathan Rosa is Assistant Professor in the Graduate School of Education, Center for Comparative Studies in Race and Ethnicity, and, by courtesy, Departments of Anthropology and Linguistics, at Stanford University.

Language and Social Justice in Practice

Edited by Netta Avineri,
Laura R. Graham, Eric J. Johnson,
Robin Conley Riner, and Jonathan Rosa

Routledge
Taylor & Francis Group

NEW YORK AND LONDON

First published 2019
by Routledge
52 Vanderbilt Avenue, New York, NY 10017

and by Routledge
2 Park Square, Milton Park, Abingdon, Oxon, OX14 4RN

Routledge is an imprint of the Taylor & Francis Group, an informa business

© 2019 Taylor & Francis

The right of Netta Avineri, Laura R. Graham, Eric J. Johnson, Robin Conley Riner, and Jonathan Rosa to be identified as authors of this work has been asserted by them in accordance with sections 77 and 78 of the Copyright, Designs and Patents Act 1988.

Library of Congress Cataloging-in-Publication Data
A catalog record for this title has been requested

ISBN: 978-1-138-06944-2 (hbk)
ISBN: 978-1-138-06945-9 (pbk)
ISBN: 978-1-315-11570-2 (ebk)

Typeset in Times New Roman
by Swales & Willis Ltd, Exeter, Devon, UK

Contents

viii *Contents*

Figures

Tables

Contributors

Suriati Abas is a PhD candidate in Literacy, Culture and Language Education at Indiana University. She is currently researching the linguistic landscape of Buenos Aires, Argentina, in the context of a commemorative event with a specific focus on understanding how images and texts communicate meanings in public spaces.

H. Samy Alim is the David O. Sears Presidential Endowed Chair in the Social Sciences and Professor of Anthropology and African American Studies at the University of California, Los Angeles, and the Founding Director of the Center for Race, Ethnicity, and Language (CREAL). His most recent books include *Raciolinguistics: How Language Shapes Our Ideas about Race* (Oxford, 2016, with John Rickford and Arnetha Ball) and *Culturally Sustaining Pedagogies: Teaching and Learning for Justice in a Changing World* (Teachers College Press, 2017, with Django Paris). He is also author of *Articulate While Black: Barack Obama, Language, and Race in the U.S.* (Oxford, 2012, with Geneva Smitherman), which addresses language and racial politics through an examination of former President Barack Obama's language use—and America's response to it. He has written extensively about Black language and hip hop culture in his books: *Street Conscious Rap* (1999), *You Know My Steez* (2004), *Roc the Mic Right* (2006), *Tha Global Cipha* (2006), *Talkin Black Talk* (2007), and *Global Linguistic Flows* (2009).

Netta Avineri is an Associate Professor in the TESOL/TFL Program at the Middlebury Institute of International Studies at Monterey (MIIS), where she serves as the Intercultural Competence Committee Chair. She also teaches Service Learning and Teacher Education courses at California State University, Monterey Bay (CSUMB). Netta is an Associate Editor for the *Heritage Language Journal*, previously served as a Core Member of the American Anthropological Association's Language and Social Justice Task Group, and currently serves as the American Association for Applied Linguistics Public Affairs and Engagement Committee Chair. Her book *Research Methods for Language Teachers: Inquiry, Process, and Synthesis* was published by Palgrave Macmillan in 2017. Her research interests include critical service-learning, community partnerships, interculturality, narrative, language and social justice, and heritage and endangered languages. Netta is committed to building collaborative environments in which societal inequities can be both explored and resisted, through the inclusion of diverse voices and ways of knowing.

Dominika Baran is Associate Professor in the English Department at Duke University. Her main research interests are in the area of language, identity, and migration; in particular, how migrant identities are formed and enacted through discourse and linguistic practices. Her book, *Language in Immigrant America*, examines language as a site for the contestation of the meanings of "immigrant" and "American" identities. Her current research project focuses on narratives of migration and belonging among former fellow refugees, and on narratives and discourse on social media.

Steven P. Black is Associate Professor of Anthropology at Georgia State University. He is on the advisory board for the journal, *Anthropology and Humanism*, and he served as chair of the Committee on Ethics for the American Anthropology Association from 2014–2017. Dr. Black is interested in verbal art, performance, ethics, health and culture, gender and sexuality, global health, and globalization, with regional expertise in South Africa, the United States, and Costa Rica.

Charles L. Briggs (PhD University of Chicago, 1981) Professor of Anthropology, Co-Director of Medical Anthropology Program, Co-Director Berkeley Center for Social Medicine, University of California, Berkeley; is the Alan Dundes Distinguished Professor in the Department of Anthropology of the University of California, Berkeley, where he teaches social/cultural, medical, and linguistic anthropology and folkloristics. He received his PhD from the University of Chicago. His books include *Making Health Public: How News Coverage Is Remaking Media, Medicine, and Contemporary Life* (with Daniel C. Hallin, Routledge, 2016) and *Tell Me Why My Children Died: Rabies, Indigenous Knowledge and Communicative Justice* (with Clara Mantini-Briggs, Duke University Press, 2016). He serves on a number of editorial boards, including the *Medical Anthropology Quarterly*.

Mary Bucholtz is Professor in the Department of Linguistics at the University of California, Santa Barbara, and the director of the Center for California Languages and Cultures; she is also affiliated with the Departments of Anthropology, Education, Feminist Studies, and Spanish and Portuguese, as well as the Comparative Literature Program and the Latin American and Iberian Studies Program. A specialist in sociocultural linguistics with a focus on language, youth, and race, she is the author of *White Kids: Language, Race, and Styles of Youth Identity* (Cambridge University Press, 2011) and co-editor of *Feeling It: Language, Race, and Affect in Latinx Youth Learning* (Routledge, 2018).

Mark Byrd is a graduate of the Masters in Social Work program from Gallaudet University. Mark Byrd has appeared in several articles regarding HIV and the Deaf community. Current articles include: "A Sign of Trouble: The HIV Crisis in the Deaf Community," "Equal Voices: The Difficult Reality of Managing HIV while Deaf," and "Accountability and Accessibility in the LGBT Community." He is currently pursuing his dream job: being a college professor. He currently lives in Ohio.

Genevieve Caffrey is a doctoral student in the Department of Learning, Teaching and Curriculum at the University of Missouri-Colombia.

Dolores Inés Casillas is Associate Professor in the Department of Chicana and Chicano Studies, and a faculty affiliate in the Department of Film and Media Studies, Applied Linguistics, and Latin American and Iberian Studies at the University of California, Santa Barbara. She is the author of *Sounds of Belonging: U.S. Spanish-language Radio and Public Advocacy* (NYU Press, 2014), co-editor of *Latina/o Media Studies* (Routledge, 2016), and co-editor of *Feeling It: Language, Race, and Affect in Latinx Youth Learning* (Routledge, 2018). She has published essays on radio humor, "accent" use within popular culture, immigration-based broadcasts, and the politics of language and is a senior contributor to the academic and activist site, *Sounding Out! A Sound Studies Blog.*

Anita Chary, MD PhD, is an anthropologist and resident physician at the Harvard Affiliated Emergency Medicine Residency. She is the Research Director of Wuqu' Kawoq | Maya Health Alliance, a non-governmental organization that provides free health care in Guatemala, and former editor-in-chief and current contributor to the Global Health Hub. She recently published (with Peter Rohloff, MD PhD) the book *Privatization and the New Medical Pluralism: Shifting Healthcare Landscapes in Guatemala.*

James S. Damico is an Associate Professor of Literacy, Culture, and Language Education at Indiana University. He is the author of many journal articles, book chapters, and is co-author of *Social Studies as New Literacies: Relational Cosmopolitanism in the Classroom* (Routledge, 2011). His teaching and research interests focus on critical literacy, inquiry-based teaching and learning, multidisciplinary curricula, and working with new texts and technologies.

Julia R. Daniels is a doctoral candidate in Curriculum and Instruction at the University of Washington and a former high school and middle school English language arts teacher. Julia's research draws from Critical Whiteness Studies, Critical Theory, and Postructuralism to examine White teachers' racialized identities and self-understandings—and the harmful consequences of those understandings for students of color. At the

University of Washington, Julia has taught courses in English language arts methods, interdisciplinary literacy instruction, and culturally and linguistically responsive teaching in the UW's secondary and elementary teacher education programs.

Mariam Durrani is Assistant Professor at Hamilton College. Her research brings together scholarship on transnational Muslim communities, migration and mobility, racial and gender-based approaches to (im)mobility, and neoliberalism and its institutions. Mariam's approach to research draws on critical engagements with semiotics, intersectionality, and multimodal and critical visual methodologies. Her work has been published in *American Anthropologist*, *Anthropology News*, and *Anthropology and Education Quarterly*.

David Flood, MD, MSc, is a physician and health services researcher at Wuqu' Kawoq | Maya Health Alliance in Tecpán, Guatemala, and at the University of Minnesota in Minneapolis, Minnesota, USA.

Laura R. Graham is Professor of Anthropology at the University of Iowa. She is Founding Chair of the Society for Linguistic Anthropology/American Anthropological Association's Task Group on Language and Social Justice. Her book publications include *Performing Dreams: Discourses of Immortality among the Xavante Indians of Central Brazil* (Texas, 1995), *Performance de Sonhos: Discursos de imortalidade Xavante* (EDUSP 2018) and *Performing Indigeneity: Global Histories and Contemporary Experiences* (with Glenn Penny, Nebraska 2014). She is author of numerous articles and book chapters on native peoples of lowland South America, and especially on Xavante and Wayuu. She is producer and co-director, with David Hernández Palmar (Wayuu) and Caimi Waiassé (Xavante), of the film *Owners of the Water: Conflict and Collaboration over Rivers* (Documentary Educational Resources, 2009).

Brent Henderson PhD is an Associate Professor of Linguistics at the University of Florida. He also serves on the editorial board for Natural Language and Linguistic Theory and as the President of the Board of Directors for Wuqu' Kawoq | Maya Health Alliance.

Kathryn I. Henderson is an Assistant Professor in the Department of Bicultural-Bilingual Studies, College of Education and Human Development at The University of Texas at San Antonio.

Adam Hodges is a Visiting Assistant Professor of English at Carnegie Mellon University in Qatar. His research examines issues of social or political concern as they play out in discursive interaction, such as the collective enactment of racism or justification of political violence. His articles on language and racism have appeared in *Language in Society, Language & Communication*, and the *Journal of Linguistic Anthropology*. His books include *The "War on Terror" Narrative: Discourse and Intertextuality in the Construction and Contestation of Sociopolitical Reality* (2011, Oxford),

Discourses of War and Peace (2013, Oxford), and (co-edited) *Discourse, War and Terrorism* (2007, Benjamins).

Quinn Holmquist graduated from Duke University with a BA with Highest Distinction in Romance Studies: Haitian Kreyòl and Spanish. His senior thesis was titled *Strange Chains: A Microanthropological Study of Non-English Speakers' Courtroom Experience.* He has extensive nonprofit work and volunteer experience in Durham, North Carolina, including at The Community Empowerment Fund, Reality Ministries, Legal Aid, and El Centro Hispano. As a Legal Aid volunteer, he interpreted for Spanish-speaking survivors of domestic violence and translated outreach materials into Haitian Kreyòl. Currently, he lives and works in the North Street Community in Durham, a neighborhood where people with and without disabilities share life.

Eric J. Johnson is an Associate Professor of Bilingual Education at Washington State University Tri-Cities. His research focuses on immigrant education contexts and examines language policies and programs in public schools. He teaches graduate and undergraduate courses on bilingual education, cultural and linguistic diversity in schools, and bilingual/ESL teaching methods. Recent articles have been published in the *Journal of Linguistic Anthropology* (2016), *Journal of Language & Literacy Education* (2016), *Journal for Multicultural Education* (2015), *Language Policy* (2015), *and International Journal of Bilingual Education and Bilingualism* (2015).

Monica Shank Lauwo is the Founder and Director of Cheche Community Library in Monduli, Tanzania, a community learning space promoting creativity, critical literacies and multilingualism. She is a graduate of OISE, University of Toronto, with an MA in Language and Literacies Education and Comparative, International and Development Education. She has experience as a teacher, teacher educator and literacy specialist in East Africa, and is trained as a Waldorf teacher. Her research interests include multilingual education, translanguaging, and critical pedagogy in East Africa.

Jin Sook Lee is Professor of Education in the Gevirtz Graduate School of Education at the University of California, Santa Barbara, where she is also an affiliate faculty member in the Department of Linguistics. Her research examines sociocultural factors that influence the learning and teaching processes of bilingual children as well as the maintenance and development of heritage languages in immigrant families. She co-edited *The Education of Language Minority Immigrants in the US* (Multilingual Matters, 2009) and *Feeling It: Language, Race, and Affect in Latinx Youth Learning* (Routledge, 2018) and serves on the editorial boards of the *International Journal of Multilingual Research, Language Arts*, and *The Journal of Asia TEFL*.

Kathryn Lindholm-Leary is professor emerita of Child and Adolescent Development at San Jose State University, where she taught for 28 years.

Kathryn has worked with over 75 two-way and developmental bilingual programs from PreK through 12 over the past 30 years and has written books, chapters, and journal articles, and has given presentations to researchers, educators, and parents on the topics of dual language education and child bilingualism. More recently, she worked with the National Academy of Sciences in their report on the development of English/Dual language learners. Kathryn has served on advisory boards or as consultant to federal and state departments of education, various professional organizations, and other agencies, school districts, and schools.

Lina Martín-Corredor is a doctoral student in the Department of Bicultural-Bilingual Studies, College of Education and Human Development at the University of Texas at San Antonio.

Martha I. Martinez received her PhD in Educational Methodology, Policy and Leadership from the University of Oregon and has over 15 years of experience working on various projects and initiatives designed to improve educational outcomes for underserved populations. Currently, Martha is the Director of Research and Evaluation for the Sobrato Early Academic Language (SEAL) model, where she oversees research activities investigating SEAL's efforts to improve educational experiences and outcomes for English Learners in Pre-Kindergarten through grade 5 in California. Prior to joining SEAL in 2017, she spent six years at the Oregon Department of Education, where she was responsible for the state's dual language programs.

Joyce Milambiling received her PhD in Linguistics and is Professor in TESOL and Applied Linguistics at the University of Northern Iowa in Cedar Falls. She has conducted research and has published on the topics of second language teacher education, language policy, and bilingualism and bilingual education. She has presented papers and conducted workshops on language policy in the U.S., the Philippines, Indonesia, and Wales; multilingualism as a resource in the language classroom; and techniques and resources in online teaching, among other subjects. Travel and reading, not necessarily in that order, are her particular passions.

Rosa G. Molina is the Executive Director of the national non-profit, the Association of Two-Way & Dual Language Education (ATDLE) in support of the professional development and expansion of Two-Way & Dual Language programs throughout the United States. Prior to this, she worked for 30 years as a K-12 educator working in various teaching and administrative positions. She completed her K-12 career by leading San Jose Unified and Ravenswood school districts as the Assistant Superintendent of Curriculum and Instruction. For over 27 years, Rosa has served as the primary TWBI program developer and promoter of Two-Way and Dual Language programs through intensive district and site leadership work, consultancies, hosting the national annual conferences, regional institutes and local contracts.

Leila Monaghan holds a PhD in linguistic anthropology from UCLA. She teaches anthropology at Northern Arizona University and has written on Deaf culture, Deaf communities and HIV/AIDS, and the history of Plains Indian women.

Bernard C. Perley is a member of the Maliseet Nation from Tobique First Nation, New Brunswick, Canada. He is an Associate Professor in the Anthropology department at the University of Wisconsin where he teaches courses in linguistic anthropology and American Indian Studies. He is a member of the Editorial Board for the *Journal of Sociolinguistics* and the Senior Editor of "Indigenous Anthropology" for the Oxford University Press *Oxford Research Encyclopedia of Anthropology*. He is a "core member" for the Language and Social Justice Group—a standing committee for the Society for Linguistic Anthropology. Perley's ongoing research is dedicated toward revitalizing Indigenous languages. Perley's Native American language advocacy is closely tied to confronting public stereotypes, name calling, and other public forms of semiotic denigration.

Luis E. Poza, PhD is Assistant Professor of Culturally and Linguistically Diverse Education at the University of Colorado Denver.

Robin Conley Riner received her PhD in anthropology from UCLA and is currently Associate Professor of Anthropology at Marshall University. Her research focuses on language and morality in the contexts of death penalty trials and military combat. Riner's book, *Confronting the Death Penalty: How Language Influences Jurors in Capital Trials*, published by Oxford University Press (2016), examines how death penalty jurors' life and death decisions are mediated by language used in capital trials. She has also published in journals including *Political and Legal Anthropology Review* and *Language in Society*. She teaches courses in linguistic and cultural anthropology, language and gender, and law and society. She regularly contributes to continuing legal education and consults on capital defense and legislation.

Peter Rohloff, MD PhD, is the Chief Medical Officer at Wuqu' Kawoq in Guatemala and an Assistant Professor of Medicine at Harvard Medical School in Boston, Massachusetts, USA.

Jonathan Rosa is Assistant Professor in the Graduate School of Education, Center for Comparative Studies in Race and Ethnicity, and, by courtesy, Departments of Anthropology and Linguistics, at Stanford University. His research analyzes the interplay between racial marginalization, linguistic stigmatization, and educational inequality. Dr. Rosa is author of *Looking Like a Language, Sounding like a Race: Raciolinguistic Ideologies and the Learning of Latinidad* (2018, Oxford). His work has appeared in scholarly journals such as the *Harvard Educational Review*, *American Ethnologist*, *American Anthropologist*, and the *Journal of Linguistic Anthropology*, as well as media outlets such as MSNBC, NPR, CNN, and Univision.

Krystal A. Smalls is Assistant Professor of Anthropology, Linguistics, and African American Studies at the University of Illinois, Urbana-Champaign. Her research examines the semiotics of race in young people's lives, with a particular focus on the African diaspora. She is developing a book manuscript titled *The Pot and the Kettle: Antiblackness and the Semiosis of Black Transnational Subjectivity in the Liberian Diaspora*. Her publications have appeared in journals such as *Language & Communication*, *Transforming Anthropology*, the *Journal of Linguistic Anthropology*, and *Anthropology & Education Quarterly*. Dr. Smalls received her PhD in Africana Studies and Educational Linguistics at the University of Pennsylvania.

Elizabeth S. Vartkessian is the Executive Director of Advancing Real Change, Inc. (ARC, Inc.), a national non-profit located in Baltimore, MD dedicated to conducting high-quality life history investigations in criminal cases. She has worked as a mitigation specialist with defense teams since 2004 in trial and post-conviction cases in state and federal jurisdictions and has served as a faculty member in federal and state-wide trainings on the collection and effective presentation of mitigating evidence, as well as the standard of care required by the defense in death penalty and juvenile cases. Dr. Vartkessian is also a Research Fellow at the University at Albany in the School of Criminal Justice where she is a researcher with the Capital Jury Project (CJP). Her publications, which include articles in law reviews and peer review journals, focus on juror receptivity to mitigating evidence. Dr. Vartkessian received her PhD in Law from the University of Oxford, a MS in Comparative Social Policy from the University of Oxford and BAs in Philosophy and Political Science from the George Washington University where she was a Presidential Scholar. In 2015 she was awarded the J. M. K. Innovation Prize for her efforts to bring mitigation to all areas of the criminal justice process.

Kara Mitchell Viesca, PhD is Associate Professor of Teaching, Learning and Teacher Education at the University of Nebraska Lincoln.

Ana Celia Zentella is a central figure in the anthro-political linguistic study of U.S. Latin@ varieties of Spanish and English, Spanglish, and language socialization in Latin@ families, and a critic of the linguistic profiling facilitated by English-only laws and anti-bilingual education legislation. Her book, *Growing up Bilingual: Puerto Rican Children in New York* (Blackwell, 1997) won awards from the British Association of Applied Linguistics, and the Association of Latina and Latino Anthropologists. Edited collections include *Building on Strength: Language and Literacy in Latino Families and Communities* (2005), and two volumes with undergraduates, *Multilingual San Diego* (2008), and *Multilingual Philadelphia* (2010). *Spanish in New York: Language Contact, Dialectal Leveling, and Structural Continuity* (2011) was co-authored with Ricardo Otheguy. In 2015, the Latino Studies Section/Latin American Studies Association honored Zentella as Public Intellectual of the Year.

Lal Zimman is Assistant Professor of Linguistics at the University of California, Santa Barbara and Editor of Oxford University Press's Series in Language, Gender, and Sexuality. His research program is broadly focused on the linguistic practices of transgender communities and includes publications on homonormativity in the coming out narrative (in the journal *Gender & Language*, 2009), the construction of biological sex among trans men (*Queer Excursions: Retheorizing Binaries in Language, Gender, and Sexuality*; *Journal of Homosexuality*, 2014), and the acoustic characteristics of the voice (*Journal of Language & Sexuality*, 2013; *Language in Society*, 2017; *Linguistics*, 2017). His co-edited volume, *Queer Excursions* was published by Oxford University Press in 2014.

Acknowledgments

The idea for this collection grew out of conversations within the joint American Anthropological Association (AAA)/Society for Linguistic Anthropology (SLA) Task Group on Language and Social Justice. We are grateful to the Task Group for the positive intellectual exchanges and collegial collaborations it offers, and to the AAA and SLA for providing institutional spaces where scholars and practitioners can engage in work focused on language and social justice. Through these various collective efforts, we were eventually able to develop our ideas for this book as a way to share with broader audiences the possibilities for language and social justice in diverse contexts. We thank the Routledge editorial staff, especially Rebecca Novack, who immediately appreciated the project's importance. We also appreciate the Routledge team's support and guidance through the publication process. It has been a real pleasure working with all of the chapter authors who have contributed to the project's success. We appreciate their responsiveness, conscientious effort and valuable work. The conversations we have shared with contributors greatly enriched our thinking and have been immensely productive. Finally, we sincerely thank each other. Working collaboratively on this project has been immensely gratifying. We have learned a great deal from each other and from working together as a collective; our contributions are equal and our names appear in alphabetical order. The opportunity to share ideas and engage in this collaborative effort has been an invaluable experience for us all.

Introduction

Reimagining Language and Social Justice

Netta Avineri, Laura R. Graham, Eric J. Johnson, Robin Conley Riner, and Jonathan Rosa

Language is a central concern in contemporary conversations surrounding social justice, as evident in issues as diverse as bilingual education, racial epithets, gendered pronouns, immigration discourses, sports team mascots, and signage in public spaces. Developed as a collaborative effort by members of the American Anthropological Association's Language and Social Justice Task Group, this volume presents case studies of language and social justice in a range of contexts spanning five thematic areas: race discourse, education, health, social activism, and law and policy. The case studies illustrate with striking detail the meaningful relationships among language, social action, and broader social change. The chapters cover a diverse set of topics in a range of global contexts, and provide concise overviews of key concepts, debates, and approaches in the examination of language and social justice. Each case can be read on its own or together with others in sets of complementary essays on a common theme or, as we hope, the volume as a whole. Essays are deliberately brief in order to facilitate access to a broad range of examples and for use in teaching. Taken together, these case studies powerfully demonstrate how language provides a crucial vantage point from which to (re)imagine, understand, and contribute to the achievement of social justice.

A broad range of U.S.-based scholarship concerned with relationships between linguistic diversity and social inequity emerged in the 1960s when sociolinguistics and the ethnography of communication diverged from strictly formal approaches to the study of language. Within these newly developed fields, scholars systematically began to focus attention on the social uses of language and linguistic variation (for example, see Erickson 1979; Gumperz 1982; Heath 1983; Hymes 1962; Labov 1966; Wolfram 1974). Moreover, the fields of linguistic anthropology and sociolinguistics (as well as related disciplines) have strongly established histories documenting the constitutive relationship among social hierarchies, linguistic difference, and social inequality. A number of these studies draw upon the work of sociologist Pierre Bourdieu (1999), for example, who used apt economic metaphors to describe ways that distinct languages, language varieties, and linguistic resources have greater or lesser "symbolic value" and thus become associated with differential access to social, economic, and political resources and power. Over 40 years of scholarship in linguistic anthropology and sociolinguistics consistently demonstrates that language is neither a neutral communicative medium nor a passive way of referring to things in the world, but rather a crucial form of social action in itself (Ahearn 2011; Austin 1962; Duranti 2011). Numerous studies highlight that language use is socially, politically, and economically consequential and that language and speech are fraught with power (Fairclough 1995; Gal 1989; Irvine 1989). Crucially, these approaches consider not only how language is implicated in the constitution and maintenance of social hierarchies and social inequities, but also in their contestation (Heller 2017; Hoffman-Dilloway 2018).

A concern with what we today call "social justice" was an implicit focus of much of the early, influential work in linguistic anthropology, discourse analysis, and sociolinguistics (Heller 2014). Despite this fact, discussions that explicitly frame linguistic diversity and language use in terms of "social justice" are relatively recent. Language-focused scholarship in the field of education has played a pioneering role in forwarding these discussions. In *Language, Minority Education and Gender: Linking Social Justice and Power*, David Corson (1993) argued that language is central to minority success in education, and educational equity is a matter of social justice. This study, and many others, counter influential socially regressive deficit arguments, such as those of "elaborated" and "restricted codes" (Bernstein 1971) and "verbal deprivation" (Bereiter and Engelmann 1966), that locate blame for differential success in education and other arenas *within* minority populations. Even so, socially disparaging deficit arguments, such as a "language gap" or immigrant populations' "failure" to speak English, persistently reassert themselves in scholarship as well as in popular discourse (Avineri et al. 2015). Chapters in this book continue the tradition of challenging these arguments by demonstrating ways that language in education and other spheres is central to social justice.

In her 2016 book, *Linguistic Diversity and Social Justice: An Introduction to Applied Sociolinguistics*, Ingrid Piller directly framed the discussion of linguistic difference in relation to social justice. Through a review of contemporary research and media reports, Piller places social justice at the center of discussions of linguistic diversity and demonstrates how linguistic participation mediates social participation. The present collection complements and extends Piller's efforts to put linguistic diversity "on the map" of social justice debates. In this diverse set of cases, scholars conceive of and explicitly frame their discussions in terms of social justice. We view social justice as a contested concept and existential problem that remains to be realized rather than a pragmatic challenge that can be reconciled in any straightforward way. As James Baldwin (1972, 149) noted long ago:

> Ask any Mexican, any Puerto Rican, any black man, any poor person—
> ask the wretched how they fare in the halls of justice, and then you will
> know, not whether or not the country is just, but whether or not it has any
> love for justice, or any concept of it.

Indeed, the hierarchical structures of power that have produced profound injustice across societal contexts are often endemic to and constitutive of these societies, such that the creation of justice requires the radical reimagination of alternative worlds instead of simply championing the legitimacy or inclusion of stigmatized populations and language practices (Salinas and Guerrero 2018; Tuck and Yang 2018). Rather than claiming there is one way to define and address social justice, the cases in this volume present a variety of perspectives on experiences of (in)justice, providing an emergent, variegated view of the concept.

The American Anthropological Association's (AAA) Language and Social Justice Task Group was founded in 2008 when linguistic anthropologists with interests in these issues (Charles Briggs, Laura R. Graham, Marco Jacquemet) converged within the Committee on Human Rights (CfHR, Graham 2009). Eventually, the Task Group evolved into the joint Society for Linguistic Anthropology (SLA)/AAA Task Group on Language and Social Justice. Today this is one of the most active, vibrant, creative, and socially engaged committees within the AAA, an international professional organization with over 10,000 members. The present volume grows out of the leadership and work of this Committee (see more below on how this collection emerged). It is a deliberately collaborative project which is characteristic of the efforts of this committee and collective scholarly thinking about ways language is implicated in social inequity and how language can be an instrument of positive social change toward a more equitable and just society. Given the book's focus on social justice, it is helpful to consider what this term means in contemporary discussions and how the concept entered into public discourse.

Social Justice

"Social Justice" became an important theme within late 19th and early 20th century political and legal philosophy, and the work of political philosopher John Rawls (1971) was particularly influential. Although there is no single, agreed upon definition of "social justice," common themes addressed in social justice scholarship include equitable distribution of resources, respect for human rights, equitable access to opportunities, political representation, cultural respect, and social recognition (Picower 2012). The concept generally entails a notion of group or collective rights as well as individual rights (see Young 1993)—though it has been applied to a variety of specific sociocultural contexts in recent decades (see Adams et al. 2013). Bell (2007, 3), who conceptualizes social justice as both a process and a goal, emphasizes that the concept entails full and equal participation of all groups in "a society that is mutually shaped to meet the[ir] needs." Efforts at social justice can be facilitated or restricted by a variety of actors, including national governments, international agencies and instruments, NGOs, individual activists, and scholars. Language, as cases in this volume demonstrate, is key to social justice and can play a powerful role in bringing about positive social change.

Social justice assumed prominence in public debates and international legal arenas during the late 20th and early 21st centuries (Capenheart and Milovanovic 2007). It has become ever more salient during the neoliberal era with its increasing disparities between those who have access to resources and those who do not (Flores 2013). In the early 20th century, social justice became central within international law, institutions, and legal instruments. The Constitution of the International Labour Organization (ILO), an entity that was established in 1919 as part of the Treaty of Versailles (and is now a United Nations agency), states, "Universal and lasting peace can be established only if it is based upon social justice" (International Labour Organization 2011, 1). In the late 1960s, the notion of "social justice" became prominent within various United Nations documents and instruments that seek to place people and equity at the center of debates about economic development (see United Nations 2006, 53).[1] Within the UN at the time, the spheres of "development, growth and equity" and "human rights" operated independently and were disconnected from each other (United Nations 2006).

Like the idea of social justice, a universal definition of "human rights" and agreements on how they should be implemented are elusive. As Wynter (2003) notes, the reference point for the human in normative conceptions of human rights is often deeply circumscribed along lines of race and gender, such that only particular human populations are indeed eligible for or guaranteed human rights. Anthropology has a uniquely conflicted history with, and relationship to, the concept (see Goodale 2009), particularly in its complicity with colonial projects that have positioned populations as more or less fully human. Despite debates, the United Nations Declaration on Human Rights (1948) and subsequent covenants provide an internationally agreed upon set of principles and standards. Accordingly, human rights pertain to individuals and include the right to life, liberty, and security, the right not to be held in slavery, servitude, or be subject to torture, inhuman or degrading treatment, as well as the right to be recognized as a person before the law and various other civil rights. Within the UN, while human rights concentrated on the rights of *individuals*, the work of development agencies focused on *societal* levels of rights violations and international cooperation for economic and social development (United Nations 2006, 53–54). "Social justice" was increasingly used to bridge this dichotomy between discourses of individual and societal rights within the UN. The Copenhagen Declaration that resulted from the 1995 World Summit for Social Development represents an attempt to present a coherent vision. It is replete with references to "social justice," and "just societies," as well as "equity "and "equality."

This volume focuses on case studies to provide a deep understanding of local contexts and to identify common threads around social justice more broadly. Therefore, we take a "bottom up" approach to our discussions of language and social justice. The topics covered here demonstrate how social justice comes to take on multiple meanings in specific contexts. Taken together, they uphold Bell's (2007) assertion that social justice is both a process and goal. Each chapter points to nuances of the term and together they illustrate the utility of the concept in terms of language and linguistic diversity and respect for language as culture and a right (for discussion of language as a human right, see May 2001; Skutnabb-Kangas and Phillipson 1995). Our discussion of language and social justice in this volume highlights the following areas: access, equity, power, privilege, and marginalization.

Language, Interaction, and Social Justice

This book explores cases in which language is central to social justice issues. While chapters present different aspects of and perspectives on language, the book overall espouses a view of language as more than a system of signs that refer to abstract ideas and things in the world. Rather, language is understood as having the capacity to change people's awareness of status quo injustices.

Here, we recognize language as social action; in other words, language and language practice can actually effect change. Obstructing linguistically minoritized groups from participating in civic and community practices in their home languages not only limits their access to broader social institutions, but also:

- limits their participation and representation in the dominant political, economic, and social institutions;
- prevents them from opportunities of self-advocacy;
- diminishes their cultural and linguistic identity;
- restricts their access to inter-generational knowledge;
- denies them from cherishing and maintaining their historical, filial, and personal connections;
- prevents them from having equal opportunities and privileges;
- denigrates their social positionality and legitimacy; and
- denies them access to content knowledge and materials reflective of their cultural norms and linguistic practices, thereby constraining their learning opportunities.
- denies humanity itself.

Language, in this view, includes interactional practices, their contexts, and participants. The social justice case studies addressed here thus recognize societal, structural, systemic, institutional, and interpersonal modes of participation in creating equitable and just spaces across contexts. In addition, the chapters highlight how certain narratives get foregrounded while others are marginalized due to harmful presumptions made about individuals, social groups and communities. As readers will note, professional roles/responsibilities and personal identities/experiences are contested in contexts in which social justice is at issue.

The book also highlights how language can serve as a critical resource in achieving social justice, as highlighted by other recent works in language education and intercultural communication (cf. Glynn and Wesely 2014; Hastings and Jacob 2016; Sorells 2013). In particular, the chapters identify how and why certain linguistic forms are situated to either perpetuate or limit access to information and networks of interaction. Language is often positioned as a barrier to or facilitator of such access. The chapters emphasize ways people use language as a means, or instrument, to bring about change. Together they demonstrate change in language, through language and beyond language. Changes *in* language and language practice can bring attention to injustice and inequities. In that social justice entails not only conceptualizations of but also ways of communicating about the fair distribution of opportunities and resources to all people, language constitutes a significant part of this process.

In serving as a resource either to stymie or enable social change, language is often understood as an attribute of a particular group or identity. Some of the cases in this book thus examine instances in which linguistic rights—or the right of a people, community, or individual to have and use a particular language variety—are pursued. Limiting access to have and use a language can serve to erase a culture, identity, or recognition of a people. However, these cases consider not only social justice efforts focused on securing linguistic rights, but also the ways in which language becomes a medium for the articulation and contestation of inequities.

Access, Equity, Power, Privilege, and Marginalization

Social justice issues often come down to access; seeking social justice involves ensuring that all people have equitable access to available resources and opportunities. Questions surrounding this understanding of social justice include who is or should be responsible for providing access to such resources? Instances of social justice include creating and implementing policies that expand access to a variety of resources and institutions, including law, education, and health care. Social justice efforts thus include making sure people are not barred from access to these institutions and support because of linguistic differences.

Issues of access necessarily entail the equitable distribution of resources so that people may live their fullest lives. This involves, for example, ensuring that minoritized languages are given equitable status and utilized in ways that demonstrate respect and value towards the speakers of those languages. Institutional action is often a critical mechanism for leveling social inequities and expanding access to valuable resources for all communities. However, it is crucial to frame efforts toward access not simply in relation to inclusion within existing institutional or broader societal frameworks, but also to the fundamental transformation of structures that have systematically privileged particular populations and marginalized others. Language is as central to inclusion as it is to such transformations.

The chapters in this volume highlight power, privilege, and marginalization in different ways. Many social justice efforts include advocating for languages and dialects, as well as communities and groups that have been historically marginalized and remain socially subordinated. An accurate portrayal of how issues of language and social justice emerge in a variety of contexts must take into consideration the existence of entrenched social hierarchies of power as well as the ideological assumptions that maintain them. Indeed, an ongoing concern in social justice efforts is the need to situate contemporary inequities in relation to historical hierarchies of power so as to identify and address root causes of various disparities. By doing so, it becomes possible to understand inequity as a systemic phenomenon rather than a specifically contemporary or narrowly pragmatic challenge. In solidarity with such efforts, the topics in this book highlight issues of oppression, power, privilege, hegemony, and identity as well as consciousness, agency, and resistance. The following descriptions provide an overview of the thematic sections covered in this book.

Part I: Language and Race

Race has been a longstanding consideration in analyses of language and social justice. Research on this topic includes considerations of the stigmatization of racialized language practices as well as discourses that perpetuate the racialization of particular populations (Labov 1966; Santa Ana 2002). Building on conceptualizations of racial formations as sociocultural and historical constructions rather than biological phenomena (Omi and Winant 1994), examinations of race, language, and what has been characterized as "sociolinguistic justice" seek to understand and unsettle entrenched societal hierarchies and power relations (Bucholtz et al. 2014, 2016; Rosa and Flores 2017). The broader goal is to connect scholarship on race and language to political struggles over access to rights, resources, and institutions.

The chapters in this part frame these issues in relation to education, media representations, and popular discourses. Daniels focuses on White public school teachers' fraught positionality in classrooms predominated by students of color. She presents teachers' reflections on their role in reproducing the racial and linguistic marginalization of their students, as well as their attempts to mitigate the potential harm they cause in these educational spaces. Hodges explores media discourses surrounding the 911 call made by George Zimmerman before he killed Trayvon Martin, an unarmed African American teenager. He powerfully demonstrates how efforts to determine whether Zimmerman uttered a racial slur frame racism as a problem of individual beliefs rather than institutional structures. Rosa focuses on efforts to eradicate the use of the term "illegal" in reference to immigration in mainstream media representations. He argues that such struggles over language must be understood not as ends in themselves but rather as part of broader projects of social change. Durrani investigates the discursive enactment of Islamophobia through instances of the profiling of race, language, and religion of perceived Muslim populations. She shows not only how anti-Muslim sentiments circulate with dire consequences for targeted populations, but also how various groups organize to communicatively contest this stigmatization. Smalls looks at the role of digital discourses in the Black Lives

Matter movement. Focusing specifically on Black Twitter, she highlights the creative ways in which social media users have transformed these platforms into profound sites of racial protest. Collectively, these chapters present a critical view of the role of language in reproducing racial injustice as well as its potential to contribute toward efforts to disrupt inequity.

Part II: Language and Education

Social justice has become a central focus in educational research and practice (see Allen and Reich 2013; Picower 2012). Intersections between language and social justice manifest across a variety of educational contexts (for examples, see Adams et al. 2007; Hastings and Jacob 2016). Articulating a cogent depiction of these intersections first necessitates viewing "education" as a process that spans a broad spectrum of sociocultural spaces and practices. Whether taking place within settings of formal schooling, community events, religious ceremonies, political movements, or the family sphere, it is essential to point out that the process of education is fundamentally mediated through language that reflects the interests of broader social structures. Thus, an accurate portrayal of how issues of language and social justice emerge within education must take into consideration the existence of entrenched social hierarchies of power as well as the ideological assumptions that maintain them.

By examining contexts where minoritized languages and/or dialects confront dominant norms of communication, we can identify how/why certain linguistic forms are situated to either perpetuate or limit access to information and networks of interaction. As demonstrated in the chapter by Viesca and Poza, instances of social justice in formal education contexts often involve creating and implementing policies that expand access to academic content by developing programs that integrate students' home languages and cultural experiences within the curriculum and classroom settings. The chapters describing contexts surrounding dual language programs (see Lindholm-Leary et al. and Henderson et al.) illustrate that while ensuring access to the language of instruction is fundamental for academic progress in formal school settings, it also has additional unfolding sociocultural repercussions.

Shank Lauwo's discussion of translanguaging practices in Tanzania demonstrates how the same social justice thrust applies to community education contexts when minoritized languages are given equitable status and utilized in ways that demonstrate respect and value towards the speakers of those languages. On one hand, when diverse languages are represented as a resource in community settings, individuals from those linguistic groups are empowered. On the other hand, when diverse languages are framed as deficits, community members often feel obligated to assimilate to dominant language norms. These two sides of the social justice spectrum are often conflated by policymakers. For example, Johnson's description of the "language gap" illustrates why some people might assume that promoting social justice involves teaching linguistically diverse communities the language, behavior, and knowledge of the dominant groups—which, in turn, influences policymakers and imple-menters to promote educational programs designed to assimilate (or transition) minoritized students into the dominant culture and language. These attempts often spawn from good intentions; however, social justice means valuing and advocating for minoritized groups—including their full cultural and linguistic identities. This involves ensuring the educational conditions for them to take ownership of their learning and make their own decisions about their own lives without having to negotiate linguistic discrimination on a daily basis.

Considering the far-reaching potential that educational contexts provide, the authors in Part II view language education as a critical mechanism for leveling social inequities and expanding access to valuable resources for all communities. Essentially, any instance of advocating for languages and dia-lects that have been historically marginalized and remain socially subordinated is an act of social justice. Educational policies and programs need to meet the linguistic needs of minoritized groups as well as the needs of their local com-munities by promoting dynamic interdependency and interrelation between schools and community settings.

Part III: Language and Health

The chapters focused on language and health foreground the roles of com-munity, equity, access, and participation in social justice efforts. All of the chapters recognize societal, structural, systemic, institutional, and interper-sonal modes of participation in creating equitable and just spaces for health care across contexts. Power, privilege, and marginalization are highlighted in different ways in every case study in this section. The chapters span foci including global health efforts in South Africa, language and healthcare in indigenous communities in Guatemala, Deaf AIDS activism in the US, and the treatment of epidemics among marginalized populations in Venezuela. All of the chapters highlight how certain narratives get foregrounded while others are marginalized due to harmful assumptions made about individuals and com-munities. As readers will note, professional roles/responsibilities and personal identities/experiences are contested in all of these health care contexts.

Black's paper focuses on multiple levels of presuppositions, power and authority, and inequity in biomedical contexts in South Africa, highlight-ing the constraints on what is possible for South Africans with HIV. Briggs examines the experiences of indigenous families in Venezuela, highlighting how (racialized) ideologies around communities and communication can have harmful and fatal consequences. Byrd and Monaghan foreground the health care experiences of one of the authors who is Deaf and HIV positive, noting that systemic inequities in language and health care can mean the difference between getting care and not getting care. Flood et al. highlight the intercon-nectedness of language revitalization and healthcare outcomes, focusing on the ways that simultaneous attention to language and health among indigenous communities can allow increased access to social goods. Overall, the chapters in Part III provide us with unique ethnographic perspectives on the experiences of marginalized individuals and communities, and the ways that intentional partnership, communication, and activism can provide pathways towards full and equitable participation across contexts.

Part IV: Language and Social Activism

Authors in this section, like others in this collection, are activist scholars who are specifically engaged in sociolinguistic activism and work toward socio-linguistic justice (Bucholtz et al. 2014). Activist scholars, as Charles Hale (2008, 96) notes, "establish an alignment with an organized group of people in struggle and accompany them on the contradictory and partly compromised path toward their political goals" (see also Low and Merry 2010). Taking strong positions in scholarship is one form of activism.

The chapters in this part explore direct relationships among language, social action, and broader social change. They emphasize ways people use language as a means, or instrument, to bring about change. Since activism is taking action to effect social change, agency is prominent in all of the essays in Part IV. The cases highlight specific ways that social actors (agents) use language to bring attention to injustice in the forms of discrimination, racism, homophobia, social and linguistic exclusion, and political and economic inequities to effect social change. Several highlight relationships among language and other communicative modalities stressing the importance of considering language within a broader semiotic field.

In their analysis of the linguistic landscape (LL) of Argentinian university campuses, Abas and Damico show how student activists use text and images on posters to make social justice issues visible to the public, stimulate critical consciousness, or *concientização*, a concept they borrow from activist-educator Paulo Freire, and promote critical reflection on past and current social, political, and economic injustices in Argentina. Bucholtz, Casillas, and Lee draw attention to ways that high school students in California resist racism and linguistic exclusion by asserting their right to speak and use Spanish and Indigenous languages in educational contexts. Through acts of sociolinguistic agency youth bring attention to sociolinguistic exclusion and in doing so become agents of social change. Zimman, in his discussion of translinguistic activism, argues that the goal of translanguage activism is "to rehaul not only language but also how people think about gender." His chapter demonstrates that ultimately trans-language activists seek to promote and affirm greater inclusivity.

Chapters in Part IV show how people may harness language and speech in efforts to dismantle existing inequities. Avineri and Perley discuss their own and others' scholarly and extra-scholarly activism in relation to the natural-ized racism against Native Americans embedded in sports teams' names and mascots. They underscore the importance of working across various semiotic platforms to present multiple and varied opportunities for turning audiences into engaged participants, and for building audience coalitions that have the potential to bring about meaningful social change. They also highlight distinctions and complementarities between awareness-raising and social change. Alim challenges readers to think about how language can be used in "ever more liberatory and transformative ways." Like activists Angela Davis and Toni Morrison, he advocates using language as more than an instrument for change. As an example of "linguistic deoccupation," Alim offers the Afrikaaps linguistic movement in Cape Town, South Africa, where Hip Hop artist-activists creatively reconfigure languages and linguistic practices that are marginalized and racialized by White South Africans to raise consciousness and disrupt and transform the legacies of apartheid. Ultimately, Alim exhorts readers to use language a means for revolution.

Insofar as authors bring attention to social injustices in the chapters of this collection, they may be considered activists or "engaged scholars." In this part and others, authors take explicitly activist positions through the forms they choose in their writing itself. They perform activism by consciously choosing to use specific forms, such as certain lexical items (words) or pronouns, that—as discussed by Zimman—make political positions explicit. For example, by using the form "Latinx," as opposed to "Latino" (generic masculine for a person who has Latin American heritage) or "Hispanic," Bucholtz et al. make a non-binary conceptualization of gender explicit in their writing. This spelling choice stands out for readers who are used to seeing the forms "Latino," "Latina," and even "Latin@" (male/female inclusive). Latinx brings attention to spelling on the page. The act of choosing Latinx denaturalizes standard spelling practice and underlying ideologies, and causes readers to reflect not only on spelling conventions but also on cisgender norms and expectations. This exemplifies the point that changes in language and language practice bring attention to injustice and that inequities are often inscribed in language, in this case cisgender expectations that are embedded in orthography.

Part V: Language, Law, and Policy

Social justice efforts involve trying to achieve a fair distribution of opportunities and resources to all people. Realizing such conditions requires institutions set up to protect individual freedoms and, at the same time, to assure that the "greatest good" is shared with the greatest number of people (Sandel 2009). Law is perhaps the primary institution tasked with achieving justice, but there is no single, fixed legal definition of justice. In fact, justice is a concept that people disagree about and may define differently.

Legal theorists identify two types of legal justice. First is substantive justice, which is the desire for our laws themselves to be just. Again, justice in this sense is not an absolute quality; it can change and usually relies on the moral principles of a time and place. The second type is formal justice, which involves making sure laws are applied equitably. This type entails assuring that similar cases are treated similarly and that biases do not influence how laws are applied. Both types of justice operate in and through legal institutions in efforts to achieve social justice. That is, to achieve social justice we must be sure that all people have the same access to and treatment under the law (formal justice) and it is in part up to our laws as written to ensure that this is achieved (substantive justice). The chapters in this section discuss instances of social justice embroiled in various legal systems, in which the ideals of social justice are far from assured. The case studies presented address social justice in two main forms: as an issue of rights and an issue of access.

Some of these cases examine instances in which linguistic rights—or the right of a people, community, or individual to have and use a particular language variety—are pursued. In these instances, social justice is understood in the context of human rights. Social justice in this sense refers to the ability for all humans to have their rights upheld and social justice action involves the mechanisms by which this this may be achieved. Even when rights are purportedly granted to people, social justice action involves ensuring that these rights are in fact recognized and enacted. These efforts at social justice can be facilitated or restricted by national governments, as in Graham's case of Brazilian indigenous peoples. Graham illustrates how indigenous activists work to attain recognition of their language by the national government, as well as the local non-indigenous population, through bilingual road signage. Efforts to ensure human rights are also often taken on by NGOs, as Milambiling discusses in regards to the International Declaration of Linguistic Rights. Graham and Milambiling argue, along with others, that limiting access to have and use a language can serve to erase a culture, identity, or recognition of a people.

Zentella's chapter addresses the issue of rights and social justice from a slightly different angle. In her discussion of the U.S. Census's categories for English language proficiency, it is not the ability to speak a language that is at issue, but the ability for speakers of languages other than English to be recognized as competent members of U.S. society. By classifying certain people as "less than proficient in English," the Census Bureau is endangering the rights of many, including limiting their access to benefits bestowed on those considered to be "true citizens" (i.e., English-only speakers) of the United States.

In that social justice entails the fair distribution of opportunities and resources to all people, language constitutes a significant part of this process. Social justice issues often come down to access; seeking social justice thus also involves maintaining access to available resources and opportunities for all people. Questions surrounding this understanding of social justice include, who is or should be responsible for providing access to such resources? Language can often serve as a barrier to or facilitator of access. Baran and Holmquist address this issue in their discussion of interpreters in North Carolina courts. Speakers of many minority languages do not have access to legal knowledge and procedures because interpreters who speak their language variety are not available. Social justice efforts should thus include making sure these people are not barred from access to the justice system simply because of linguistic differences. Riner and Vartkessian also address access within the legal system as mediated by language. The death penalty trials they investigate require a unique kind of legal language—mitigation narratives—in order for defendants' lives to be fully considered during the sentencing phases of their trials. Attorneys' proficiency (or lack thereof) in this narrative form can affect whether defendants receive the full consideration they are entitled to by the Constitution.

Underlying the varied law and policy issues explored in these chapters are ideologies of language that classify certain people as undeserving of rights and opportunities that should be afforded to all. Addressing social justice in these contexts thus involves not merely a critique of specific rules and laws, but also of the insidious ideologies that sustain inequitable institutions and their policies.

How the Book Came into Being

The chapters in this book provide us with unique ethnographic perspectives on the experiences of marginalized individuals and communities, and the ways that intentional partnership, communication, and activism can provide pathways towards full and equitable participation across contexts. The idea of bringing together a collection of brief essays to illustrate the broad range of ways contemporary scholars are engaging with language and social justice was born in meetings of the AAA's Task Group on Language and Social Justice. Discussion among members and leaders over time eventually led to the suggestion of compiling a variety of language and social justice topics into a volume. The five editors responded to an invitation posted on the Task Group listserv and engaged in a series of dialogues regarding how to approach the project.

We drafted a call for abstracts and solicited abstracts through a variety of platforms in efforts to ensure contributions representing a diverse set of perspectives, contributors, and social justice issues both in and outside academia. Once a set of essays was agreed upon, themes were identified and each editor assumed the role of coordinating one of the five parts. This involved curating chapters, managing peer review, and collaborating with contributing authors (which entailed facilitating a dialogue among the authors in each part to identify both shared insights and points of distinction). Through our collaborative approach toward presenting a range of language and social justice case studies, we envision the process of creating this book as an enactment of social justice principles and commitments discussed in the chapters that follow. The case studies point to social justice as a contested potentiality that critical perspectives on language can help us to interrogate and reimagine. Our hope is that the volume as a whole provides opportunities for critical dialogue and collaboration around the important issues of language and social justice highlighted here.

Note

1 "Social justice" first appears in an official UN Document within the Declaration on Social Progress and Development (United Nations 1969).

References

Adams, Maurianne, Lee Anne Bell, and Pat Griffin. 2007. *Teaching for Diversity and Social Justice*. New York: Routledge.

Adams, Maurianne, Warren J. Blumenfeld, Carmelita Castaneda, Heather W. Hackman, Madeline L. Peters, and Ximena Zuniga. 2013. *Readings for Diversity and Social Justice*. New York: Routledge.

Ahearn, Laura. 2011. *Living Language: An Introduction to Linguistic Anthropology*. Malden, MA: Wiley-Blackwell.

Allen, Danielle, and Rob Reich (Eds.). 2013. *Education, Justice, and Democracy*. Chicago, IL: University of Chicago Press.

Austin, John. 1962. *How to Do Things with Words*. Oxford: Clarendon Press.

Avineri, Netta, Eric Johnson, Shirley Brice-Heath, Teresa McCarty, Elinor Ochs, Tamar Kremer-Sadlik, Susan Blum, Ana Celia Zentella, Jonathan Rosa, Nelson Flores, H. Samy Alim, and Django Paris. 2015. "Invited Forum: Bridging the 'Language Gap.'" *Journal of Linguistic Anthropology* 25 (1): 66–86.

Baldwin, James. 1972. *No Name in the Street*. New York: The Dial Press.

Bell, Lee Anne. 2007. "Theoretical Frameworks for Social Justice Education." In *Teaching for Diversity and Social Justice: A Sourcebook*, edited by M. Adams, L. A. Bell, and P. Giffin, 3–15. New York: Routledge.

Bereiter, Carl, and Siegfried Engelmann. 1966. *Teaching Disadvantaged Children in the Preschool*. Englewood Cliffs, NJ: Prentice Hall.

Bernstein, Basil. 1971. *Class, Codes and Control: Theoretical Studies Towards a Sociology of Language*. New York: Schocken Books.

Bourdieu, Pierre. 1999. *Language and Symbolic Power*. Cambridge, MA: Harvard University Press.

Bucholtz, Mary, Audrey Lopez, Allina Mojarro, Elena Skapoulli, Christopher VanderStouwe, Shawn Warner-Garcia. 2014. "Sociolinguistic Justice in the Schools: Student researchers as linguistic experts." *Language and Linguistics Compass* 8 (4):144–157.

Bucholtz, Mary, Dolores Ines Casillas, and Jin Sook Lee. 2016. "Beyond empowerment: Accompaniment and Sociolinguistic Justice in a Youth Research Program." In *Sociolinguistic Research: Application and Impact*, edited by R. Lawson and D. Sayers, 25–44. New York: Routledge.

Capenheart, Loretta and Dragan Milovanovic. 2007. *Social Justice: Theories, Issues, and Movements*. New Brunswick, NJ: Rutgers University Press.

Corson, David. 1993. *Language, Minority Education and Gender: Linking Social Justice and Power*. Clevendon: Multilingual Matters/Toronto: Ontario Institute for the Study of Language.

Duranti, Alessandro. 2011. "Linguistic Anthropology: Language as a Non-Neutral Medium." In *The Cambridge Handbook of Sociolinguistics*, edited by Raj Mesthrie, 28–46. Cambridge: Cambridge University Press.

Erickson, F. 1979. "Talking Down: Some Cultural Sources of Miscommunication in Interracial Interviews." In *Nonverbal Behaviour*, edited by A. Wolfgang, 99–126. New York: Academic Press.

Fairclough, Norman. 1995. *Critical Discourse Analysis: The Critical Study of Language*. Harlow: Longman.

Flores, Nelson. 2013. "The Unexamined Relationship Between Neoliberalism and Plurilingualism: A Cautionary Tale." *TESOL Quarterly* 47 (3): 500–520.

Gal, Susan. 1989. "Language and Political Economy." *Annual Review of Anthropology* 18: 345–367.

Glynn, Cassandra, and Pamela Wesely. 2014. *Words and Actions: Teaching Languages through the Lens of Social Justice*. Alexandria: ACTFL.

Goodale, Mark. 2009. *Human Rights: An Anthropological Reader*. Malden, MA: Wiley-Blackwell.

Graham, Laura R. 2009. "Language and Social Justice: Report from the CfHR Task Group." *Anthropology News* 50 (4): 51–52.

Gumperz, John. 1982. *Discourse Strategies*. Cambridge: Cambridge University Press.

Hale, Charles. 2008. "Activist Research v. Cultural Critique: Indigenous Land Rights and the Contradictions of Politically Engaged Anthropology." *Cultural Anthropology* 21(1): 96–120.

Hastings, Christopher, and Laura Jacob. 2016. *Social Justice in English Language Teaching*. Alexandria, VA: TESOL Press.

Heath, Shirley Brice. 1983. *Ways with Words: Language, Life, and Work in Communities and Classrooms*. New York: Cambridge University Press.

Heller, Monica. 2014. "Gumperz and Social Justice." *Journal of Linguistic Anthropology* 23 (3): 192–198.

Heller, Monica. 2017. "Dr. Esperanto, or Anthropology as Alternative Worlds." *American Anthropologist* 119 (1): 12–22.

Hoffman-Dilloway, Erika. 2018. "Linguistic Anthropology in 2018: It Could Be Otherwise." *American Anthropologist* 120 (2): 278–290.

Hymes, Dell. 1962. "The Ethnography of Speaking." In *Anthropology and Human Behavior*, edited by T. Gladwin and W. C. Sturtevant, 13–53. Washington, DC: Anthropology Society of Washington.

International Labour Organization. 2011. *The International Labour Organization and Social Justice*. Accessed May 24, 2018. https://whycare.ie/images/Resources/ILOsocialjustice2013.pdf

Irvine, Judith T. 1989. "When Talk Isn't Cheap: Language and Political Economy." *American Ethnologist* 16 (2): 248–267.

Labov, William. 1966. *The Social Stratification of English in New York City*. Arlington, VA: Center for Applied Linguistics.

Low, Setha M., and Sally Engle Merry. 2010. "Engaged Anthropology: Diversity and Dilemmas: An Introduction to Supplement 2." *Current Anthropology* 51 (supplement 2): S203–S226.

May, Stephen. 2001. *Language and Minority Rights: Ethnicity, Nationalism and the Politics of Language*. Harlow: Pearson Education.

Omi, Michael, and Howard Winant. 1994. *Racial Formation in the United States from the 1960s to the 1990s*. New York: Routledge.

Picower, Bree. 2012. *Practice What You Teach: Social Justice Education in the Classroom and Streets*. New York: Routledge.

Piller, Ingrid. 2016. *Linguistic Diversity and Social Justice: An introduction to Applied Sociolinguistics*. Oxford: Oxford University Press.

Rawls, John. 1971. *A Theory of Justice*. Cambridge, MA: Belknap Press of Harvard University

Rosa, Jonathan, and Nelson Flores. 2017. "Unsettling Race and Language: Toward a Raciolinguistic Perspective." *Language in Society* 46: 621–647.

Salinas Jr., Cristobal, and Valerie A. Guerrero. 2018. "Tokenizing Social Justice in Higher Education." In *Colleges at the Crossroads: Taking Sides on Contested Issues*, edited by J.L. DeVitis and P.A. Sasso, 161–180. New York: Peter Lang.

Sandel, Michael, J. 2009. *Justice: What's the Right Thing to Do?* New York: Farrar, Straus and Giroux.

Santa Ana, Otto. 2002. *Brown Tide Rising: Metaphors of Latinos in Contemporary American Public Discourse*. Austin, TX: University of Texas Press.

Skutnabb-Kangas, Tove, and Robert Phillipson, eds. 1995. *Linguistic Human Rights: Overcoming Linguistic Discrimination*. New York: Mouton de Gruyter.

Sorells, Kathryn. 2013. *Intercultural Communication: Globalization and Social Justice*. London: Sage.

Tuck, Eve, and K. Wayne Yang, eds. 2018. *Toward What Justice? Describing Diverse Dreams of Justice in Education*. New York: Routledge.

United Nations. 1948. "United Nations Declaration of Human Rights." Accessed May 25, 2018. www.un.org/en/universal-declaration-human-rights.

United Nations. 1969. "General Assembly Resolution 2542 (XXIV)." December. Accessed June 28, 2018. www.un-documents.net/a24r2542.htm.

United Nations. 2006. *Social Justice in an Open World: The Role of the United Nations*. New York: United Nations. Accessed June 28, 2018. www.un.org/esa/socdev/docu ments/ifsd/SocialJustice.pdf.

Wolfram, Walt. 1974. *Sociolinguistic Aspects of Assimilation: Puerto Rican English in New York City*. Arlington, VA: Center for Applied Linguistics.

Wynter, Sylvia. 2003. "Unsettling the Coloniality of Being/Power/Truth/Freedom: Towards the Human, After Man, Its Overrepresentation—An Argument." *CR: The New Centennial Review* 3 (3): 257–337.

Young, Iris. 1993. Together in Difference: Transforming the Logic of Group Political Conflict. In *Principled Positions: Postmodernism and the rediscovery of Value*, edited by J. Squires, 121–150. Cambridge, MA: MIT Press.

Part I

Language and Race

Introduction

The chapters in this section approach race as a central consideration in analyses of language and social justice. Research on this topic includes of the stigmatization of racialized language practices as well as discourses that perpetuate the racialization of particular populations. These examinations of race and language seek to understand and unsettle entrenched societal hierarchies and power relations. The broader goal is to connect scholarship on race and language to political struggles over access to rights, resources, and institutions. The chapters in this section frame these issues in relation to education, media representations, and popular discourses. The case studies focus on White public school teachers' fraught positionality in classrooms predominated by students of color, media discourses surrounding the 911 call made by George Zimmerman before he killed Trayvon Martin, an unarmed African American teenager, efforts to eradicate the use of the term "illegal" in reference to immigration in mainstream media representations, the discursive enactment of Islamophobia through instances of the profiling of race, language, and religion of perceived Muslim populations, and the role of digital discourses in the Black Lives Matter movement. Collectively, these chapters present a critical view of the role of language in reproducing racial injustice as well as its potential to contribute toward efforts to disrupt inequity.

Critical Questions

As you read these cases, we encourage you to consider the following questions:

1 What is the relationship between the linguistic enactment of racism on interpersonal and institutional levels?
2 How are racial and linguistic stereotypes linked to one another?
3 How can language alternately reproduce and contest racial hierarchies?

1 "Never Tell Me How to Say It"

Race, Language Ideologies, and Harm Reduction in Secondary English Classrooms

Julia R. Daniels

On an early morning in April of my third year teaching high school English, I sat at my desk with a young student. Elizabeth was a tall ninth-grader with blue braces and short hair, always ready to laugh or speak out in defense of a friend. Elizabeth and I talked about her grade for a few minutes—then her other classes and the peer who annoyed her in my morning class. Eventually we settled on the essay she had recently written analyzing Sherman Alexie's (2007) novel, *Flight*, and the comments I had written on her paper. Elizabeth turned to me: "Don't ever tell me how to talk or change my writing like that, Ms. Daniels. Never tell me how to say it. That shouldn't be your job."

As a White[1] high school English teacher I taught at a school that served exclusively students of Color. My students—including Elizabeth, who identified as Chicana and a speaker of English, Spanish, and Spanglish—spoke, wrote, and read in a variety of languages. Almost all of the teachers at my school were White and, like me, identified as monolingual English speakers. My discussion with Elizabeth, and the ensuing conversations students and I had in our classes, dramatically reshaped my understanding of language and school-based language pedagogies—and, especially, my understanding of my "job" as a White high school English teacher who taught students of Color.

In this chapter, I rely on my own experiences as a White high school English teacher and later, teacher educator and educational researcher, to explicate the often-"invisiblized" (Lipsitz 1998) ideologies of schooling-based language practices that ignore the mutually constitutive relationship between race and language (Alim and Reyes 2011; Aneja 2016; Bucholtz and Hall 2005; Fairclough 2003; Valdes 2016; Young 2009). I argue that our raciolinguistic (Flores and Rosa 2015) identities are always implicated in the work of teaching or talking about language. My identity as a White woman and my students' identities as people of Color and speakers of multiple languages and language varieties shaped our experiences of the language pedagogies and practices that I enforced and that students resisted and contested. I focus specifically on the commonly accepted schooling practice of teaching code switching to students of Color—or, as Elizabeth might have argued, of teaching students "how to say it." I use the phenomenon of White teachers teaching students of Color to code switch into a Standardized English (Charity-Hudley and Mallinson 2010) as a prism through which to explicate the relationship between race and language.

Throughout my analysis, I draw from the public health tradition of harm reduction in order to situate my analysis within broader struggles for racial and linguistic justice. Harm reduction allows us to name and work to mitigate injustice without fundamentally altering the conditions that created such injustice in the first place—even as we acknowledge the profound inadequacy of such an approach (Karoll 2010; Roberts and Marlatt 1999; Wodak 2003). In this case, harm reduction allowed me to engage with the urgency of the racialized harm that White teachers perpetuate through our language pedagogies—while also naming the inadequacy of that engagement and the profound need for more fundamental change in teacher demographics and language ideologies.

The Raciolinguistic Ideologies of Teaching Code-Switching

Secondary English classrooms are powerful laboratories for explorations of raciolinguistic ideologies—ideologies that cast speaking subjects according to their racialized positions as opposed to any objective language practices (Flores and Rosa 2015). Secondary English classrooms produce, reflect, and contest dominant raciolinguistic ideologies—as well as the particular raciolinguistic ideologies of the often White teachers who make up 80 percent of public school teachers (Charity-Hudley and Mallinson 2010; National Center for Educational Statistics 2012; Wheeler and Swords 2006). As a White teacher, I believed it was my responsibility to teach students of Color to code switch: to speak and write in Standardized English in schools. According to the ideological perspectives to which I subscribed, Standardized English was both static and aracial: a fixed language form that opened doors for whoever spoke or wrote according to its rules, regardless of their racialized identities (Rosa 2016). My commitment to teaching code-switching to students of Color rested on powerful ideological assumptions about the separation of race and language and the fixedness of language itself (Aneja 2016; Valdes 2016).

Code switching typically refers to "the use of two or more languages or varieties of a language in the same speech situation" (Kamwangamalu 2010, 116). However, the term is commonly used in the context of schooling to refer to an "appropriateness-based" pedagogy and approach to language education (Flores and Rosa 2015). As a teacher I relied on this common conception of code-switching: I taught my students that while "nonstandard varieties of English and nonstandard varieties of languages other than English . . . are appropriate for out-of-school contexts," students must learn to employ "standard conventions [in schools] . . . because these linguistic practices are appropriate for a school setting" (Flores and Rosa 2015, 153).

The teaching of code switching is a commonly accepted practice in schools and is often framed as a uniformly positive, necessary, and racially neutral teaching practice (Godley, Reaser, and Moore 2016; Delpit 2006; Wheeler and Swords 2006). Young (2009) points out that teachers are often encouraged to avoid making connections between race and language when teaching students to code switch: Wheeler and Swords (2006) write that teachers should "refrain from referring to race when describing code-switching. It's not about race," (161). Advocates of teaching code switching frame it as an "asset-based" alternative to "deficit approaches" to language teaching that focus on the "inadequacies" of nonstandardized languages and language varieties (Godley et al. 2006). For proponents, the teaching of code-switching does not send students the message that nonstandardized language varieties are inferior—only that nonstandardized language varieties are "inappropriate" for school contexts (Flores and Rosa 2015). Within my own classroom, I explicitly taught students that code-switching was necessary because it would allow them access to institutions of higher education and the formal education necessary to fight for a more socially just world.

There are numerous assumptions underlying the above statements and belief in the importance of teaching students of Color to code switch. As Flores and Rosa (2015) argue, teaching students of Color to code switch rests on the false assumption that employing particular language practices will necessarily alter the ways that a student is heard by a "White listening subject." In other words, the authors argue that teaching students of Color to employ particular language practices ignores the reality that students will often be racialized in harmful ways regardless of the language practices they employ. Teaching students of Color to code switch with the hope of giving them the language necessary to enact social change, then, ignores the ways in which racism will work against student of Color regardless of the language varieties they employ (Rosa 2016).

At the same time, Flores and Rosa (2015) point out the ways that an "appropriateness-based" language pedagogy relies on an understanding of language as static and a refusal to engage with the mutually constitutive relationship between race and language (Alim and Reyes 2011; Aneja 2016; Bucholtz and Hall 2005; Fairclough 2003; Valdes 2016; Young 2009): "notions such as 'standard language' or 'academic language' and the discourse of appropriateness in which they both are embedded must be conceptualized as racialized ideological perceptions rather than objective linguistic categories" (Flores and Rosa 2015, 152). If we understand Standardized English as a fixed and "objective" target toward which students' language practices should move, then we ignore the ways in which Standardized English is in fact a dynamic and constructed linguistic form that depends on the racial identity—the Whiteness—of its speaker in order to make itself true (Aneja 2016; Flores and Rosa 2015; Valdes 2016). As a White teacher, I ignored the ways in which my speech was always already identified as standardized regardless of the particular linguistic forms I employed; my students' language practices, however, were always read as racially and linguistically "deviant" (Aneja 2016; Davila 2012; Flores and Rosa 2015; Hill 1998; Urciuoli 1996).

At the same time, my commitment to teaching code switching to students of Color as a White woman erased the consequences of my Whiteness as a fundamental part of my teaching—and my students' experiences of being taught. Like many teachers, I focused on what I believed my students needed to know—not on what my students of Color needed to learn from me, given my Whiteness.

I believed that my students needed to know how to employ Standardized English. In doing this, I ignored the potential consequences of teaching students of Color to speak and write in particular ways—and, in fact, policing their language—as a White woman, and the racialized histories upon which my teaching necessarily built. When I crossed out the words in Elizabeth's paper, I built on a history of White people shaming and policing the language practices of people of Color. Regardless of my justification and my belief that Elizabeth needed to write in a Standardized English in order to get into college and effect a more just world, my position as a White person in power defined the impact of crossing out Elizabeth's words—of telling her "how to say it."

"Do I Have to Say it for a White Person?"

In my third year of teaching, I stopped teaching my students to code-switch to particular linguistic forms. While this choice did not absolve my classroom of its raciolinguistic complexity, it revealed and engaged that complexity, pushing me to name the harmful contradictions in my teaching and—perhaps—to mitigate some of that harm.

The vast majority of teachers at my school were White and I came to understood our very presence in positions of power as harmful to students of Color. The discourses of Whiteness center and normalize within classrooms particular experiences, knowledges, languages, feelings, and ways of being while marginalizing others (Foster 2013; Frankenberg 1993; McIntyre 2002). Classrooms lead by White teachers mirror the circumstances under which people of Color are forced to develop a painful double consciousness (DuBois 1903): contexts in which people of Color are made to see and imagine themselves seen through the eyes of White people because those White people wield significant power and police narrow ways of being. In considering my work as a White teacher, I began to borrow from the public health tradition of harm reduction in which any work meant to reduce harm must first acknowledge that it is incapable of eliminating that harm. Given that I could not immediately change the broader demographic trends of teachers, the teacher demographics of my school, or remove myself instantaneously from the classroom without abandoning my students to daily substitutes, I considered how I might acknowledge and mitigate the racialized harm that I perpetuated in my own classroom—and, in particular, how I might do that through my language pedagogies.

After my conversation with Elizabeth—and numerous conversations with students, colleagues, and former students—my students and I embarked on an exploration of the language choices and pedagogies that might do the least harm given the racialized and linguicized power dynamics in our classroom. After much discussion and research—reading texts by Lisa Delpit (2006) exploring the merits of code switching as well as texts like Gloria Anzaldua's (1987) *Borderlands/La Frontera* and June Jordan's (1988) essay, "Nobody mean more to me than you and the future life of Willie Jordan" that refused to abide by "appropriateness-based" (Flores and Rosa 2015) language expectations—my students and I developed a set of questions that accompanied any assignment in our class: "What language(s) and/or language variety(ies) did you choose to use in this assignment? What register(s) and/or jargon(s) did you use? Why did you make these choices? How did those choices reflect your purpose and your intended audience? Did those choices give you power? Why or why not?"

These questions and the discussions they provoked forced our class to explicitly engage with the ways that race and language were tangled up with each other, both reproduced and contested in our classroom. My students and I examined my language practices: the language I chose to use when writing assignments, when describing my upbringing or family, when sending letters home to students' families, and when expressing frustration at students. Students pointed out the ways that I asserted or avoided claiming my Whiteness through language: affecting racialized linguistic forms, for instance, in attempts to "connect with" or erase the differences between myself and my students of Color (Ruth-Gordon 2011). Similarly, students shared their choices and experiences in examining their own language practices and the racialized consequences of those practices in our classroom and in the world. "I don't think you heard me because of how I said it," my students would sometimes tell me. "Do I have to say it for a White person?"

The Raciolinguistic Ideologies of Whiteness

As a teacher educator and educational researcher, I have continued to engage with harm reduction as a guiding principle. Essential research examines how we might shift the demographics of the increasingly White and monolingual teaching force (National Center for Educational Statistics 2012). Powerful work explores the language practices and pedagogies of teachers of Color and the ways that teachers of Color are uniquely able to support students of Color and multilingual students in essential explorations of their raciolinguistic identities (Haddix 2012; Monzo and Rueda 2003; Sanchez and Ek 2009). At the same time, it is important to consider how we might help current White teachers—an overwhelming percentage of the teaching force—to perpetuate less racism and do less harm in classrooms and to students of Color. Language is a powerful vehicle and incubator for racism, a site at and through which we normalize Whiteness and domination—and so we must examine the role of language and language pedagogies in White teachers' practice.

In conversations about teaching code switching with White teachers, I am often met with responses that mirror my own resistance and tendencies as a White teacher. The ideological tensions that arise in our conversations about the raciolinguistic complexities of teaching English reveal the teachers' commitment to code switching as a neutral, uniformly positive classroom expectation (Delpit 2006; Godley, Reaser, and Moore 2016; Wheeler and Swords 2006). For many White teachers, their commitment to the pure beneficence of teaching code switching is untouched by the power dynamic between their own and their students' raciolinguistic identities. At the same time, however, White teachers rely on their students' experiences of raciolinguistic marginalization to justify teaching code switching (arguing that marginalized students need standardized language practices in order to access higher education)—while simultaneously erasing the effects of their own Whiteness on language, language pedagogy, and language learning.

The task of engaging with the raciolinguistic ideologies of Whiteness demands that we look at schools—and secondary English classrooms, in particular—as one of the sites at which raciolinguistic ideologies are created, perpetuated, and rendered invisible. White teachers participate in the construction of a fixed, racially neutral Standardized English toward which they insist their students of Color constantly move. Their insistence renders invisible the ways that teaching code switching perpetuates an understanding of language as an objective, racially neutral terrain through which students can fight racism—rather than seeing language as a currency of racism itself.

How then, might we push White teachers to complicate and racialize their understandings of language? How might we help White English teachers to see classrooms as sites at which raciolinguistic ideologies are perpetuated and potentially contested? The questions my students and I developed did not neutralize the raciolinguistic ideologies at work in our classroom. Rather, they afforded us the space to articulate how those ideologies worked within and through us. The questions forced me to engage with the consequences of my own raciolingusitic identities: to see my Whiteness at work in my language practices and pedagogies.

In my work as a teacher educator, I have begun to ask a series of questions to the White teachers with whom I work—most of whom have expressed a commitment to the neutrality and importance of teaching students of Color to code switch: How is your raciolinguistic identity implicated in your pedagogies? What histories of racial and linguistic domination and resistance are you building upon or disrupting in your pedagogies? What assumptions about the relationship between race and language are implicated in your pedagogies? What language choices are you making and in what ways might those choices serve and protect your raciolinguistic identity? These questions do not, of course, neutralize the harm that White teachers perpetuate in classrooms through our language pedagogies. Rather, in the tradition of harm reduction, these questions work to name the ways that injustice is perpetuated in classrooms and begin the necessary and always insufficient work of engaging with that injustice.

Note

1 While there is little consensus regarding capitalization in the fields of Whiteness Studies or Critical Race Theory, I capitalize "White" and "Whiteness" to highlight their role in shaping White individuals' and communities' identities – and their profound effects on individuals and communities of Color.

References

Alexie, Sherman. 2007. *Flight*. New York: Black Cat.

Alim, H. Samy, and Angela Reyes. 2011. "Complicating Race: Articulating Race Across Multiple Dimensions." *Discourse and Society* 22(4): 379–384.

Aneja, Geeta. 2016. "(Non)native Speakered: Rethinking (Non)nativeness and Teacher Identity in TESOL Teacher Education." *TESOL Quarterly* 50(3): 572–596.

Anzaldua, Gloria. 1987. *Borderlands/La Frontera: The New Mestiza*. San Francisco, CA: Spinsters/Aunt Lute.

Bucholtz, Mary, and Kira Hall. 2005. "Identity and Interaction: A Sociocultural Linguistic Approach." *Discourse Studies* 7(4–5): 585–614.

Charity-Hudley, Anne, and Christine Mallinson. 2010. *Understanding English Language Variation in U.S. Schools*. New York: Teachers College Press.

Davila, Bethany. 2012. "Indexicality and 'Standard' Edited American English: Examining the Link Between Conceptions of Standardness and Perceived Authorial Identity." *Written Communication* 29(2): 180–207.

Delpit, Lisa. 2006. *Other People's Children: Culture Conflict in the Classroom*. New York: The New Press.

DuBois, William E. B. 1903. *The Souls of Black Folk*. New York: Bantam.

Fairclough, Norman. 2003. *Analyzing Discourse: Textual Analysis for Social Research*. New York: Routledge

Flores, Nelson, and Jonathan Rosa. 2015. "Undoing Appropriateness: Raciolinguistic Ideologies and Language Diversity in Education." *Harvard Education Review* 85(2): 149–172.

Foster, John D. 2013. *White Race Discourse: Preserving Racial Privilege in a Post-Racial Society*. Plymouth: Lexington Books.

Frankenberg, Ruth. 1993. *White Women, Race Matters: The Social Construction of Whiteness*. Minneapolis, MN: University of Minnesota Press.

Godley, Amanda, Jeffrey Reaser, and Kaylan Moore. 2016. "Pre-service English Language Arts Teachers' Development of Critical Language Awareness for Teaching." *Linguistics and Education* 32: 41–54.

Godley, Amanda, Julie Sweetland, Rebecca Wheeler, Angela Minnici, and Brian Carpenter. 2006. "Preparing Teachers for Dialectically Diverse Classrooms." *Educational Researcher* 35(8): 30–37.

Haddix, Marcelle. 2012. "Talkin' in the Company of my Sistas: The Counterlanguages and Deliberate Silences of Black Female Students in Teacher Education." *Linguistics and Education* 23(2): 169–181.

Hill, Jane. 1998. "Language, Race, and White Public Space." *American Anthropologist* 100(3): 680–689.

Jordan, Jordan. 1988. "Nobody Mean More to Me than You and the Future Life of Willie Jordan." *Harvard Educational Review* 58(3): 363–375.

Kamwangamalu, Nkonko. 2010. "Multilingualism and Codeswitching in Education." In *Sociolinguistics and Language Education*, edited by Nancy Hornberger and Sandra Lee McKay, 116–142. New York: Multilingual Matters

Karoll, Brad. 2010. "Applying Social Work Approaches, Harm Reduction, and Practice Wisdom to Better Serve Those with Alcohol and Drug Disorders." *Journal of Social Work* 10(3): 363–281.

Lipsitz, George. 1998. *The Possessive Investment in Whiteness: How White People Benefit from Identity Politics*. Philadelphia, PA: Temple University Press.

McIntyre, Alice. 2002. "Exploring Whiteness and Multicultural Education with Prospective Teachers." *Curriculum Inquiry* 32 (1): 31–49.

Monzo, Lilia, and Robert Rueda. 2003. "Shaping Education through Diverse Funds of Knowledge: A Look at One Latina Paraeducator's Lived Experiences, Beliefs, and Teaching Practice." *Anthropology and Education Quarterly* 34(1): 72–95.

National Center for Educational Statistics. 2012. *School and staffing survey, 1987–88 through 2011–2012.* Washington, DC: U.S. Department of Education.

Roberts, Lisa J., and G. Alan Marlatt. 1999. "Harm Reduction." In *Sourcebook on Substance Abuse: Etiology, Epidemiology, Assessment, and Treatment*, edited by Peggy Ott, Ralph Tarter, and Robert Ammerman, 389–398. Boston, MA: Allyn and Bacon.

Rosa, Jonathan. 2016. "Standardization, Racialization, Languagelessness: Raciolinguistic Ideologies Across Communicative Contexts." *Journal of Linguistic Anthropology* 26(2): 162–183.

Ruth-Gordon, Jennifer. 2011. "Discipline and Disorder in the Whiteness of Mock Spanish." *Journal of Linguistic Anthropology* 21(2): 211–229.

Sanchez, Patricia, and Lucila Ek. 2009. "Escuchando a las Maestras/os: Immigration Politics and Latina/o Preservice Bilingual Educators." *Bilingual Research Journal* 31(1–2): 271–294.

Urciuoli, Bonnie. 1996. *Exposing Prejudice: Puerto Rican Experiences of Language, Race, and Class.* Boulder, CO: Westview Press.

Valdes, Guadalupe. 2016. "Latin@s and the Intergenerational Continuity of Spanish: The Challenges of Curricularizing Language." *International Multilingual Research Journal* 9: 253–273.

Wheeler, R. and Swords, R. 2006. *Code-switching: Teaching Standard English in Urban Classrooms.* Chicago, IL: National Council of Teachers of English.

Wodak, Alex. 2003. "Harm Reduction as an Approach to Treatment." In *Principles of Addiction Medicine*, edited by Allan Graham, Terry Schultz, Michael Mayo-Smith, Richard Ries, and Bonnie Wilford, 533–534. Chevy Chase, MD: American Society of Addiction Medicine.

Young, Vershawn. 2009. "Nah, We Straight: An Argument Against Code Switching." *Journal of Advanced Composition* 29(1–2): 49–76.

2 Identifying "Racists" While Ignoring Racism

The Case of the Alleged Slur on George Zimmerman's 911 Tape

Adam Hodges

Introduction

Publicized cases of state-sanctioned violence against African Americans have forced US society to visibly grapple with its enduring problem of racism. Yet, as I illustrate in this chapter, the way media outlets cover such incidents can constitute a significant barrier to dealing with the systemic racism that undergirds the incidents. *Systemic racism* encompasses the "white-racist ideologies, attitudes, emotions, images, actions, and institutions of this society" (Feagin 2010). To say racism is systemic is to recognize that discrimination runs throughout the entire social body. It is deeply embedded in the workings of institutional power (*institutional racism*), acting as a foundational norm that guides institutions like the criminal justice system and activities like policing.

Media reportage typically filters reactions to racial events through a narrow understanding of racism. That narrow understanding privileges individual racism at the expense of systemic racism, defining racism simply as individual bigotry. Accordingly, discussions of racism tend to revolve around highly visible acts of racial animus where an individual's bigotry is clearly on display—for example, in the use of racist language. Incidents that do not neatly accord with this narrow definition of racism tend to be dismissed as having nothing to do with race. The collective and structural dimensions of racism are thereby minimized or brushed aside. By constraining the discourse surrounding racial events, the narrow definition of racism perpetuates a willful ignorance of the complex nature of racism, which effectively serves to maintain the dominant racial structure rather than to challenge it.

I explore this phenomenon through the case of media coverage of an alleged slur uttered by George Zimmerman in a 911 call he made before killing Trayvon Martin. I show how the narrow definition of racism guided reactions to the incident, and I argue that the narrow focus on individual racism shifted attention away from the systemic racism that underpinned the incident—frustrating attempts by racial justice advocates to attain justice for Trayvon. Begun in the wake of the incident, the Black Lives Matter (n.d.) movement has continued to grapple with the privileged position of individual racism over systemic racism in US discourse—a substantial barrier to racial justice insofar as institutional patterns of racism continue to be willfully ignored by many white Americans. This occurs even as "most whites of all political persuasions will say they are opposed to racism" (Feagin 2010, 190). This chapter aims to raise awareness of the dominant assumptions and language ideologies that often guide mainstream discussions of racism in an effort to push systemic racism to the forefront of more conversations. The ideas and case study discussed in this chapter are further detailed in Hodges (2015, 2016a, 2016b).

The Case Study

The events that took place on the evening of February 26, 2012 in Sanford, Florida have become well known around the world. Those events, of course, involved the shooting death of Trayvon Martin, an unarmed African American high school student, by a neighborhood watch volunteer named George Zimmerman. On that rainy night, Zimmerman began following Martin as he returned from a local convenience store to the home of his father's fiancée. Seeing Martin walking through the neighborhood, Zimmerman perceived in him a threat—a threat in line with the cultural stereotype of young black men as criminals. Zimmerman made a 911 call to report, in his words, a "suspicious guy" walking through the neighborhood. He then continued to follow Martin despite the explicit admonition from the 911 dispatcher that "we don't need you to do that." Before a police car arrived, a confrontation occurred between the two with Martin ending up dead, shot by Zimmerman, who was carrying a gun. The immediate handling of the incident by the Sanford police gave Zimmerman, who claimed self-defense, the benefit of doubt—a benefit of doubt in line with historical patterns of institutional racism. Those patterns of racism have failed to value the lives of young black men and have inverted racial vulnerability by obscuring the racial violence enacted on people of color. Zimmerman was let go that night without an arrest or further action. It wasn't until the Martin family held a press conference and the national media began to cover the case that further investigation was undertaken.

As national media struggled in the aftermath of the shooting death of Trayvon Martin to provide the necessary contextualization to understand the racial dimensions of the incident, focus soon turned to what Zimmerman may have said during his 911 call. Words are often looked to as harbingers of a person's intent. This stems from what linguistic anthropologists term the language ideology of personalism. A language ideology is a set of beliefs or ideas about language and its use; and the language ideology of personalism "holds that the most important part of linguistic meaning comes from the beliefs and intentions of the speaker" (Hill 2008, 38). If Zimmerman could be heard uttering overtly racist words in the background of his 911 call, then it would be an obvious way to connect race to the incident. Branding him a "racist" would overcome the many objections that race had nothing to do with it. In other words, uncovering a racist slur would allow commentators to straightforwardly recognize that race factored into the incident without having to delve into more complex aspects of racism that include cultural stereotypes, unconscious bias, and historical patterns of state-sanctioned violence against African Americans.

The media reactions provide an interesting case study for understanding the way the concept of *racism* is conveyed in mainstream discourse. In particular, I am interested in three episodes of the CNN news show *Anderson Cooper 360 Degrees*, which aired in 2012 on March 21, March 26, and April 4. In each of these shows, journalists subjected Zimmerman's 911 call to various audio enhancements as they isolated and repeatedly replayed a 1.6-second segment of the tape in an effort to determine whether a difficult-to-decipher sound attributed to Zimmerman could be interpreted as a racist slur (see Hodges 2016b for an in-depth analysis of these replays). It is through this case of journalists intently looking for a racist slur that we find taken-for-granted assumptions about the nature of racism that undergird mainstream American discourse. These assumptions place the focus on individual and overt acts of racism, and thereby obscure the relevance of structural and covert forms of racism. This leads to the idea that determining the relevance of racism in an incident like the shooting death of Trayvon Martin comes down to whether the shooter said something racist. If not, according to those assumptions, he is not a "racist" and racism could be deemed irrelevant.

Understanding Racism

At issue in this case study is the way racism is differently defined and understood. As Americans come together to discuss racial events, *racism* can mean different things to different speakers. It is not that the meanings necessarily conflict. Rather, it is that the meaning underlying much of the mainstream discourse about racism is selectively narrow and incomplete. As Eduardo Bonilla-Silva argues:

> One reason why, in general terms, whites and people of color cannot agree on racial matters is because they conceive terms such as "racism" very differently. Whereas for most whites racism is prejudice, for most people of color racism is systemic or institutionalized.
>
> (Bonilla-Silva 2013, 8)

The popular conception of racism that dominates much mainstream discourse in US society focuses on the way racism can be embodied in the "beliefs, intentions, and actions" (Hill 2008, 6) of bigoted individuals. Racism is assumed to manifest itself in overt or highly visible actions. Overt forms of discrimination, such as Jim Crow laws, conform to this conceptualization of racism. Visible words of hate, such as racial epithets or slurs, also conform to this understanding. The archetypical "racist" per the popular conception of racism can be seen in the Archie Bunker type characters that espouse bigoted views or the popular image of a Ku Klux Klan member dressed in his white robe. This uncritical view, which widely informs the way Americans think and talk about racial events, provides a decidedly narrow understanding of racism that constrains the discourse surrounding racial events. According to this view, overcoming racism merely consists of changing bigoted views so that the eradication of personal prejudice equates to the eradication of racial disparities.

Of course, the popular view operates upon a theory of change that fails to acknowledge the deep entrenchment of institutionalized racism, and the way structural racism can operate side-by-side disavowals of individual racial animus. As Feagin (2010, 27) notes, it "overlooks the point that the prejudices held by individuals are still rooted firmly in an extensive system of racism." But, racism is not confined to a few societal outliers with bigoted beliefs who can be dismissed as remnants of a by-gone era (Hodges 2016a). Racism is much broader and more complex than the popular conception professes. As the Black Lives Matter (n.d.) movement spotlights, there are numerous "ways in which Black people are intentionally left powerless at the hands of the state." Systemic racism, as described by Feagin (2006, xii), "encompasses a broad range of racialized dimensions" that include "extensive racist institutions developed over centuries by whites." This involves the criminal justice system and the way it gives the benefit of doubt to shooters of unarmed black men, casting black men as inherently "suspicious," and rationalizing a fear of black men as a justifiable legal defense.

A more complete view of racism, one widely recognized by sociologists and critical race scholars, emphasizes that racism is a system of power. As such, racism is institutionalized and systemic (Feagin 2006, 2010). It is collectively constructed and perpetuated through a set of cultural projects that create or maintain structures of domination (Hill 2008; Omi and Winant 1994). Moreover, although it can be overt and visible, as society evolves to widely denounce overt forms of prejudice and bigotry, racism increasingly manifests itself in covert and less visible ways. Today's racism, as Bonilla-Silva (2013) explains, is "colorblind." It exists side by side with widespread denunciations of overt racism. As social psychologists have shown (e.g. Eberhardt et al. 2004), the manifestation of racism need not always be conscious, as when it is overtly expressed through racist language. Rather, it often operates through ingrained racial biases we carry around with us—racial biases that stem from the cultural stereotypes that have been foundational to establishing and maintaining "the totality of the social relations and practices that reinforce white privilege" (Bonilla-Silva 2013, 9). As a system of power, racism therefore serves to uphold a racial structure that benefits those categorized as white at the expense of people of color.

This broader conception of racism provides a more complete view, recognizing the historical, social, and cultural processes that have led to the establishment and perpetuation of the racial hierarchy. This broader conception also provides a positive critical stance from which to understand the case study under consideration here. When racism is conceptualized merely as individual utterances and acts of bigotry per the popular understanding, then the subtler workings of racism that produce and maintain the racial hierarchy are erased from view—these include the historical patterns of institutionalized injustice emanating from police departments organized by and for white Americans to the ingrained racial biases that we all carry around with us as a result of early socialization patterns (Eberhardt et al. 2004, inter alia).

Hunting for "Racists"

As CNN journalists engaged in their scrutiny of the 911 tape, they forwarded a narrow understanding of racism as explicitly bigoted utterances. This narrow understanding of racism serves to perpetuate the current racial structure, obscuring a broader understanding of racism that could better inform the conversation about race surrounding the death of Trayvon Martin.

The narrow understanding of racism arises through a particular pattern of communication that I term the "hunting for 'racists' language game" (Hodges 2016a, 2016b). This is an interactional routine that identifies individuals as "racists," separating them from the rest of society. This pattern of communication can be seen to operate every time a well-known figure is caught on tape having uttered a slur or racist remark. Reactions to racist remarks made in 2014 by Donald Sterling, the owner of the Los Angeles Clippers basketball team, and Cliven Bundy, a rancher caught up in a dispute with the federal government over grazing fees, are prime examples of the way public discourse gravitates toward cases that are easy to identify as racism by narrowly conceptualizing racism as individual bigotry (Hodges 2016a). In such cases, racism is made visible through language use. The hunting for "racists" language game allows people to claim: *As long as I don't say overt racist things then I'm not contributing to racism.* It separates people who do use racist language from the people playing the language game, thus rendering those playing the game innocent.

Given the complex nature of the many dimensions of racism underlying the shooting death of Trayvon Martin, it is therefore not surprising that mainstream journalists would gravitate toward a more obvious and visible sign of racism to explain the case. Namely, this sign came in the form of what some perceived to be a racist slur uttered as an aside in the background of Zimmerman's 911 call. Identifying a racist slur would allow journalists to frame racial justice in terms of the eradication of bigoted language rather than systemic institutional change.

At issue was a 1.6-second segment of the 911 call. In that segment, it is alleged that Zimmerman uttered two words—words obscured by wind and background noise, making them difficult to decipher. As CNN journalist Anderson Cooper stated in the introduction to his show on March 21, "Some hear an ugly racial insult and an expletive, others hear nothing of the sort." So, CNN journalist Gary Tuchman met with audio engineer Rick Sierra in a sound studio to try to uncover what exactly might have been uttered by Zimmerman during that moment. Tuchman and Sierra began their investigation by playing a 12-second portion of the four-minute 911 call. During those 12 seconds, the dispatcher asks Zimmerman a question about which entrance of the neighborhood Martin was heading towards. Zimmerman responds, "The back entrance." Then there is a three-second pause followed by the indecipherable 1.6-second utterance made by Zimmerman, muttered under his breath and apparently not directed to the dispatcher. With the surrounding context established, the remainder of the sound room session on the March 21 show replayed the segment in question numerous times. At first, the journalists looped in repeated succession the full 1.6-second segment corresponding to two alleged words. Then, they zeroed in on the last part of the segment corresponding to the alleged slur, looping the indecipherable sound five times over the period of about six seconds. A similar sound studio routine took place on the April 4 show, only this time Tuchman met with a different audio engineer, Brian Stone, as they further isolated and enhanced the sound quality of the tape in an effort to uncover what Zimmerman might have said. The original sound room session from the March 21 show was also replayed on the March 26 and April 4 shows.

The ultimate decision made by the journalists or the television viewers on what Zimmerman might have uttered is irrelevant to the effectiveness of this interactional routine in narrowing the public's understanding of racism. For the record, Tuchman and Sierra leaned toward hearing a slur in the March 21 show, but Tuchman along with Stone took an opposing stance on the April 4 show. Regardless, both positions—for or against believing that Zimmerman uttered a slur—are premised on an understanding of racism where individuals can be clearly delineated in binary terms as racists or non-racists. The process of setting up this binary opposition allows journalists and viewers to engage in the fantasy that racism can be cleanly isolated in individual "racists" and that those individuals can be easily identified by uncovering and attributing hateful words to them. From this perspective, anti-racism efforts consist of identifying "racists," and separating those individuals as outliers or anachronisms in a modern society that has supposedly moved beyond racism. If Zimmerman could be heard uttering a racist slur, then he could be clearly marked as a "racist." As such, that act of characterizing him would allow journalists to easily explain the role racism played in the shooting death of Trayvon Martin. After all, according to the underlying assumption of the popular conceptualization of racism, racism is only seen as occurring in this instance if explicit racist language was used.

This process of differentiating between racists, on the one hand, and the rest of society, on the other, serves to maintain the current racial hierarchy by preserving the illusion that racism is a problem confined to what are popularly described as "uneducated, marginal, and backward individuals" (Hill 2008, 62–63). Racism is thought to exist merely in the attitudes of those individuals, and those attitudes are rendered visible through instances of explicit racist language. The underlying logic of identifying and separating those individuals, as described by Hill (2008), allows others who benefit from the privileges associated with being at the top of the racial hierarchy to claim, "I am a good and normal mainstream sort of White person. I am not a racist, because racists are bad and marginal people" (180). By implication, society as a whole putatively remains untainted by the racism now isolated in those individual outliers.

Interestingly, the process of supplanting the complete understanding of racism is achieved through a pattern of communication that masquerades as anti-racist discourse. By engaging in the "hunting for 'racists' language game," well-intentioned whites can ostensibly take a stand against racism by calling out racists and abhorring their actions. Crucially, this can be done while ignoring their own privilege or the role they play—even if unintentionally—in perpetuating the racial structure.

Conclusion

In examining the case of the media's scrutiny of George Zimmerman's 911 call on the night he killed Trayvon Martin, this chapter has argued that the type of discursive routine employed in this case—the hunting for "racists" language game—draws from and reinforces an overly narrow understanding of racism that supplants a more complete understanding of racism as a system of power. Public discourse that ignores systemic and institutional racism in such incidents misses an opportunity to critically discuss the way racism contributes to the construction and perpetuation of the US racial hierarchy—a hierarchy in which "young black men are 21 times as likely as their white peers to be killed by police" (Gabrielson, Jones, and Sagara 2014).

To move toward racial justice, discussants need to recognize the systemic and institutional dimensions of racism. Given that the unmarked understanding of racism simply equates it with bigotry and personal prejudice, moving the conversation forward requires calling attention to the assumptions that under-lie the unmarked meaning of the term in everyday talk. Discussants can shine light on the systemic dimensions of racism by explicitly defining the term in more complete terms as a starting point for discussions. Ultimately, achieving racial justice and dismantling racism as a system of power requires dismantling the taken-for-granted assumptions that obscure the workings of that system.

References

Black Lives Matter. n.d. "About the Black Lives Matter Network." Retrieved from http://blacklivesmatter.com/about.

Bonilla-Silva, Eduardo. 2013. *Racism Without Racists*. Plymouth: Rowman & Littlefield.

Eberhardt, Jennifer, Phillip Atiba Goff, Valerie Purdie, and Paul Davies. 2004. "Seeing Black: Race, Crime, and Visual Processing." *Journal of Personality and Social Psychology* 87(6): 876–893.

Feagin, Joe. 2006. *Systemic Racism*. New York: Routledge.

Feagin, Joe. 2010. *Racist America*. New York: Routledge.

Gabrielson, Ryan, Ryann Grochowski Jones, and Eric Sagara. 2014. "Deadly Force, In Black and White." *ProPublica*, October 10. Retrieved from www.propublica.org/article/deadly-force-in-black-and-white.

Hill, Jane. 2008. *The Everyday Language of White Racism*. Malden, MA: Wiley-Blackwell.

Hodges, Adam. 2015. "Ideologies of Language and Race in US Media Discourse about the Trayvon Martin Shooting." *Language in Society* 44(3): 401–423.

Hodges, Adam. 2016a. "Accusatory and Exculpatory Moves in the Hunting for 'Racists' Language Game." *Language & Communication* 47: 1–14.

Hodges, Adam. 2016b. "Hunting for 'Racists': Tape Fetishism and the Intertextual Enactment and Reproduction of the Dominant Understanding of Racism in US Society." *Journal of Linguistic Anthropology* 25(3): 26–40.

Omi, Michael, and Howard Winant. 1994. *Racial Formation in the United States*. New York: Routledge.

3 Contesting Representations of Migrant "Illegality" through the Drop the I-Word Campaign

Rethinking Language Change and Social Change

Jonathan Rosa

Language plays a key role in global public debates about migration, citizenship, and various forms of diversity. This chapter focuses on one particular debate surrounding representations of migrant "illegality" in the United States, examining how language can simultaneously provide a crucial vantage point from which to understand and contest the stigmatization of particular populations' mobility, as well as the ways that language can function deceptively as a sign of exclusion and inequality. I explore the "Drop the I-Word Campaign," a language and social justice initiative that calls for media outlets and broader publics to refrain from using the term "illegal" in representations of (im) migration. The "Drop the I-Word" campaign resonates with a central tenet of linguistic anthropology: language is not merely a passive way of referring to or describing things in the world, but a crucial form of social action itself. While language change is not necessarily equivalent to broader social change, struggles over representations of (im)migration can contribute to efforts toward imagining and establishing migration as a fundamental human right.

In September 2010, the racial justice organization Race Forward initiated the "Drop the I-Word" campaign in efforts to eradicate the use of the term "illegal" in reference to immigration, particularly among mainstream media outlets. They argued that, despite the word's widely embraced usage, the language of illegality is an incorrect and stigmatizing way of representing immigration. A video that was released as part of the campaign states:

> Calling a person "illegal" takes away their humanity. We can join our voices to ask media and government to drop the I-word now. The I-word derails real conversation about immigration and human rights ... it's racially charged, legally inaccurate, and morally wrong.
>
> (Drop the I-Word 2011)

As the campaign picked up steam, members of the Society for Linguistic Anthropology's Language and Social Justice Committee entered into dialogue with the creators of the Drop the I-Word campaign about the possibility of drafting a statement in support of their efforts. As a committee, we believed it was our responsibility to challenge problematic claims that the use of the term "illegal" in reference to immigration among mainstream media is unbiased, neutral, or accurate.

In the explanation that accompanied a 2011 update to the Associated Press Stylebook, widely regarded as the U.S. news media industry standard, Deputy Standards Editor David Minthorn suggested that "illegal immigrant" should be the preferred term because it is "accurate and neutral for news stories" (Novoa 2011b). Similarly, the Public Editor of the *New York Times* drew on this logic in a column titled "Readers Won't Benefit if Times Bans the Term 'Illegal Immigrant'" (Sullivan 2012). She argued that the phrase "illegal immigrant"

> is clear and accurate; it gets its job done in two words that are easily understood. The same cannot be said of the most frequently suggested alternatives—"unauthorized," "immigrants without legal status," "undocumented." Undocumented . . . has "a new currency" because of a federal policy change involving immigrants who came here as children 15 and under, so the word may be useful in that context.
>
> (Sullivan 2012)

However, scholarship focused on this issue points out that "legal immigrant" is a redundant concept and "illegal immigrant" is oxymoronic, since the U.S. Immigration and Nationality Act defines immigrants as people who have been lawfully admitted for permanent residence (Plascencia 2009). My use of the term "migrant" throughout this chapter reflects this insight.

The language of illegality is far from neutral, and conservative political consultants have actively promoted its use. Recognizing the nefarious criminalization of particular racialized migrants, organizations such as the Society of Professional Journalists have described "illegal immigrant" as a "politically charged" phrase that should be reevaluated for its potential violation of the widely embraced journalistic practice of assuming innocence until guilt is proven (Novoa 2011a). Others have made the related case that "illegal" is at best a misleading generalization, at worst a slur (Garcia 2012). A person diagnosed with cancer is not described as cancerous; however, "illegal" becomes a way of characterizing not just one's migration status, but also one's entire person. This perspective galvanized the campaign to "Drop the I-Word."

From a linguistic anthropological and language and social justice perspective, we might consider what forms of social action take place in and through language used in popular representations of immigration. One of the most noteworthy characteristics of immigration discourses is their naturalization of concepts such as "illegality" and the construction of immigration laws as rigid, unchanging phenomena (Santa Ana 2002; Dick 2011). These discourses frame migration status as a matter of individual choice rather than historically situated policies that have shifted over time. Dramatic shifts in immigration laws throughout U.S. history have created straightforward pathways to citizenship for some groups, but lengthy, laborious, or fruitless roads for others (De Genova 2004). This is also true globally, where particular populations' mobility is seen as legitimate and even celebrated and other populations' mobility is highly surveilled or restricted altogether. Ngai (2004) shows how throughout U.S. history, policies such as the Chinese Exclusion Act of 1882, the Asiatic Barred Zone Act of 1917, the Johnson–Reed Act of 1924, and the Hart–Cellar Act of 1965 have strategically and nefariously made various migrants illegal based on particular historical, political, and economic circumstances. The dynamic nature of this history is obscured by the assumption that migrants simply opt to be legal or illegal. In fact, authorization should be understood primarily as a matter of political will rather than the individual choices of migrants themselves.

The misleading construction of illegality is tied to the circulation of troublesome stereotypes about the migration status of different marginalized groups. Specifically, assessments of illegality are often associated with unreliable signs of one's migration status, such as language, religion, and physical appearance. These presumptions lead not only to law enforcers' regular misidentification of people's migration status based on wrongful assumptions about signs of difference, but also to the broader public stigmatization of those signs. Thus, notions of illegality are not simply innocuous characterizations of migration status, but highly stigmatizing conceptions that are perilously mapped onto entire populations. Seemingly euphemistic invocations of illegality, such as in "illegal alien hunting permit" bumper stickers, are all too literal for people who have been targeted based on presumptions about their so-called "illegal immigrant" status. The terrifying raids that are frequently carried out by Immigration and Customs Enforcement, modes of detention and deportation, the separation of migrant families, and border militarization demonstrate that "illegal immigrant hunting" is an actual practice (Hernández 2007; Marquez 2012). Marcelo Lucero and Luis Ramirez were both killed in separate incidents in which groups of mostly white teenagers sought to "hunt an illegal" (Hing 2009). These violent practices are patterned; rates of anti-Latinx hate crimes have surged in recent years (Romero 2016). Constructions of illegality are thus anything but accurate or neutral.

Taking into account these various perspectives, the Language and Social Justice Committee drafted a statement that was endorsed by dozens of linguistic anthropologists, published in Anthropology News (Rosa 2012), and mentioned by mainstream media outlets such as ABC News/Univision (Costantini 2012), CNN (Rodriguez 2013), and NPR (Demby 2013). Shortly thereafter, media outlets such as the Associated Press (Costantini 2013), USA Today (Planas 2013), LA Times (King 2013), and many others, changed their style guidelines, essentially dropping the I-word. In response, Race Forward, the organization that spearheaded the Drop the I-Word campaign, released a new video reporting these successes and reaffirming "the dignity and humanity of immigrants" (Race Forward 2015).

While on one level the Language and Social Justice Committee viewed this as a great success, as linguistic anthropologists we also knew that the eradication of this word alone should not be equated with the kinds of broader social change for which pro-immigration reform activists had been advocating. This was evident in many media outlets' questions about what term to use instead of "illegal." Rather than simply replacing "illegal" with a less stigmatizing term, we must call into question the legitimacy of restrictive migration policies altogether such that there would no longer be a criminalized form of migration in need of a label. An engaging discussion took place among members of the Language and Social Justice Committee about whether to explicitly endorse an alternative term to the I-word, since this would likely be the most pressing concern for journalists and the broader public. For example, "undocumented" is a commonly preferred alternative to "illegal." However, cultural anthropologist Luis Plascencia argues that the usage of "'undocumented' migrant . . . shares common assumptions with the term 'illegal' migrant, and thus it is also complicit in promoting the 'illegalization' that its development and deployment was seeking to negate" (Plascencia 2009, 413).

In linguistic anthropological parlance, Plascencia's analysis speaks to the ways that ideologies of referentialism often miss the point in debates about terminology (Hill 2008). From a referentialist ideological perspective, each word refers to a concept in a unique way, so if that word is no longer used, then that concept is no longer referred to. However, many different words can in fact have similar social functions depending on the context of their use. Thus, a new word might in fact invoke conceptions of illegality and thus function in stigmatizing ways just as much as if not more powerfully than the term "illegal." While referentialist ideologies might lead one to think that the term itself is the problem, simply replacing "illegal" with another term will not eradicate the aforementioned legal conflations, historical erasures, racial and linguistic profiling, and acts of violence. We must recognize that this debate is not merely a matter of policing language, or deciding whether one word or phrase is better than another. The declaration that "no human being is illegal" is not just a claim about language (Ngai 2006; Gambino 2015).

Longstanding histories of migrant illegalization demonstrate the ways that anxieties surrounding migrant mobility and their diversities are by no means new phenomena. This point seems lost in much of the recent work on so-called "super-diversity" in a range of language-related fields (Blommaert and Rampton 2011). This framework is based on the premise that we are witnessing a proliferation of "categories of migrants" and diverse language practices dramatically superseding that of previous historical moments. In contrast, Reyes (2014) suggests that "this speaker focus neglects a thorough conceptualization and interrogation of the listening subject: how change may not in fact begin with speaking subjects (migrants) but may be brought into being by listening subjects (those authorized to speak about migrants) and whatever anxieties and desires motivate the circulation of representations of speakers" (2014, 368). For Reyes, it is crucial to interrogate the ideologies of Otherness that inform gradations of diversity, positioning some populations as the norm and Others as "diverse" or "super-diverse." Reyes argues that we must locate the production of linguistic "super-diversity" in the politics of positionality that structures perceptions of difference rather than in the empirical practices of migrant populations within a globalizing world. Other scholars warn that "if we approach globalization naively. . .we overlook the fact that words like 'global' and globalization' in their most current use were first broadcast most aggressively by marketing agents and marketing schools" (Trouillot 2001, 128). From this perspective, "super-diversity" is part of a broader set of narratives about globalization that "not only silence histories of the world but also veil our understanding of the present" (ibid., 128). Building from these insights, we might interrogate the ways that the sentiments that inform the perception of super-diversity are linked to Otherizing discourses such as illegality.

We can also locate debates about "illegality" alongside previous domestic struggles over language used to characterize minoritized and marginalized populations. A more example, the website nohomophobes.com, tracks the use of homophobic epithets in new media in real time. While such enumerations might be imprecise (e.g., by not distinguishing between pejorative usages versus potentially critical or revalorized usages), they serve as an opportunity to challenge modes of linguistic stigmatization. Such struggles over language serve as opportunities to imagine and enact counter-hegemonic realities. Thus, the call to "Drop the I-Word" is a means to a much greater end.

We should also pay attention to the ways that the "Drop the I-Word" campaign is linked to other contemporary debates, including the troublesome call to "Drop the T" (Marcus 2015) from LGBT by mainstream gay (i.e., specifically cis white male) activists who seek to separate their identities from the increasingly emergent recognition of transgender populations.[1] "Drop the T" advocates operate from a zero-sum perspective in which newly gained visibility and rights for transgender individuals are understood to come at the expense of cisgender lesbian, gay, and bisexual groups. This view contradicts longstanding efforts toward building solidarity across marginalized populations, as well as intersectional approaches to understanding the ways that people simultaneously experience a range of identities in relation to matrices of domination. The irony of invoking the Drop the I-Word Campaign in efforts to Drop the T from LGBT was perhaps most glaringly evident when, in the summer of 2015, Jennicet Gutiérrez, an undocumented trans Latina activist, interrupted President Obama at a White House event celebrating LGBT Pride Month to draw attention to the administration's record-setting rates of deportation (Rivas 2015). Drawing on an intersectional analysis of migration rights and queer liberation, Gutiérrez and others have noted that while privileged lesbian and gay populations might be enjoying increased access to marriage rights and other forms of societal inclusion, many queer people of color—especially trans people of color—face systematic forms of marginalization that are linked to the targeting and stigmatization of particular racialized migrant groups. Thus, for an undocumented trans Latina activist such as Gutiérrez, Obama's record of deporting more than 2.5 million people during his two-term presidency—more than any other U.S. President in history—has earned him the moniker "deporter in chief" (Marshall 2016). In fact, more people were deported by Obama than the combined total of all 19 U.S. presidents from 1892–2000 (Rogers 2016). The inhumanity of this record has reached new levels in recent years, in which the targets for deportation are increasingly women and children asylum-seekers fleeing violence in Central America. Of course it is important to note the history of U.S. political, economic, and military intervention in Central America, such that the presence of these asylum seekers is no coincidence, but rather, as journalist Juán González (2000) puts it, the "harvest of empire." These histories were ignored in many of the public responses to the anti-Muslim migration orders that President Donald Trump issued during his first few weeks in office. It is important to see Trump's efforts—including the profoundly inhumane policy of separating migrant children from their parents at the border—as the rearticulation of long-standing forms of racism and xenophobic migration policies rather than as exceptional or new phenomena.

In the context of the current political moment, we might also consider how seemingly opposing framings of "anchor babies" and "DREAMers" become linked to notions of illegality. From many progressive points of view, anchor baby is a highly stigmatizing term for a U.S.-born child of an unauthorized migrant parent and dreamer is a positive term for unauthorized migrant youth who have grown up in the U.S. for the majority of their lives. Through the invocation of the American Dream—which has, in fact, continually been a nightmare for various populations—and a blame the parent, not the child perspective, "DREAMer" discourses could inadvertently participate in the reproduction of notions of illegality and the broader forms of stigmatization to which they correspond. In order to stake a claim to authorized resident status or a so-called pathway to citizenship, these young people are recruited to simultaneously embrace the notion of the "American dream" and disavow their parents, doubling-down on their characterization as illegal aliens; that is, they must distinguish themselves from their families and promote the false notion of the American Dream. What, exactly, is the meaningfulness of the American dream and citizenship in the context of mass incarceration, mass deportation, extrajudicial violence, and extreme socioeconomic precarity?

In light of the emergence of movements such as #BlackLivesMatter and other efforts toward addressing profound structural disparities including extrajudicial violence, state-sanctioned violence, and the mass incarceration of African Americans in particular, it is curious that questions about the significance of citizenship are rarely posed. These forms of marginalization and violence are clear examples of the ways that populations can possess citizenship and yet still be positioned as second, third, or fourth class citizens. Connecting #BlackLivesMatter to the immigration debate, what reason do we have to believe that simply granting citizenship to the undocumented will do anything but position them as abject citizens, similar to African Americans, Native Americans, and other groups throughout the nation? For example, we must remember that there are millions of Latinxs who are U.S. citizens and yet still face profound forms of marginalization across societal contexts, including employment, housing, education, the criminal justice system, and access to health care. These insights demand an analysis of the relationship between forms of incarceration, detention, exclusion, and expulsion as part of a broader, racialized process of disposability, dispossession, abandonment, and rightlessness. Rather than simply advocating for access to U.S. citizenship within a settler colonial state (re)produced through racial capitalism, we must continually seek to imagine and enact alternative political and economic orders.

These various discourses and debates highlight ways that language and social justice efforts can inform scholarly and popular understandings of communication, context, power, reproduction, and transformation. However, as I have sought to show in this chapter, there are a range of pitfalls associated with these efforts, not the least of which is the tendency to equate linguistic change with broader social change in straightforward ways. Thus, we remain faced with the task of drawing critical connections between communication and social transformation. This challenging undertaking will require interdisciplinary collaborations drawing on a range of critical approaches to the study of language, as well as community collaborations in contexts where forms of linguistic discrimination are most acutely experienced.

Note

1 Intertextuality and interdiscursivity have been important features of other intersectional campaigns, such as Pulitzer Prize winning journalist and undocumented queer activist José Antonio Vargas' call for undocumented people to "come out." This combines the slogan of "coming out of the closet" associated with queer communities, with the slogan of "coming out of the shadows" associated with undocumented communities.

References

Blommaert, Jan, and Ben Rampton. 2011. "Language and Superdiversity." *Diversities* 13(2): 1–21.

Costantini, Cristina. 2012. "Linguists Tell New York Times that 'Illegal' is Neither 'Neutral' nor 'Accurate." *ABC News/Univision*, October 1. Accessed February 17, 2017, at http://abcnews.go.com/ABC_Univision/linguists-york-times-illegal-neutral-%20accurate/story?id=17366512.

Costantini, Cristina. 2013. "Associated Press Drops 'Illegal Immigrant' from Stylebook." *ABC News/Univision*, April 2, accessed February 17, 2017, at https://abcnews.go.com/ABC_Univision/press-drops-illegal-immigrant-standards-book/story?id=18862824.

De Genova, Nicholas. 2004. "The Legal Production of Mexican/Migrant 'Illegality.'" *Latino Studies*, 2(2): 160–185.

Demby, Gene. 2013. "In Immigration Debate, 'Undocumented' Vs. 'Illegal' is More than Just Semantics." *NPR*, January 30. Accessed February 17, 2017, at www.npr.org/blogs/itsallpolitics/2013/01/30/170677880/in-immigration- debate-undocumented-vs-illegal-is-more-than-just-semantics.

Dick, Hilary. 2011. "Making Immigrants Illegal in Small-Town USA." *Journal of Linguistic Anthropology* 21(S1): E35–E55.

Drop the I-Word. 2011. "Drop the I-Word. No Human Being is Illegal." YouTube video, 0:46, posted by "Drop the I-word." May 18. Accessed February 17, 2017, at www.youtube.com/watch?v=ebs6SCPf_dU.

Gambino, Lauren. 2015. "'No Human Being is Illegal': Linguists Argue Against Mislabeling of Immigrants." *The Guardian*, December 6. Accessed February 17, 2017, at www.theguardian.com/us-news/2015/dec/06/illegal-immigrant-label-offe nsive-wrong-activists-say.

Garcia, Charles. 2012. "Why 'Illegal Immigrant' is a Slur." *CNN*, July 6. Accessed February 17, 2017, at www.cnn.com/2012/07/05/opinion/garcia-illegal-immigrants/.

González, Juan. 2000. *Harvest of Empire: A History of Latinos in America*. New York: Penguin Books.

Hernández, David. 2007. "Pursuant to Deportation: Latinos and Immigrant Detention." *Latino Studies* 6(1): 35–63.

Hill, Jane. 2008. *The Everyday Language of White Racism*. Malden, MA: Blackwell.

Hing, Julianne. 2009. "Luis Ramierez, Marcelo Lucero, and the White Boys We Can't Bring Ourselves to Convict." *Colorlines*, August 19. Accessed February 17, 2017, at www.colorlines.com/articles/luis-ramirez-marcelo-lucero-and-white-boys-we-cant-bring-ourselves-convict.

King, Jamilah. 2017. "Los Angeles Times Drops 'Illegal Immigrant,'" *Colorlines*, May 2, 2013, accessed February 17, at www.colorlines.com/articles/los-angeles-times-drops-illegal-immigrant.

Marcus, David. 2015. "Exclusive: Gay Man Explains His Initiative to Drop the T in LGBT." *The Federalist*, November 9, accessed February 18, 2017, at http://thefederalist.com/2015/11/09/exclusive-gay-man-explains-his-petition-to-drop-the-t-in-lgbt.

Marquez, John. 2012. "Latinos as the 'Living Dead': Raciality, Expendability, and Border Militarization." *Latino Studies* 10(4): 473–498.

Marshall, Serena. 2016. "Obama Has Deported More People Than Any Other President." *ABC News*, August 29, accessed February 18, 2017, at http://abcnews. go.com/Politics/obamas-deportation-policy-numbers/story?id=41715661.

Ngai, Mae. 2004. *Impossible Subjects: Illegal Aliens and the Making of Modern America*. Princeton, NJ: Princeton University Press.

Ngai, Mae. 2006. "No Human Being Is Illegal." *Women's Studies Quarterly* 34(3–4): 291–295.

Novoa, Mónica. 2011a. "Society of Professional Journalists Votes to Drop the I-Word." *Colorlines*, October 4. Accessed February 17, 2017, at www.colorlines.com/articles/society-professional-journalists-votes-drop-i-word.

Novoa, Mónica. 2011b. "The Associated Press Updates Its Stylebook, Still Clings to I-Word." *Colorlines*, November 10. Accessed February 17, 2017, at www.colorlines. com/articles/associated-press-updates-its-stylebook-still-clings-i-word.

Planas, Roque. 2013. "USA Today Drops 'Illegal Immigrant'." *The Huffington Post*, April 11. Accessed February 17, 2017, at www.huffingtonpost.com/2013/04/11/usa-today-illegal-immigrant_n_3062479.html.

Plascencia, Luis. 2009. "The 'Undocumented' Mexican Migrant Question: Re-examining the Framing of Law and Illegalization in the United States." *Urban Anthropology* 38(2–4): 375–434.

Race Forward. 2015. "Why We Should Drop The I-Word." YouTube video, 2:34, posted on October 28. Accessed February 17, 2017, at www.youtube.com/watch?lis t=PL4ruTyc9FHOXIiw7XW1kF424I4wRPGRo8&v=K4KObY2tqe4.

Reyes, Angela. 2014. "Linguistic Anthropology in 2013: Super-New-Big." *American Anthropologist* 116(2): 366–378.

Rivas, Jorge. 2015. "Meet Jennicet, One Month after She Interrupted President Obama." August 3. Accessed February 18, 2017, at http://fusion.net/story/175990/ jennicet-gutierrez-interrupted-president-obama.

Rodriguez, Cindy Y. 2013. "Language like 'Illegal Immigrant' Seen as a Challenge During Immigration Debate." *CNN*, April 4. Accessed February 17, 2017, at www. cnn.com/2013/04/04/us/illegal-immigrant-term-still-a-challenge.

Rogers, Tim. 2016. "Obama has Deported More People than Any Other President. Now He's Running up the Score." January 7. Accessed February 18, 2017, at http:// fusion.net/story/252637/obama-has-deported-more-immigrants-than-any-other-president-now-hes-running-up-the-score/.

Romero, Dennis. 2016. "In the Era of Trump, Anti-Latino Hate Crimes Jumped 69% in L.A." L.A. Weekly, September 29. Accessed February 17, 2017, at www.laweekly. com/news/in-the-era-of-trump-anti-latino-hate-crimes-jumped-69-in-la-7443401.

Rosa, Jonathan. 2012. "Contesting Representations of Immigration." *Anthropology News* 53(8): S13–S14.

Santa Ana, Otto. 2002. *Brown Tide Rising: Metaphors of Latinos in Contemporary American Public Discourse.* Austin: University of Texas Press.

Sullivan, Margaret. 2012. "Readers Won't Benefit if Times Bans the Term 'Illegal Immigrant'." *New York Times*, October 2. Accessed February 17, 2017, at https:// publiceditor.blogs.nytimes.com/2012/10/02/readers-wont-benefit-if-times-bans-the-term-illegal-immigrant/?_r=0.

Trouillot, Michel Rolph. 2001. "The Anthropology of the State in the Age of Globalization: Close Encounters of the Deceptive Kind." *Current Anthropology* 42(1): 125–138.

4   Communicating and Contesting Islamophobia

Mariam Durrani

Introduction

In recent years, peoples, practices, and objects perceived as "Muslim" have been stereotyped by some people, groups, and state systems as representative of an existential threat to American national security. For example, certain kinds of language use that sounds "Muslim" has led to people being removed from planes and buses despite no immediate threat or justifiable reason. On April 6, 2016 Khair-ul-deen Makhzoomi was taken off a Southwest Airlines flight at LAX after speaking *Inshallah* ["God willing" in Arabic] while speaking on the phone. The airline had the Berkeley student removed from the plane based on a non-Arabic speaker's complaint (Revesz 2016). The language need not be Arabic—spoken in many Muslim majority countries. In fact, it can be Punjabi spoken while wearing a turban, as was the case for two Sikh-American men on a Greyhound bus in Texas (Wang 2016); or it might be Arabic numerals, such as when a math professor wrote differential equations in his notebook, garnering the fear of a fellow passenger for what she thought was Arabic (Rampell 2016). In each of these situations, the perception of language use as "Muslim" or "foreign" leads to bias and discrimination against Muslims and non-Muslims alike.

The use of Arabic in school assignments has also been perceived as suspicious. In December 2015, the Augusta County School District in Virginia closed due to security concerns following a worksheet assignment asking students to copy Arabic calligraphy. On social media, a caustic discussion erupted about religion, specifically Islam, in education (Brumfield 2015). This incident is part of a larger trend of anti-Muslim, anti-Arab, anti-immigrant bias in US schools. A 2013 study of Muslim American students in California found that one in five young women experienced bullying for wearing a headscarf to school. This report found that over 50 percent of Muslim American students in California have been bullied verbally and more than 10 percent reported physical bullying (CAIR 2013).

The recurring phenomenon across these events is that the language and, more importantly, the person using it, is perceived as "foreign," a foreignness that is synonymous with the category of "Muslim" and/or "Islam." These examples of bias are demonstrative of discriminatory linguistic profiling which is based on auditory and orthographic cues that may include racial identification (Baugh 2003). Unfortunately anti-Muslim bias is pervasive across American society, including schools, and it has crystalized in responses to the use of "Muslim-sounding" languages, seen as threatening and representative of terrorist sympathy or action. In some cases, simply possessing Muslim-sounding names is heard as evidence of crimality (Thanagaraj under review). Moreover the co-occurrence of racially ambiguous brown and Black *bodies* using Muslim-sounding *speech forms* becomes representative of a strategically constructed Muslim bogeyman—dangerous to an American body politic.

This unfounded fear of and systemic discrimination against Muslims is referred to as *Islamophobia* and is observable in everyday actions—mosque vandalism, hate speech and hate crimes—and structural discrimination—the sensationalist meida coverage of the "Muslim threat," selective policing and surveillance of Muslim communities, and the use of Islamophobic ideologies in election campaigns, including when Obama was erroneously said to be a Muslim (Shyrock 2010). Some scholars have argued that rather than using "Islamophobia" to understand the current political climate for Muslim minorities in non-Muslim societies, we should consider the term "anti-Muslim racism" as a discriminatory set of practices for the racialized Muslim subject (Carr 2016). Others argue that despite its shortcomings, Islamophobia retains currency in the public sphere and thus remains useful (Beydoun 2018).

This chapter contextualizes how these contemporary formulations of the Muslim figure as Other are situated within a larger sociohistorical frame and draws attention to the micro-level linguistic phenomena to consider how new raciolinguistic formulations about Muslims take shape.

The Racialization of "Muslims" in America

While the category of "Muslim" does not fit into the categories of race as defined by the US census, racial demographics are a poor gauge to understand new racial formations. The emergent racial formation of "Muslim" relies on both the biological constructions of the "race" concept, drawing on darker phenotypic features, and the perceptions and stereotypes of Muslim "culture," such as visible Muslim-ness, i.e. wearing the hijab, and the use of "Muslim-sounding" languages (Omi and Winant 2015; Hall 1997). Furthermore the historicity of the "Muslim" subject as a racialized figure originates in the ways that religion has been key to the historical development of the "race" concept (Rana 2011). "The "raceing" of Islam has taken place not in a vacuum but within the context of specific sociohistorical relationships" (ibid., 48). Elsewhere Prashad (2001) explains that the "immigrant" category is racialized through xenophobic sentiments that place blame on migrants for larger societal deficiencies. To understand the historical context for anti-Muslim racism in contemporary America, we should consider the governmental mechanisms that have evolved alongside the ideological biases against the imagined "Muslim" figure. Said's *Orientalism* (1978) illustrated how centuries of representing the Oriental figure—or Muslim Other—as "weak, decadent, depraved, irrational, and fanatical" operated as a kind of self-flattery to say that the West was the opposite, i.e. civilized, dynamic, and superior, and that this influenced official colonial and later national policies (Grewal 2013, 5). Beydoun expounds on this: "Islamophobia is a modern extension and articulation of an old system that branded Muslims as inherently suspicious and unassimilable and cast Islam as a rival ideology at odds with American values, society, and national identity" (Beydoun 2018, 18). Despite the presence of Muslims in the Americas, which predates independence, many Americans have inherited and perpetuated this worldview of Muslims as Other and foreign.

Muslim-Americans are often racialized based on stereotypes that link physical presentation, sartorial choices, and language use. Despite cultural, ethnic, religious, and racial heterogeneities, Muslim and Muslim-"appearing" individuals experience forms of anti-Muslim racism, anti-Black racism, and/or anti-immigrant racism. Muslims may be categorized as Black, Hispanic, Asian, or White in the census, but as discussed, they are also racialized as the Muslim Other in everyday interactions and official policies. To better understand this process, we turn to transracialization, a framework that explains how the same body is raced and re-raced into multiple racial formations (Alim 2016). Transracialization considers not only how individuals might move across these racial formations but also to question dominant ideas about race and language *and* the relationship between language and phenotype. Across events of the discriminatory linguistic profiling of Muslim-sounding speech, the listener/ observer dehumanizes the individual of personhood. Instead the listener/ observer imposes a racialized type based on some combination of phenotypic features, sartorial presentation, and linguistic usage that draws on pre-existing racisms against the Brown or Black body and then racializes this person as a dangerous Muslim Other.

In Hill's (1998) analysis of Whites using Spanish in White public spaces, in which Whites (here speakers of standard American English) are the invisible normal, Spanish becomes a marker of racialized language practice. Hill explicates the various ways that White racism is ever-present in our everyday language practices in terms of what practices are marked as a deviation from acceptable language use in predominantly White public spaces. In relation to our discussion here, the mere mention of *Islam* or *Muslim* in White public spaces has come to function as a kind of *shifter* that indexes a condemnation, defense, or ambiguous value judgment about the racialized "Muslim" subject. Here, "shifter" is defined as a linguistic term used to denote words that combine both a referential and indexical function in speech (Jakobson 1971; Silverstein 1976). In its referential function, a shifter denotes a word that stands independent of the particular speech utterance. Used in its referential capacity, the term *Islam* can refer to a religious practice with about 1.6 billion followers worldwide. It can also have multiple meanings that are geographically specific or class-based. For example, the Islam practiced by adherents living in Jeddah is likely different than that practiced by Latinx Muslims in San Diego. And yet for both, those who claim a Muslim identity are all followers of Islam, referentially understood as a religion. In contrast, the indexical function of a shifter means that it can be understood through the context of the specific use, where meaning can shift based on the context. When we see the form *Islam* in a phrase like *radical Islam* or *Islamic terrorism*, the referential function is eclipsed by an indexical meaning of Islam as a negative, threatening, and even dangerous religion by linking the word *Islam* to "radicalism," "extremism," "terrorism." Some right-wing extremists argue that Islam is not a religion but a political ideology. The increasing use of "Islam" with *radical* or *extremism* in political speeches and platforms has altered its referential meaning within mainstream American media. For those convinced Islam and Muslims pose a threat to "western civilization," echoing Huntington's (1993) treatise, the words can denote a contemporary bogeyman—the dangerous, foreign Other—reproducing racist and colonialist logics in contemporary White public spaces. What is most troubling about this change in referential meaning from a religious group/faith to dangerous Other is that White public audiences do not require a particular interactional context to index this latter, more problematic interpretation. The mere use of Islam, Muslim, Arabic, or Muslim-sounding languages, as discussed earlier, can create a sense of paranoia and alarm, leading to bias, discrimination, and possibly violence.

Phonetic/Phonemic Distinctions of Islam/Muslim

We can consider the referential distinctions from a phonetically-based perspective. This allows for an analysis of how certain terms are pronounced by Muslim and non-Muslim speakers in the US and the metapragmatic commentary about these pronunciations. For some speakers and listeners, we can observe a marked differences between pronouncing Muslim as /mʊs-lɪm/ (Moos-lim) versus /mʊz-lɪm/ (Muz-lim), and perhaps even more so with an extended initial vowel /mʌz-ləm/ or /mʌs-ləm/. This is also manifested in the phonemic differences between /isˈläm/ (IS-lam) and /izˈläm/ (IZ-lam). In other words, one may pronounce it with either the voiced (/z/) or voiceless (/s/) form of the alveolar fricative consonant. The pronunciation of Muslim/Islam varies widely among speakers, and these variations understandably stem from the speakers' linguistic repertoires. In other words, there is no homogeneity within Muslim-only communities for what lexeme refers to a person who adheres to Islam since Muslims come from many different linguistic communities. The use of the voiceless /s/ consonant is most frequently used by Muslim speakers whose first language might be Arabic, Farsi, Urdu/Hindi, Malay, Bangla, and others. This is still true for speakers who use "Musalman" as a synonym for Muslim that has been modified from Arabic. Other speakers may use other variations such as MaSilamsi (Xhosa), Musilimi (Amhari), and Musulimi (Yoruba). While the fact that people pronounce the same denotational content in multiple ways is not remarkable, what is notable is when the decision to use one pronunciation or the other functions as a shifter indexing political values or ideological positions.

In all these variations, the voiceless consonant is used but for English speakers, specifically during colonial encounters with Muslim populations, the voiced consonant appears more prevalent. The use of the voiced consonant co-occurs with the use of the orthographic form, "Moslem," a term that was used during the colonial period into the twentieth century. However both the spelling and pronunciation of "Moslem" was perceived as insulting by some Muslims, in part because the term had a colonialist context, essentially mispronounciation, but also in that /mʊz-ləm/ [مظلم] translates to "dark," "black," or "very evil" in Arabic compared to /mʊs-lɪm/ [مسلم], translated as "one who accepts/submits." Based on a discourse analysis of British newspapers from 1998–2009, researchers found that while "Muslim" and "Islam" were used almost 200,000 times, Moslem/Moslems had 7,009 references with 97 percent of those between 1998 and 2003 (Baker, Gabrielatos, and McEnery 2013). In England, several daily newspapers adamantly held on to "Moslem" until 2004 when British Muslim groups, including the Media Committee of the Muslim Council of Britain, asked the media to stop using it (Baker 2010, cited in Baker, Gabrielatos, and McEnery 2013). These phonetic and orthographic distinctions between a voiced or voiceless consonant, as well as the larger speech segments these words were used in, were understood as an indexical marker of political affiliation or immigrant sympathies. If using the voiceless consonant, orthographically marked by "Moslem," indexes someone who aligns favorably with immigrant Muslims/the "Other", then the decision to use a voiced consonant takes on the opposite signification, i.e. rejection/condemnation of the foreigner/Other. In each, the speaker is orienting to possible interpretations by listeners, and thus the subsequent discourse may question or critique the speaker's allegiance to social and political values, i.e. the speaker's position on immigration, the travel ban on seven Muslim-majority countries, or violent extremism.

During one of the 2016 Democratic Presidential Debates (November 14, 2015), presidential candidates Sanders, Clinton, and O"Malley debated whether or not the US was at war with Islam. In this debate, all three used the voiceless consonant, /ɪsˈläm/. In contrast during an interview with ABC News" George Stephanopoulos, Republican presidential candidate Marco Rubio explains that America is at war with radical Islam, using the voiced consonant /ɪzˈläm/ (Oprea 2016). The co-occurrence of the voiced consonant in constructions where Islam is preceded by "radical" and followed by "terrorism" such as Trump's first speech to Congress on February 28, 2017 where the one time he mentioned Islam was in its adjectival form to describe criminal behavior: "Our obligation is to serve, protect, and defend the citizens of the United States. We are also taking strong measures to protect our Nation from Radical Islamic Terrorism" (Trump 2017). These individually-produced phonemic differences are embedded in digitally recorded videos, posted on various internet platforms and websites, and shared by media users, functioning as indexical markers of political values to the broader White digital public sphere. On right-wing media outlets, some argued that the voiceless consonant was evidence of pro-Muslim, pro-immigrant, and even un-American sentiments (Oprea 2016). When we cross-analyze this metacommentary on pronunciation with the larger media story about Islam/Muslims, the substance and form often focuses on how the foreign, immigrant "Muslim" subject is only relevant to immigration and foreign policy issues, specifically regarding the ongoing War on Terror.

A final example for how this operates is when Hoda Katebi, a Muslim-American fashion blogger, was interviewed on Chicago's WGN News to speak about her book *Tehran Streetstyle* (LeSavage 2018). The interviewer then switched to asking about nuclear weapons and Iran, to which Katebi offered a critical response that acknowledged the legacy of imperialism and colonization in the Middle East. To this, the interviewer stated: "A lot of Americans might take offense to that. You're an American, you don't sound like an American when you say [that]." Here a young woman was told she did not *sound* American, despite having a standard American accent, because her political ideologies might be offensive to "a lot of Americans," i.e. the larger White public sphere.

Interventions on the Figure of the "Muslim" in America

Many individuals, think tanks, non-profit organizations, and media companies have focused their work on countering the negative and racist stereotypes about Muslim figure circulating in media, politics, and education. For example, the Institute for Social Policy and Understanding develop research projects that empower "American Muslims to develop their community and fully contribute to democracy and pluralism in the United States." Through this work, they hope to offer media and policymakers evidence-based strategies to counter Islamophobia. Focusing on the Black Muslim experience, Sapelo Square develops online materials that "celebrate and analyze the experiences of Black Muslims in the United States to create new understandings of who they are, what they have done, and why that matters." The Yaqeen Institute for Islamic Research, conducts research and public outreach work to counter claims by both Islamophobes and extremists that Islam is incompatible with modernity. Within these and other organizations, people speak publicly about countering anti-Muslim racism. Linda Sarsour, a Palestinian-American activist and co-organizer of the 2017 Women's March, speaks against anti-Muslim racism but also contributes to the national progressive movement through the organization MPower Change, a Muslim grassroots movement. Activist Amani Al-Khatahtbeh created her website (MuslimGirl.com) to give young Muslim women a platform for their experiences of living and working in America. The Nexus Fund, a secular think tank, is developing efforts to counter hate speech in the US, with the concern that certain populations such as women, LGBTQIA persons, and Muslims are especially vulnerable. Their "Dangerous Speech Global Fund" supports work to understand and counter hate speech that can catalyze mass violence in communities around the world – including the United States.

Conclusion

Since 2016, Americans have experienced intense political and ideological divisiveness. In this context, positions on the Muslim question become a litmus test for political allegiance. For Muslims, it is particularly precarious as we must address daily encounters with discrimination in a panoptic climate, where one's name, language use, dress, words or action can be seen as anti-American and threatening to national security. In other words, Muslims living in America experience a kind of conditional citizenship that hinges on a continuous process of transracialization, of where they must prove their loyalty to the state or be racialized as an aggressor/enemy of the state. The challenge for social justice scholars and activists is critiquing this emergent racial formation and by highlighting the hypocrisies of anti-Muslim racism and connecting this phenomenon to other forms of racism, anti-Semitism, and xenophobia..

References

Alim, Samy. (2016). "Who's Afraid of the Transracial Subject?: Raciolinguistics and the Political Project of Transracialization." In *Raciolinguistics: How Language Shapes our Ideas about Race*, edited by Samy Alim, John Rickford, and Aretha Ball, 33–50. New York: Oxford University Press.

Baker, Paul, Gabrielatos, Costas, and Tony McEnery. (2013). *Discourse Analysis and Media Attitudes: The Representation of Islam in the British Press*. Cambridge: Cambridge University Press.

Baugh, John. (2003). Linguistic Profiling. In *Black Linguistics: Language Society and Politics in Africa and the Americas*, edited by Sinfree Makoni, Geneva Smitherman, Arnetha F. Ball and Arthur K. Spears, 155–168. London: Routledge.

Beydoun, Khalid. (2018). *American Islamophobia: Understanding the roots and rise of fear*. Oakland: University of California University Press.

Brumfield, Ben. (2015). "All Schools Shut Down in Augusta County, Virginia, Over Islam Homework." *CNN*, 19 December. Retrieved from http://edition.cnn. com/2015/12/18/us/virginia-school-shut-islam-homework.

CAIR. (2013). "Growing in Faith: California Muslim Youth Experiences with Bullying, Harassment and Religious Accommodation in Schools." Retrieved from http:// ca.cair.com/downloads/GrowingInFaith.pdf.

Carr, James. (2016). *Experiences of Islamophobia: Living with Racism in a Neoliberal era*. London: Routledge.

Grewal, Zareena. (2013). *Islam Is a Foreign Country: American Muslims and the Global Crisis of Authority*. New York: New York University Press.

Hall, Stuart. (1997). "Race, The Floating Signifier." Media Education Foundation. Retrieved from www.mediaed.org/transcripts/Stuart-Hall-Race-the-Floating-Signifier-Transcript.pdf.

Hill, Jane. (1998). "Language, Race, and White Public Space." *American Anthropologist* 100(3): 680–689.

Huntington, Samuel. (1993). "The Clash of Civilizations?" *Foreign Affairs* 72(3): 22–49.

Jakobson, Roman. (1971). *Selected Writings, vol. 2: Word and Language*. The Hague: Mouton.

LeSavage, Halie. (2018). "Fashion Blogger Hoda Katebi on Her Viral WGN News Interview: 'This Happens All the Time' (Updated)." *Glamour*, 16 February. Retrieved from www.glamour.com/story/hoda-katebi-blogger-wgn-news-interview.

Omi, Michael and Howard Winant. (2015). *Racial Formation in the United States* (3rd ed.). New York: Routledge.

Oprea, M. G. (2016). "How You Pronounce "Muslim" Says A Lot About Your Politics." *The Federalist*, 6 January. Retrieved from http://thefederalist.com/2016/01/06/how-you-pronounce-muslim-says-a-lot-about-your-politics/#disqus_thread.

Prashad, Vijay. (2001). *Everybody Was Kung Fu Fighting: Afro-Asian Connections and the Myth of Cultural Purity*. Boston, MA: Beacon Press.

Rampell, Catherine. (2016). "Ivy League Economist Ethnically Profiled, Interrogated for Doing Math on American Airlines Flight." *The Washington Post*, 7 May. Retrieved from www.washingtonpost.com/news/rampage/wp/2016/05/07/ivy-league-economist-interrogated-for-doing-math-on-american-airlines-flight/?utm_term=.c5b503 8c73ba.

Rana, Junaid. (2011). *Terrifying Muslims*. Durham: Duke University Press.

Revesz, Rachel. (2016). "Southwest Airlines kicks Muslim off a plane for saying "inshallah," meaning "God willing" in Arabic." *Independent*, 5 October. Retrieved from www.independent.co.uk/news/world/americas/muslim-passenger-southwest-airlines-khairuldeen-makhzoom-arabic-phone-uncle-baghdad-cair-statement-a7347311.html.

Said, Edward. (1978). *Orientalism*. New York: Pantheon Books.

Shyrock, Andrew. (2010). "Introduction: Islam as an Object of Fear and Affection." In *Islamophobia/Islamophilia: Beyond the Politics of Enemy and Friend*, edited by Andrew Shyrock, 1–28. Bloomington, IN: Indiana University Press.

Silverstein, Michael. (1976). "Shifters, Linguistic Categories, and Cultural Description." In *Meaning in Anthropology*, edited by Keith H. Basso and Henry A. Selby, 11–55. Albuquerque, NM: University of New Mexico Press.

Thanagaraj, Stanley. (Under review). "Between White and Islam: Contradictory Kurdish American Performances of Difference." *American Quarterly*.

Trump, Donald. (2017). "Donald Trump's Congress Speech (Full Text)." Retrieved from www.cnn.com/2017/02/28/politics/donald-trump-speech-transcript-full-text/index.html.

Wang, Frances Kai-Hwa. (2016). "Sikh Man Falsely Accused of Terrorism Demands Accountability for Accusers." *NBC News*, 29 October. Retrieved from www.nbcnews.com/news/asian-america/sikh-man-falsely-accused-terrorism-demands-accountability-accusers-n564311.

5 Languages of Liberation
Digital Discourses of Emphatic Blackness

Krystal A. Smalls

Introduction

In the careful naming of Black Lives Matter (BLM) and the Movement for Black Lives,, we glimpse the articulation of an emphatic and insurgent mode of blackness that is hardly new but that has found categorically new technologies of signification. Through its hashtag circulation, the unambiguous statement of, and demand for, value is unadorned yet fundamentally upsetting in a world that raucously declares the darkest bodies the least valuable. Just the utterance of this phrase can excavate deeply buried anxieties and resentments, even as it exposes carefully entombed black pain and rage. But beyond its appellation and the necessary signifying that it does, the movement itself has engendered structural transformation in U.S. polities large and small and has provided the social justice organizing blueprint for a generation. And, in tandem with its other ideological and material feats, BLM has prompted and provided the tools for the cultivation of a new kind of black public space—digital space (Taylor 2016).

The kind of digital space discussed in this chapter is widely referred to as "social media," or websites and applications that allow users to directly communicate with one another. From the deeply esoteric to the easily translatable, the language of black social media (the discourses, lexicons, dialects [textually demonstrated through phonologically accurate spelling conventions]) is frequently used for veritable acts of protest. The following pages explore such uses of identifiably black, and often "unrespectable," language (African American English, Jamaican Patois, Ghanaian Pidgin, racialized youth slangs, etc.) and examine how these uses employ verbal and visual texts to affirm the value of black bodies, minds, and hearts through productions of a sincere (Jackson 2005) and emphatic blackness, which I define as widely recognizable and emphasized racialized practices. The analysis demonstrates how these linguistic and discursive acts of protest, whether through indirect humor or very direct censure, collectively fashion black public space where black voices and lives indubitably matter.

"Black Twitter"

The image shown in Figure 5.1 was created by scholar-artist John Jennings and "remixes" (to use the artist's phrasing; Howard 2015) what most would

Figure 5.1 John Jennings' "Remixed" Twitter Bird.

agree are two examples of iconic imagery (in the parochial sense and in the most scholarly semiotic sense): the logo for the social media site Twitter and "the raised fist." Each image invokes power in different ways, bringing to the fore the complex ways it is reproduced, mediated, experienced, challenged and transformed.

The "Twitter bird" is the logo for a social media powerhouse that, via 140 characters or less, has helped to change the courses of many people's careers and personal lives. It boasts more than one billion user accounts, of which more than 300 million are actually logged into each month. But it is the immediate and successive "uptake" (Agha 2011), or reception, of tweets that makes Twitter such an important mediator of culture and politics. Scholars of new media studies, including those who conduct digital ethnography, take seriously the individual and collective impact of the uptake of media artifacts from Twitter and other major platforms like Youtube, Instagram, Tumblr, Snapchat, Vine, Reddit, Worldstar Hip Hop, and Facebook –some of which have vastly wider networks of circulation. For example, Facebook is reported to host more than 1.5 billion monthly active users (MAUs) and Youtube is said to host just around 1 billion (Protalinksi 2016; Muruganandam 2016).

The other component of this mash-up—the raised fist—is iconic (i.e., literally representative) of physical strength and indexical (i.e., contextually referential) of political resistance for most. For the artist, myself, and many others, the raised fist, and the recoloring of the logo, also index an enduring social movement of black liberation that originated in a particular historical moment in the United States: a moment when young activists cleaved from a broader Civil Rights Movement and began agitating not for inclusion in an unethical political structure, but for the fundamental dismantling of said structure. The merging of the oft-recycled symbol of the Black Power Movement with the neoteric Twitter bird visually signifies how that past period of concentrated insurgence and unrest is inextricable from the present. It declares this moment a present in which those myriad exigencies of the 1960s and 70s that threatened black life and well-being are very much intact, even if reconfigured. The persistence of these exigencies has been made excruciatingly clear by the increase of viral footage of unarmed black people being killed by police (from Michael Brown in Ferguson, Missouri in 2014 to Terence Crutcher's murder in Oklahoma in the fall of 2016). However, this particular piece, Jennings said, was specifically inspired by the horrific mass shooting of nine people in a Charleston Church in June 2015 by a young white supremacist vigilante (Gunn 2016). He explained that the tragedy moved him to create and share an "open-source icon that could be used as a symbol of solidarity" (ibid.).

The visual remix Jennings created also signifies a present that we may understand as a markedly new moment: a moment when "hashtag activism," or social media activism, becomes an essential component of some of the most important social justice movements of our time—from the "Arab Spring" in 2011 to BLM since 2013 to Standing Rock since 2016. Yarimar Bonilla and Jonathan Rosa assess the impact of social media activism and consider the ways new technologies engender different kinds of sociality. In particular, they illuminate how our changing engagement with space and time via digital technology helps to produce "a shared political temporality," or a sense of connection and involvement in "real-time" (Bonilla and Rosa 2015, 4) that is chronologically situated in an unfolding history of racialized oppression.

In many episodes of its digital dissemination, it was suggested that Jennings had successfully created the emblem of the epiphenomenon "Black Twitter." To be clear, Black Twitter is not a distinct digital platform but, rather, a virtual network of mostly US-based, black-identified, multiethnic social media users that functions within extensive platforms like, but not only, Twitter. This repurposing of a largely "white public space" (Hill 1998) like Twitter or Facebook to perform blackness and produce anti-racist political discourse follows a long tradition of subjugated black peoples politicizing and re-racializing places and practices in pursuit of joy and liberation (Hartman 1997).

"Black Twitter," which for many is shorthand for "black social media" writ large is a dynamic virtual space that is constantly created and experienced through digitized conversation between and about black people. These conversations span everything from gossiping about celebrities, to identifying and commiserating about "microaggressions" (i.e., racism or sexism) at work, to collecting signatures for petitions, to organizing die-ins and other collective acts of protest. It is also the launch pad for countless hashtags, emojis, and memes related to the black experience.

Most significantly, Black Twitter is, effectively, the birthplace of BLM. One component of the broader Movement for Black Lives network, the Black Lives Matter movement was the innovation of organizers Alicia Garza, Patrisse Cullors, and Opal Tometti and that took form through the creation and circulation of the blacklivesmatter hashtag after the acquittal of 17-year-old Trayvon Martin's murderer in 2013. Their hashtag and myriad projects coalesced into a contemporary "freedom ride" to Ferguson, Missouri after 18-year-old unarmed

Michael Brown was killed by police officer Darryl Wilson and protestors took to the streets.

In their description of the political and cultural disruption that was immediately historicized as "Ferguson," Bonilla and Rosa (2015) explain that "[d]uring the initial week of protests, over 3.6 million posts appeared on Twitter documenting and reflecting on the emerging details surrounding Michael Brown's death; by the end of the month, "#Ferguson" had appeared more than eight million times on the Twitter platform." Prodded by the video-recorded extrajuridical murders of Eric Garner, Walter Scott, Laquan McDonald, Tamir Rice, and Walter Scott, along with the recorded inhumane treatment of Sandra Bland before her highly suspicious and tragic death, numerous digital derivatives of #BlackLivesMatter and #BLM have emerged since the summer of 2014, and have been passionately deployed to affirm the value of black life. Some of these included an emoji of a surrendering silhouette and the hashtags #HandsUpDontShoot, #NotOneMore, #ICantBreathe, #SayHerName, and #IfIDieInPoliceCustody.

This chapter briefly explores some examples of digitized multimodal conversations, or digital discourses, that are directly and indirectly connected to a current racial justice movement. Specifically, I introduce and apply the concept of "emphatic blackness" to help read such discourses as a performative racial schema and as part of an enduring mode of survival that is being transformed vis-à-vis new art forms and new technologies of expression and sociality. I then present examples of digital significations of emphatic blackness and finally, I underscore the significance (and sacredness) of this kind of work by positioning it as the legitimate and thriving offspring of earlier racial justice movements.

Public Emphatic Blackness

When examining the following examples of stigmatized black languaging in digital discourse, we must consider the ways digital space is always already a "white public space" and how "public" has historically been correlated with whiteness, exposure, and danger. Discursively, this sensibility has been conveyed in many African American communities by discussing what is and is not appropriate in "mixed company," proverbializing the black community as "home" (and therefore as part of the private sphere), and reciting the dangers of airing our collective dirty laundry in public, for example.

The whiteness of public space is plainly evident linguistically, according to Jane Hill (1998). She explains that white public space is made in part by the policing and hypervisibility of verbal language produced by non-white people and by the simultaneous normalization and invisibility of verbal language produced by white people. When we also consider that white public space, virtual and physical, can be truly treacherous because it engenders a social and political climate in which one may lose their rights or life at any moment, then conscious uses of black language in white space are not simply "inappropriate" but could be considered subversive in many cases.

Specifically, using stigmatized/marginalized/othered language varieties that are widely indexical of particular models of blackness (Alim and Smitherman 2012; Delpit 2013; Matory 2015; Rickford 2002; Smitherman 1977, 2006) in social media is one important modality of emphatic blackness. By and large, these statuses and circulated memes use varieties either deemed "creoles" or "dialects" that were created by black people in conditions of subjugation and that partly functioned as means of survival (Morgan 1993; Spears 1999). In the most generous of metalinguistic discourses produced—mostly by non-speakers— these varieties are regarded as simplified or entertaining or indicative of a kind of romanticized authenticity—and in the worst discourses, they are regarded as abominable, unintelligent, and *unintelligible*. For many, regardless of hue, a rubric of antiblackness often renders these ways of speaking "unrespectable" at the very least, especially in white public space.

I understand the following examples of language from various social media posts (often the text of photographic memes) as performative acts of emphatic blackness:

1　*"Dis is some bullshit"* (African American English)
　　"This is some bullshit"

2　*"Niggas trippin"*
　　"People are acting crazy"

3　*"Tenki tenki fa all de blessin and support hunnuh da gee we!"* (Gullah/ Geechee)
　　"Thank you thank you for all the blessings and support you have given us!"

4　*"Tek di what and leave di what?"* (Jamaican Patois)
　　"Take the what and leave the what?"

5　*"Da real bad luck we see in Liberia oh!!!"* (Liberian English)
　　"We"re having really bad luck in Liberia, oh!"

6　*"You say wetin?"* (Liberian English)
　　"What did you say?"

To reiterate, public emphatic blackness is hardly new, as historical figures like Amiri Baraka, Nina Simone, Huey P. Newton, or even Petey Green make clear, and many of the critiques those figures endured are being revived for the BLM generation. In many evaluations of their performative schemas we hear a concern about what white people might think (or, feel), and also a profound and well-warranted fear of how substantiations of stereotypes could be transmuted into actions with material consequences (the loss of employment, the invitation of state-sanctioned violence, social alienation, voter suppression, etc.). Protection from such material consequences provided the fundamental rationale for a "politics of respectability" since the early years of the Civil Rights Movement, as Evelyn Brooks Higginbotham (1993) has explained. She and others describe respectability politics as a cogent strategy for being legible as people who are worthy of civic rights like voting. Further applications of the theory help us understand how dressing, eating, worshipping, family planning, walking, and talking in "respectable" ways also aid in one's legibility as human, and thereby help position one as deserving of basic human rights like not being lynched or raped or beaten or shot with impunity, as well as the right to adequate living conditions. However, the censuring and censoring that much respectability politics metes out onto those black lives that can't or won't meet its measures—especially, gender non-binary and transgender black people—has been a justifiable cause for urgent concern and action for many people.

In addition to "anti-respectable" memes affirming a macroscopic black trans humanity, some posts by black social media users openly critique whiteness, and even white *people* specifically, enlisting verbal registers that range from the most erudite to the most stigmatized. For example, the hashtag "#wypipo" ("white people") gained popularity in 2016 and articulates a deliberately exaggerated African American English phonology. Significantly, *wypipo* illustrates the ongoing creation of "shallow" orthographic-conventions (Rickford 1999) in social media that signify more accurate African American English pronunciations (not taking regional variation into account) of certain lexemes—such as *lawd* ("Lord"), *lawt* ("Lord"), *bruh* ("bro," i.e. "brother"—and phrasal contractions—such as *ima* ("I'm going to"), *talmbout* ("talking about") and *ion* ("I don't"). Also, some users report using *wypipo* as a resourceful attempt to thwart censorship by social media platforms like Facebook that prohibit what it deems to be hate speech.

Other posts, such as one "selfie" (a self-shot photograph of oneself) of a shirtless full-figured, brown-skinned feminine person wearing an expansive afro hairstyle, employ bodies as semiotic texts to help digitally mediate emphatic blackness. Through such images, which semiotically render black bodies as corporeal texts that are read alongside verbal and other visual co-text, we see (or hear) individuals scream a grammar of difference that was written onto the black body many centuries ago (Fanon [1952]2008).

Discussion

These visual and linguistic significations are moored to a tradition of intellectual and political resistance and continue the project of countering European modernity's racial logics—those illogical logics that have created the "racializing assemblages" (Weheliye 2014) of the modern state that effectively prohibit black bodies from full citizenship and that leave them dangling from the bottom rung of humanity, as Sylvia Wynter has told it (2003). Like their predecessors, these young digital dissenters are not asking for permission to speak and they are not privileging white comfort over black freedom, collective or personal. Where they tend to depart from their forebears, however, is in *how* they speak this freedom in different contexts. The practice of using the "n-word," African American English, or Nigerian Pidgin English, for example, in the presence of "mixed company," is not so much a practice of inappropriateness and anti-sociality, but a practice of refusal. Specifically, these usages can be read as refusals of the performances of respectability demanded by white supremacy vis-à-vis white normativity (Simpson 2014). In effect, many of these emphatically black agitators are simply refusing to translate themselves, even though they know some audience members may not find their words or humanity intelligible.

In many ways, these individuals are not only countering and interrupting, but are also performatively disrupting dominant racial logics when they simultaneously deploy linguistic, discursive, musical, kinesthetic, sartorial and other kinds of signs that have been racialized as categorically, and often unrespectably, black in tandem with deafening declarations of an uncontested humanity. Thusly, they are insisting that all manner of black *ways of being* survive white supremacy.

These digital "acts of identity" (LePage and Tabouret-Keller 1985), or "semiotic acts of identification" (Bucholtz and Hall 2005), externalize some aspect of the ways these young people may be experiencing themselves: as categorically black and indisputably human. True to a radical tradition, their identity work and, presumably, their political agenda, if aligned with the BLM movement, is not *proving* black humanity to an irrational white supremacy, but is simply demanding fundamental changes necessary for black humanity to be realized (Taylor 2016). In some of these acts of performative dissent, one tacit demand is for a raciolinguistic ideological restructuring that decouples certain linguistic practices from certain notions about black personhood (Flores and Rosa 2015; Smalls 2010).

Conclusion

These digitally mediated words and images are more than just provocative tidbits of popular culture and they are more than demonstrations of the dialogism between individual agency and structural power. When articulated through individuals whose bodies have been raced as black and who understand themselves (and their histories and communities) through or against dominant antiblack racial logics, these posts are also more than the communicative expressions of millennials but may be something closer to verbal significations of subversion and survival.

I have read particular discursive acts of emphatic blackness on social media as largely intentional and informed attempts to survive and push against antiblackness. From that stance, I encourage reconsiderations of what some have neatly bundled as behaviors reflecting self-hate, or internalized racism, or ignorance, and that others have dismissed as "merely" symbolic or gossamer attempts at social justice.

Altogether, their digitally mediated grimaces, discomforting language, visible rage, unapologetic self-love, candid self-loathing, deviant disregard, and so on, compel all of us to continue grappling with the complexities of black subjectivity and the ways it transpires in the afterlife of slavery (Hartman 1997). And, in this particular moment of that long afterlife, when digital sociality is no longer a tangential or optional mode of being for so many black young people around the world, we must bear witness to their intensely public mediation of a subjectivity that is emphatically human *and* emphatically black, and consider how such significations may alter the dominant grammar of humanity over time.

References

Agha, Asif. 2011. "Meet Mediatization." *Language and Communication* 31(3): 163–70. https://doi.org/10.1016/j.langcom.2011.03.006.

Alim, H. Samy, and Geneva Smitherman. 2012. *Articulate While Black: Barack Obama, Language, and Race in the U.S.* Oxford: Oxford University Press.

Bonilla, Yarimar, and Jonathan Rosa. 2015. "#Ferguson: Digital Protest, Hashtag Ethnography, and the Racial Politics of Social Media in the United States." *American Ethnologist* 42(1): 4–17.

Bucholtz, Mary, and Kira Hall. 2005. "Identity and Interaction: A Sociocultural Linguistic Approach." *Discourse Studies* 7(4–5): 585–614. https://doi.org/10.1177/1461445605054407.

Delpit, Lisa. 2013. *The Skin That We Speak: Thoughts on Language and Culture in the Classroom.* New York: New Press.

Fanon, Frantz. [1952]2008. *Black Skin, White Masks.* Translated by Richard Philcox. Revised edition. New York: Grove Press.

Flores, Nelson, and Jonathan Rosa. 2015. "Undoing Appropriateness: Raciolinguistic Ideologies and Language Diversity in Education." *Harvard Educational Review* 85(2): 149–171.

Gunn, Seven. 2016. "John Jennings on Graphic Arts and Afrocentricism." Accessed January 20, 2017 at www.chicagonow.com/seven-gunn-says/2016/12/john-jennings-on-graphic-arts-and-afrocentricism.

Hartman, Saidiya V. 1997. *Scenes of Subjection: Terror, Slavery, and Self-Making in Nineteenth-Century America.* Oxford: Oxford University Press.

Higginbotham, Evelyn Brooks. 1993. *Righteous Discontent: The Women's Movement in the Black Baptist Church, 1880–1920.* Cambridge, MA: Harvard University Press.

Hill, Jane H. 1998. "Language, Race, and White Public Space." *American Anthropologist* 100(3): 680–89. https://doi.org/10.1525/aa.1998.100.3.680.

Howard, Sheena C. 2015. "Black Art: Why The Artistic Commentary of John Jennings Is So Important." *Huffington Post* (blog). December 30, 2015. Accessed at www.huffingtonpost.com/sheena-c-howard/post_10765_b_8892290.html.

Jackson, John L. 2005. *Real Black: Adventures in Racial Sincerity.* Chicago, IL: University of Chicago Press.

LePage, Robert Brock, and Andrée Tabouret-Keller. 1985. *Acts of Identity: Creole-Based Approaches to Language and Ethnicity.* Cambridge: Cambridge University Press.

Matory, J. Lorand. 2015. *Stigma and Culture: Last-Place Anxiety in Black America*. Chicago, IL: University of Chicago Press.

Morgan, Marcyliena. 1993. "The Africanness of Counterlanguage among Afro-Americans." In *Africanisms in Afro-American Language Varieties*, edited by Salikoko Mufwene and Nancy Condon, 423–435. Athens, GA: University of Georgia Press.

Muruganandam, Cent. 2016. "Social Media Monthly Active Users for 2016—Infographic." *Your Escape From 9 to 5* (blog). January 26. Accessed at https://yourescapefrom9to5.com/social-media-monthly-active-users-infographic.

Protalinksi, Emil. 2016. "Facebook Passes 1.65 Billion Monthly Active Users, 54% Access the Service Only on Mobile." VentureBeat. Accessed at users-54-access-the-service-only-on-mobile/.

Rickford, John Russell. 1999. *African American Vernacular English: Features, Evolution, Educational Implications*. Hoboken, NJ: Wiley-Blackwell.

Rickford, John R. 2002. *Spoken Soul: The Story of Black English*. Hoboken, NJ: Wiley.

Simpson, Audra. 2014. *Mohawk Interruptus: Political Life across the Borders of Settler States*. Durham, NC: Duke University Press.

Smalls, Krystal A. 2010. "Flipping the Script: (Re)constructing Personhood through Hip Hop Languaging in a U.S. High School." *Working Papers in Educational Linguistics* 25(2): 35–54.

Smitherman, Geneva. 1977. *Talkin and Testifyin: The Language of Black America*. Detroit, MI: Wayne State University Press.

Smitherman, Geneva. 2006. *Word from the Mother: Language and African Americans*. New York: Routledge.

Spears, Arthur Kean. 1999. *Race and Ideology: Language, Symbolism, and Popular Culture*. Detroit, MI: Wayne State University Press.

Taylor, Keeanga-Yamahtta. 2016. *From #BlackLivesMatter to Black Liberation*. Chicago, IL: Haymarket Books.

Weheliye, Alexander G. 2014. *Habeas Viscus: Racializing Assemblages, Biopolitics, and Black Feminist Theories of the Human*. Durham, NC: Duke University Press.

Wynter, Sylvia. 2003. "Unsettling the Coloniality of Being/Power/Truth/Freedom: Towards the Human, After Man, Its Overrepresentation—An Argument." *CR: The New Centennial Review* 3(3): 257–337.

Part II

Language and Education

Introduction

The chapters in this section emphasize language education as a critical mechanism for leveling social inequities and expanding access to valuable resources for all communities. The ways in which the authors portray the intersection of language, education, and social justice illustrate the existence of social hierarchies of power as well as the ideological assumptions that maintain them. By examining contexts where minoritized languages and/or dialects confront dominant norms of communication, the authors in this section point out how/why certain linguistic forms are situated to either perpetuate or limit access to information, civic participation, and networks of interaction. The case studies here describe a variety of ways that language emerges as a central focus of educational policies and programs, spanning formal classroom/school settings to community-based education efforts. Specific topics include: promoting equity through dual language programs; analyzing legislation to expand heritage language literacy programs; illustrating the social influence of the "language gap" concept; and highlighting the impact of translanguaging in a community library. Collectively, these examples demonstrate that a social justice approach to language and education requires developing programs and policies that meet the linguistic and educational needs of minoritized groups while also honoring the language patterns of local communities. This process involves providing communities the tools and conditions to take ownership of their learning and make their own decisions without facing linguistic discrimination.

Critical Questions

As you read these cases, we encourage you to consider the following questions:

1   Why is language a critical element for accessing education?
2   How is language use regulated to either increase or limit access to education?
3   In what ways has your own language background shaped your educational experiences?

6   Issues of Equity in Dual Language Bilingual Education

Kathryn I. Henderson, Lina Martín-Corredor, and Genevieve Caffrey

Because the United States is a country of immigrants, children bring rich, complex ways of speaking into our schools. Students arrive to classrooms with varying levels of competency in their native language, English, and other communicative patterns that utilize their native language and English, such as "Spanglish." A long tradition of educational scholarship demonstrates that sustained native language education increases children's self-esteem and confidence, enhances motivation for learning, increases cognition and academic achievement, strengthens family relationships, and provides a strong basis for learning a second language (Callahan and Gándara 2014; Cummins 1984). More recent education research demonstrates the importance of valuing *all* kinds of student language practices, including non-standard vernaculars, in classrooms for academic success and socio-emotional well-being (García, Johnson and Seltzer 2016). Bilingual education is a social justice issue because of its potential to provide a meaningful, equitable education for linguistically diverse children, promote the status of minoritized languages, discontinue segregation, and improve appreciation of diverse cultures (García 2009). However, schools in the U.S. continue to struggle with responding to the linguistic complexities children bring to classrooms and implementing programs in a socially just way.

Numerous education policies seek to assimilate linguistically diverse children—often referred to as English Learners (ELs)—by prohibiting, limiting or devaluing the use of their native language in schools. ELs did not receive legal support until 1974 when the Supreme Court decided in *Lau v. Nichols* that schools violated the Civil Rights Act of 1964 because classroom instruction and curriculum did not serve ELs effectively. This decision paved the way for the development of bilingual education programs across the country in which teachers provide academic instruction in both English and the ELs' native language. Nonetheless, the goal of many bilingual education programs still aims to "transition" students to the exclusive use of English as quickly as possible (García 2009). In contrast, *Dual Language Bilingual Education* (DLBE) programs seek to promote student bilingualism, biliteracy, and biculturalism. DLBE programs consider speaking multiple languages as a right, rather than a problem (Ruiz 1984). "One-way" DLBE programs (also called maintenance programs) serve ELs only while "two-way" DLBE programs integrate ELs and native English speakers. DLBE represents an approach to education with considerable potential for social justice, specifically the valuing of cultural and linguistic diversity.

Although DLBE programs have proved successful in many contexts (Collier and Thomas 2004), historical and current events continue to create challenges and tensions. In 2002, the U.S. Congress passed the No Child Left Behind (NCLB) Act, which removed the term "bilingual" from national educational legislation. Around the same time, California, Massachusetts, and Arizona passed propositions banning bilingual education. The election of Donald Trump and an increase in anti-immigrant rhetoric creates new challenges for DLBE programs. Furthermore, bilingual education researchers continue to discover ways in which two-way DLBE program implementation disproportionately serves native English speakers, and, in some instances, reproduces and reinforces societal inequalities rather than disrupts them (Cervantes-Soon 2014; Valdés 1997). Now, more than ever, it is imperative to protect and promote DLBE programs and ensure that they are implemented in equitable and socially just ways.

Social justice promotes the examination of the learning conditions and barriers that students from low-income and racially/ethnically minoritized backgrounds encounter at school in order to effectively promote all students' active and full participation in a democratic society (Villegas 2007). Unfortunately, there are multiple obstacles and issues of equity in DLBE. High-stakes standardized testing often undermines two-way DLBE programs because ELs have to take the same English language assessments as their native English-speaking classmates, which results in skewed perceptions of ELs' knowledge and abilities" (Menken 2008). Additionally, enrollment and admission policies disproportionately favor white English-speakers (Palmer 2010; Pimentel et al. 2008).

Furthermore, ELs do not usually receive equal access to instruction and instructional materials in their native language (Torres-Guzmán et al. 2005), which increases English speakers' ability to dominate classroom conversation (Palmer 2009), and decreases ELs' opportunities for bilingual development (Bearse and de Jong 2008). Finally, not enough DLBE teachers are bilingual themselves, nor sufficiently trained in how to critically understand and serve their linguistically diverse population or provide equitable instruction to all of their students (Palmer and Martínez 2013). Teachers often limit classroom spaces for the use of non-standard varieties such as Spanglish or African American Vernacular, which devalues students' home, family, and community languages (García 2009). In sum, DLBE programs are at high risk to reinforce the very societal inequalities that bilingual education sought out to diminish.

Here, we seek to illuminate social justice issues in DLBE from a teacher-oriented perspective. We address the following question: How do DLBE teachers identify and discuss issues of equity in a DLBE program implementation?

The Case: Issues of Equity in District-Wide DLBE Implementation in Texas

Our case takes place in a large urban district in Texas in its fourth year implementing a district-wide DLBE program in over 60 schools. We surveyed, interviewed, and observed teachers in the DLBE programs in their schools and recorded/documented their theories about language. Several equity issues emerged in our data, which we categorize into four main themes: (a) student participation; (b) parent involvement; (c) assessment; and (d) language standardization. We discuss each of these themes in the section below.

Student Participation: "The Dual Language Classrooms had the Crème de la Crème"

A central issue of equity in DLBE is the method by which educators place children in the programs (Pimentel et al. 2008). Some teachers expressed concern that student placement practices in DLBE can be problematic and lead to segregation. Two-way DLBE pre-K teacher, Janice, noted the unfair selection process, "pre-K dual language was not open to everybody. Students were pulled from the population who had 'good' verbal skills, who had no behavior issues, who were not Special Ed." Janice warned her principal that this selection process promoted segregation.

A third grade teacher, Rose, similarly recognized that the native English speakers participating in the two-way DLBE program at her school were predominantly white and wealthy, which resulted in inequitable treatment of different classrooms in the same school, "he [the principal] specifically planned to have this group excel and didn't worry about the other ones." Students scored higher in the two-way DLBE classroom than all other classrooms. Rose explained, "all of a sudden their scores got skewed. The dual language kids, the dual language classrooms had the crème de la crème of the population." Educators intended to improve student academic experiences with DLBE implementation, yet segregationist placement practices exacerbated existing differences in student performance.

Parent Involvement: "Some of the Parents Feel that They are Being Pushed Out"

Parental involvement in a child's education is crucial for academic success. For culturally and linguistically diverse students, parental involvement is highly contingent upon the school's ability to make parents feel as if they are valued members of the school community (Nieto 2010). While one teacher in our study noted administrators' concerted efforts to include and value parents of ELs, a majority of the two-way DLBE teachers observed some form of parental exclusion or "benevolent racism" by the white, English-speaking families reflecting a "we-know-what's-best" attitude, positioning the language minoritized parents as lacking and inferior or needy (Villenas 2001, 4). Third-grade two-way DLBE teacher Tammy grappled with the effects of the economic dichotomy DLBE brought to her school:

> A lot of our parents don't feel as welcomed here as they used to. They are not as involved as they used to be . . . It used to be a more even playing field despite language, and now there is a lot more disparity socioeconomically that has brought a whole bunch of new challenges for us as a campus.

Tammy reported that several teachers and parents felt the wealthy families were not understanding of the socioeconomic differences.

Pre-K teacher, María, celebrated her school's efforts to value Spanish-speaking families by organizing ESL classes and Hispanic Heritage Nights; however, upon closer examination of María's comments and the schools' practices, we detected the same sense of benevolent racism as English-speaking parents controlled the events. Despite the efforts, María reported a decline in Spanish-speaking parent involvement: "I've noticed that the lower income, Spanish-speaking parents have kind of fallen to the side." This case demonstrates that mere event planning does not create a fully inclusive community.

Assessment: "The Test Wins, Period"

Multiple studies demonstrate the harmful effects of standardized testing as results are often used to make punitive decisions such as decreasing school funding, decreasing teacher salary, or preventing student graduation (Delgado 2014). Standardized testing is entirely in English and, thus, it can have a particularly harmful effect on ELs (Shohamy 2011). The participants in our study repeatedly claimed that testing was the main obstacle to the program and hindered the potential for equity in DLBE. Second grade teacher, Samantha, supported this assertion: "I think a lot of people would like it [DLBE] if we were truly doing what we needed to do for these kids, but it doesn't happen, and it never will, because the test wins, period." Also, teachers reported that DLBE was not being implemented the way it should be because of assessment pressure. Chrissy, a second-grade teacher, described her frustration with testing-related modifications: "They want me to go ahead and teach everybody in my class English for the rest of the year, and I think it's wrong." Teachers described additional harmful effects of testing on the program, including premature test emphasis (i.e., from Kindergarten), transition to English, concerns about punitive consequences, mismatches between language of instruction and language of assessment, and the generally unfair nature of ELs' assessments. Only one teacher, Samantha, a second-grade teacher, mentioned refusing to increase English instruction. The majority of teachers in this district identified negative effects of standardized testing, but felt no agency to change it.

Language Standardization: "You Can't Use Spanglish"

A more nuanced finding involved teacher beliefs about the role of nonstandard language varieties in equitable instructional practices. Most teachers felt that the program could only serve students justly by providing access to standard forms of English and Spanish. For example, Jill, a pre-K teacher, stated: "If you are going to teach Spanish, you need to the right way. You can't use Spanglish with the kids, you shouldn't . . . You want them to compete in the job market, right?" Jill's comment reflects the concern that using non-standard language practices will inhibit standard language acquisition, which research has thoroughly debunked (García 2009; Martínez 2010). Jill was dedicated to teaching Spanish "the right way," but this perspective implies the oppression and diminishment of students' home language variations. Indeed, more than three-quarters of the teachers interviewed described code-switching as something that needed to be "corrected." Three teachers articulated the perspective that students who engage predominantly in code-switching or Spanglish have "no language," calling into question these students' linguistic competency in their home language, and only legitimizing school-based language patterns.

While negative perceptions of non-standard languages were dominant in the district, some teachers displayed critical language views, and recognized the importance of valuing student home and community language practices, including Spanglish, for equity in DLBE (Sayer 2013). Maria, a Pre-K teacher said:

> They [DLBE programs] are designed for communities that already have a mixture of languages in the community, and want to try to include everyone, and make sure that this idea of an official language of the country or that you only need to speak English is not present.

Maria recognizes the "mixture of languages" in her school's community and directly challenges assimilationist ideologies. Third grade teacher, Michael, positions himself as a "major fan of code-switching" and deliberately uses Spanglish in the classroom to develop skills that allow students to analyze language. In Maria and Michael's opinion, the DLBE programs, and consequently, teachers, have the social responsibility to include all kinds of languages and language varieties in academic and social practices.

Implications for DLBE and Social Justice

The social justice issues that teachers identified in our research support prior work on issues of equity in DLBE. Student participation, parent involvement, assessment, and language standardization were central themes in our data that researchers have found as issues in other studies (Cervantes-Soon et al. 2017). Our work illuminates ways that these issues operate at the local level from educators' perspectives. The issues teachers identify in our study have the following policy implications for DLBE and social justice.

Fight for Equitable Student Participation

DLBE program implementation must deliberately address student participation from a social justice lens. Some teachers felt that certain students were systemically denied access to the program; this is illegal according to Chapter 89 in the Texas state policy and should be dealt with accordingly through legal avenues. Yet, in other cases, the inequitable student participation appeared to be based on variation in parent treatment and interest. In order to ensure that DLBE programs serve all students equitably, attention should be focused on recruitment practices and program implementation strategies that target to serve traditionally marginalized children, involving ELs and heritage language speakers.

Confront Familial Disparities and Break Down Barriers

The socioeconomic and racial disparities that often exist between families in DLBE programs need to be consciously confronted from a social justice perspective. Instead of assuming how minoritized parents should be involved, members of dominant groups need to be challenged to reflect critically on how their actions and attitudes, no matter how well intentioned, can silence and marginalize families. The definition of parental involvement must be expanded, and dominant group members need to listen carefully to minoritized families' concerns, as well as value and validate families' funds of knowledge (Moll et al. 1992). School community members must collaboratively problem solve on how to break down participation barriers, such as through home visits or using a participatory approach to parent workshops, to create a more inclusive, just community.

Recognize and Challenge the Monolingual Norms of Standardized Testing

Teachers in our study know that standardized testing is unfair, but many felt disenfranchised and unable to do anything about it. Teachers can investigate local opt-out testing policies and family rights to provide options to families. Teachers can also be introduced to Literacy Squared, a research-based teaching model that promotes biliteracy, and up-to-date research on bilingual theories to assess ELs on the combination of their language skills, rather than in just one language (Escamilla et al. 2014). Perhaps introducing the vision of a more equitable assessment format can provide a pathway to channel frustration and promote advocacy.

Promote Critical Language Awareness and Respect for Language Variation

The majority of teachers in our study believe that teaching standard academic language forms to EL students requires correcting and discouragement of the use of vernacular language varieties. Yet, fostering this linguistic environment in classrooms does not reflect students' sociolinguistic reality, particularly in the context of Texas (Sayer 2013). Professional development can empower teachers to reflect on their own language ideologies by introducing educators to research-based techniques that value and use language variation as a resource. A free, online handbook is available with instructional strategies (www. nysieb.ws.gc.cuny.edu) as well as teacher-oriented guides (García, Johnson and Seltzer 2016). Furthermore, teachers such as Mariana and Michael who value linguistic diversity can be identified in a school or district community to share ideas and approaches, which should be disseminated not only through meetings and informal conversations, but also publications and conferences.

Empower DLBE Teachers

One avenue to empower DLBE teachers is through continuous professional development rooted in a bottom-up approach that positions teachers as change agents to act upon the injustices they have detected. Professional development should emphasize teachers' central role as policymakers who interpret, negotiate, resist, and (re)create language policy (Menken and García 2010). In order for teachers to address inequalities in their classrooms, they need to develop a critical consciousness, which involves problematizing the history, culture, and societal configurations that brought particular students together in the first place and interrogate the role of power in the formation of oppressive conditions (Cervantes-Soon et al. 2017). Creating spaces for teachers to critically reflect on how to serve linguistically, socioeconomically, and racially diverse parents and students is of vital importance to provide equitable DLBE implementation and instruction for all students.

In the Texas district described here, access to instruction in more than one language was not always equitable, nor did it always result in educational equity or the creation of transformative spaces. In order for DLBE programs to disrupt existing power structures, policy makers must continue to listen to practicing DLBE teachers and empower them to critically reflect and take action.

References

Bearse, Carol, and Ester J. de Jong. 2008. "Cultural and Linguistic Investment: Adolescents in a Secondary Two-Way Immersion Program." *Equity & Excellence in Education* 41(3): 325–340.

Callahan, Rebecca M., and Patricia C. Gándara, eds. 2014. *The Bilingual Advantage: Language, Literacy and the US Labor Market*. Clevedon: Multilingual Matters.

Cervantes-Soon, Claudia G. 2014. "A Critical Look at Dual Language Immersion in the New Latin@ Diaspora." *Bilingual Research Journal* 37(1): 64–82.

Cervantes-Soon, Claudia. G., Lisa Dorner, Deborah Palmer, Dan Heiman, Rebecca Schwerdtfeger, and Jinmyung Choi. 2017. "Combating Inequalities in Two-Way

Language Immersion Programs: Toward Critical Consciousness in Bilingual Education Spaces." *Review of Research in Education* 41(1): 403–427.

Collier, Virginia P., and Wayne P. Thomas. 2004. "The Astounding Effectiveness of Dual Language Education for All." *NABE Journal of Research and Practice* 2(1): 1–20.

Cummins, Jim. 1984. *Bilingualism and Special Education: Issues in Assessment and Pedagogy*. Clevedon: Multilingual Matters.

Delgado, Richard. 2014. "Standardized Testing as Discrimination: A Reply to Dan Subotnik." *University of Massachusetts Law Review* 9(1): 100–107.

Escamilla, Kathy, Susan Hopewell, Sandra Butvilofsky, Wendy Sparrow, Lucinda Soltero-González, Olivia Ruiz-Figueroa, and Manuel Escamilla. 2014. *Biliteracy from the Start: Literacy Squared in Action*. Philadelphia, PA: Caslon Publishing.

García, Ofelia. 2009. *Bilingual Education in the 21st Century: A Global Perspective*. Malden, MA: Wiley-Blackwell.

García, Ofelia, Susana Johnson, and Kate Seltzer. 2016. *The Translanguaging Classroom: Leveraging Student Bilingualism for Learning*. Philadelphia, PA: Caslon Publishing.

Martínez, Ramón Antonio. 2010. "'Spanglish' as Literacy Tool: Toward an Understanding of the Potential Role of Spanish-English Code-Switching in the Development of Academic Literacy." *Research in the Teaching of English* 45(2): 124–149.

Menken, Kate. 2008. *English Language Learners Left Behind: Standardized Testing as Language Policy*. Clevedon: Multilingual Matters.

Menken, Kate, and Ofelia García, eds. 2010. *Negotiating Language Policies in Schools: Educators as Policymakers*. New York: Routledge.

Moll, Luis C., Cathy Amanti, Deborah Neff, and Norma Gonzalez. 1992. "Funds of Knowledge for Teaching: Using a Qualitative Approach to Connect Homes and Classrooms." *Theory into Practice* 31(2): 132–141.

Nieto, Sonia. 2010. *Language, Culture, and Teaching: Critical Perspectives*. New York: Routledge.

Palmer, Deborah. 2009. "Middle-Class English Speakers in a Two-Way Immersion Bilingual Classroom: 'Everybody Should Be Listening to Jonathan Right Now . . .'" *TESOL Quarterly* 43(2): 177–202.

Palmer, Deborah. 2010. "Race, Power, and Equity in a Multiethnic Urban Elementary School with a Dual Language "Strand" Program." *Anthropology and Education Quarterly* 41(1): 94–114.

Palmer, Deborah, and Ramón Antonio Martínez. 2013. "Teacher Agency in Bilingual Spaces: A Fresh Look at Preparing Teachers to Educate Latina/o Bilingual Children." *Review of Research in Education* 37: 269–297.

Pimentel, Charise, Lourdes Diaz-Soto, Octavio Pimentel, and Luis Urrieta. 2008. "The Dual Language Dualism: ¿Quiénes Ganan?" *Texas Association for Bilingual Education Journal* 10(1): 200–223.

Ruiz, Richard. 1984. "Orientations in Language Planning." *National Association for Bilingual Education Journal* 8(2): 15–34.

Sayer, Peter. 2013. "Translanguaging, TexMex, and Bilingual Pedagogy: Emergent Bilinguals Learning through the Vernacular." *TESOL Quarterly* 47(1): 63–88.

Shohamy, Elana. 2011. "Assessing Multilingual Competencies: Adopting Construct Assessment Policies." *The Modern Language Journal* 95(3): 418–429.

Torres-Guzmán, María E., Tatyana Kleyn, Stella Morales-Rodríguez, and Annie Han. 2005. "Self-designated Dual-language Programs: Is There a Gap between Labeling and Implementation?" *Bilingual Research Journal* 29(2): 453–474.

Valdés, Guadalupe. 1997. "Dual Language Immersion Programs: A Cautionary Note Concerning the Education of Language-minority Students." *Harvard Educational Review* 67(3): 391–429.

Villegas, Ana María. 2007. "Dispositions in Teacher Education: A Look at Social Justice." *Journal of Teacher Education* 58(5): 370–380.

Villenas, Sofia. 2001. "Latina Mothers and Small-town Racisms: Creating Narratives of Dignity and Moral Education in North Carolina." *Anthropology & Education Quarterly* 32(1): 3–28.

7 Colorado's READ Act

A Case Study in Policy Advocacy against Monolingual Normativity

Kara Mitchell Viesca and Luis E. Poza

Emergent bilinguals, students learning English in the U.S. school system, are often ignored in planning, developing, and implementing new educational policies. This is a major social justice issue as their education is often only accounted for *after* new policies have been put into place, thus limiting policy effectiveness and at times even actively harming emergent bilinguals, their teachers, and their families. Even in situations where there may have been some attempt to reasonably account for the education of emergent bilinguals at the outset of policy development and implementation, without being informed by relevant research and expertise, the policies can create additional problems for emergent bilinguals and their teachers. The following illustrates this issue via a literacy law passed in Colorado.

This case shows how researchers and practitioners formed a strong collaborative network engaged in policy advocacy in pursuit of social justice against regulation that would devalue bilingualism and discourage schools from offering bilingual programming. Social justice for emergent bilinguals in the context of their education is multifaceted and involves seeking equity and excellence across all aspects of education, including curriculum, instruction, communication with parents, and placement decisions. Here, we focus on social justice as it pertains to the policies and approaches that affirm and sustain bilingual language development, since these are most effective in supporting emergent bilinguals (Genesee et al. 2005; Umansky and Reardon 2014). We also illustrate the social justice challenges grounded in policy and practice guided by the assumption that English monolingualism is the normal and optimal outcome of schooling, or monolingual normativity.

Overview of READ Act

In 2012, the Colorado Reading to Ensure Academic Development Act (READ Act, HB 12–1238) was ratified into state law. The READ Act requires that all K-3 students be assessed with an instrument approved by the State Board of Education to determine the presence of a Significant Reading Deficiency (SRD). If a child is labeled with an SRD, an individualized READ Plan is to be developed and followed for that student. Such a plan could result in the student being removed from class for additional reading support or other interventions that are deemed appropriate. The law explicitly protects students still in the process of learning English such that their growing English abilities are not confused for an SRD. Yet, even with such protections, the first set of READ Act rules passed by the State Board of Education required that all SRD determinations be made with State Board approved literacy assessments in English.

Due to the substantial likelihood that students at the lower levels of English proficiency would be over-identified as having an SRD, local practitioners and researchers called attention to this disconnect between the law and the rules. The resulting collaboration between researchers, educators, and community members provided suggestions for improvements in the rules and arguments for resisting certain Board Members' attacks on bilingual education, with the aims of providing fair assessment and optimal educational programming for emergent bilinguals. The victories and setbacks for this collaboration for social justice and effective language-in-education policy are chronicled later in this work, following a brief overview of the benefits of bilingual education.

Research on the Education of Bilingual Learners

In the U.S. today, the education of bilingual students who live their daily lives in more than one language is not a widely successful enterprise (Goldenberg and Coleman 2010). In fact, bilingual students at the lower levels of English proficiency who are classified as "English language learners" (ELLs) by schools and districts, a group we refer to as "emergent bilinguals," are consistently the lowest performing sub-group in the US (Slama 2014). Students, families, communities, and teachers face several challenges as they strive to improve the education of bilingual students.

First, current federal and state policies rarely take the reality of bilingual language development into account in terms of assessment and accountability. For instance, Thompson (2015) examined nine years of data from one of the largest districts in the U.S. and found that emergent bilinguals required between four and seven years to obtain academic proficiency in English. However, assessment and accountability policies typically only allow 1–2 years before student test scores are taken into account in various high-stakes assessment and accountability schemes (e.g., school accreditation policies, teacher evaluation practices, etc.). Additionally, since the passage of No Child Left Behind in 2002 (a federal law requiring annual assessments in math and English in grades 3–8 and once in high school), major assessment programs have been in place to continually assess the English language development of emergent bilinguals.

Data are collected annually on all emergent bilingual students in U.S. public schools related to their English language development in speaking, listening, reading, and writing. These data are also used for accountability purposes and are reasonable to consider in terms of what schools are and are not accomplishing as they work with emergent bilingual students. Unfortunately, the data schools collect regarding grade level content development is typically collected only in English through challenging standardized tests. These tests are unable to demonstrate what students at the lowest levels of English proficiency know and can do in relation to the content being assessed (Abedi and Gándara 2006).

Second, a bias toward English monolingualism informs the education of bilingual learners and often positions home languages other than English as problems to overcome rather than as assets that students can continue to develop (García 2014; Mitchell 2012, 2013). This perspective informs the commonly used label to identify emergent bilingual students: *English language learner*. It also informs the development of programs, policies, and practices aimed at quickly remedying students' deficiencies in English, reclassifying students as "proficient" (removing the ELL label), and then treating students as if they were monolingual for the remainder of their educational career. These actions posit that English-is-all-that-matters based on monolingual normativity, which creates several problems in policy and practice.

Specifically, planning policies and programs from the perspective of monolingual normativity diminishes the opportunities for bilingual students to use their full bilingual repertoire to support their learning in school. Monolingual normativity also impacts the research we have on bilingual learners and the programs that are designed for them. For instance, multiple studies find that by fourth grade, Spanish speaking bilingual students who are instructed in English-only or a combination of English and Spanish have no significant difference in their English literacy scores (Cheung and Slavin 2012; Slavin et al 2011). The researchers thus conclude that the language of instruction is not as important as the quality of instruction. While it is difficult to argue that the quality of instruction, regardless of language, is not important, it is a major flaw to assess the value of bilingual instruction in terms of the outcomes in English only.

A major benefit of bilingual education is the opportunity to further develop and support bilingualism and biliteracy for bilingual students (Proctor et al. 2010). Substantial research suggests the value of bilingualism and biliteracy across multiple factors including educational attainment and lifetime earning potential. One study looking at two different large U.S. datasets found that students who were "balanced bilinguals" (while no bilingual is truly "native-like" in both languages, these language users are comparably fluent in English and in their home language) had significantly higher incomes as adults than students from bilingual backgrounds who became dominant in English only (Agirdag 2014). Similarly, Lutz (2004) found that biliterate students were more likely to attend college, and Garcia (2014) found that they were also more likely to graduate from college than their English-dominant peers. Additionally, research that examines the bilingual/biliteracy development of students consistently shows positive outcomes for students in quality bilingual programs, including strong English proficiency (Genesee et al. 2005; Goldenberg 2008).

Taking a long-term view of bilingual students and their achievement can support bilingual perspectives and development whereas focusing on short term outcomes in English only does not. A recent longitudinal study found that when a long-view is taken of bilingual programming, student outcomes in English language arts and Mathematics were higher for students in bilingual programs than in English-only programs (Valentino and Reardon 2015). Similarly, Umansky and Reardon (2014) examined 12 years of data from a large district and found that students in bilingual programs attained higher English proficiency and academic thresholds by the end of high school than those in English-only programs. From a perspective that values bilingualism, biliteracy, and the long-term development of students on multiple factors, the research is clear that bilingual programming offers better outcomes in both English, the additional language of instruction, and in content areas.

However, due to monolingual normativity and the prevalence of the English-is-all-that-matters narrative, not all policymakers or educators make decisions in alignment with this expansive and strong body of research. From the perspective that English-is-all-that-matters, decisions often focus on the quick attainment of English outside the parameters of what the research suggests is reasonable, desirable or even possible. These major issues in providing a quality education for bilingual students in the U.S. surfaced in the case of the Colorado READ Act.

Timeline/Narrative of Major Events

In 2012, legislators signed into law the READ Act that required monitoring of students in grades K-3 for "Significant Reading Deficiencies" (SRDs). Where SRDs were found, the law called for supportive plans to be put into place. The READ Act repeatedly states that children must read at grade level by grade four. It also allows for students to be held back a year if they have an SRD. The READ Act hardly mentions bilingual learners. However, the law does state that provisions for SRD classification shall not apply if "the student is a student with limited English proficiency . . . and the student's significant reading deficiency is due primarily to the student's language skills" (READ Act 2012, 13). Spanish is mentioned as a language in which assessments related to the regulations of the READ Act should be available.

After the law was initially passed, the Department of Education and the State Board of Education drafted rules for implementation of the new law. In March of 2013, the Board of Education voted to pass these rules. As is common with education, policy makers paid no attention to bilingualism or bilingual language development; the original rules required that all of the assessments of a child's reading ability be conducted in English.

During the summer of 2013, the Department of Education convened an English Literacy Task Force to advise on the development of guidelines for districts as they implemented the new law and its rules with bilingual learners. Task force members quickly brought the serious flaw of the rules to the attention of the state. Nowhere in the law does it require that students be assessed in English only. Further, the law explicitly points out that bilingual students whose reading deficiency is due to their lower levels of English proficiency should not be labeled as having an SRD. The State Commissioner of Education requested a ruling from the Attorney General as there was no consensus regarding whether or not all the assessments for the READ Act had to be conducted in English. In August of 2014, the Attorney General affirmed, "The purpose of the READ Act is to ensure that students become proficient in the skill of reading. There are provisions of law that seek to encourage and test proficiency in understanding the English language, but the READ Act's focus is on the skill, not the language in which it is employed" (Suthers 2014, 2–3).

After this opinion was issued, the Department of Education convened a new group called the "Spanish Literacy Group," comprised by members of the earlier Task Force and some new contributors. The purpose of this group was to suggest changes to the rules to account for the Attorney General's opinion. The group recommended minimal changes, but they included deleting references to English in terms of determining SRDs and adding the phrase "language of instruction" to a section on instruction. The starkest recommended change was to delete part of a sentence referencing the assessments that were allowed to be used. The change was to suggest that assessments in Spanish could be used to supplement, but not replace English assessments.

In April 2015, the Board of Education reviewed these suggested rule changes, heard public comment, and discussed the changes. The discussion the Board of Education held after public comment was illustrative of the prevalence of monolingual normativity in that several Board Members questioned the need for the proposed changes, and the majority voted not to pass the new rules. A final vote on the issue was pushed to the May 2015 meeting.

Between the April and May meetings, several members of the community from local organizations that support bilingual learners met with Board Members to help inform them of the need for these new rules, especially to ensure that fewer emergent bilinguals would be erroneously identified as having an SRD. In May, the new rules narrowly passed with a one-vote majority. The Spanish Literacy Group continued to work to support the improvement of the guidelines released by the Department of Education to include the new rules.

In December 2015, a notice was offered to the public regarding new rules for the administration of the READ Act. Members of the Board who opposed the new rules proposed additional changes that would require students in bilingual programs who have SRDs and are being served by the READ Act be assessed at least once annually in English literacy.

Several members of the Spanish Literacy Task force were concerned with the newly proposed rules because of the unnecessary testing burden they required as well as the fact that students are already tested annually regarding their English language development in reading and writing outside of the READ Act per federal law. Many members of the Spanish Literacy Group and other local stakeholders submitted written and public comment against the new rules. Nevertheless, the new rules requiring an annual literacy assessment in English for students in bilingual programs with SRDs passed in March 2016

Table 7.1 Overall Results of READ Act Testing.

Year	Percentage students with SRD
2013	16.5%
2014	14.4%
2015	13.8%

Table 7.2 Significant Reading Deficiency Identification for Emergent Bilinguals.

Year	Percentage students with SRD who are emergent bilinguals
2013	38.5%
2014	35.5%
2015	36%

despite substantial opposition from the field including members of the Spanish Literacy Group.

In May 2016, the Department of Education convened the Spanish Literacy Group and shared the first available data regarding the administration of the READ Act. Table 7.1 includes the "overall results" that were presented.

The state presented these results as a success since the number of overall students identified with SRDs decreased annually. However, despite this data presentation occurring for the Spanish Literacy Group, no data analyses were presented regarding the percentage of emergent bilinguals identified with SRDs. The group asked for this data and it was supplied by the end of the meeting (see Table 7.2).

When emergent bilinguals are only 10 percent of the population in Colorado, it is considered an overrepresentation for them to consist of 36 percent of students labeled as having SRDs. These data suggest that emergent bilinguals are likely being identified as having an SRD when in fact they are still just learning English.

Due to the insistence of the Literacy Task Force and other stakeholders in the aforementioned coalitions, this overrepresentation was taken up by the Board of Education for consideration. In October of 2017, the Board passed a compromise measure with respect to READ Act regulations that reinstated district autonomy in selecting the language of assessment for emergent bilingual students receiving their literacy instruction in the home language. While parents could still request assessment in English, double (and unreliable) testing would no longer be an inherent requirement of the policy, marking an important victory for advocates and, above all, bilingual learners.

Discussion

The case of the READ Act in Colorado in relationship to bilingual learners is both an example of social justice in action through policy advocacy and collaboration (the work of the Literacy Task Force and Spanish Literacy Group in calling attention to the issues and collaborating to pass more favorable rules) as well as how monolingual normativity creates issues wrought with prejudice against bilingual learners. This case provides evidence of both challenges and (eventual) victories in seeking social justice against monolingual normativity. Optimists could highlight the collaboration among researchers across institutions of higher education (who are often in competition over student enrollments, grant funding, and so on) alongside educators and community organizations for the benefit of bilingual children (Viesca, Amayo, Chávez and Esser 2015). By leveraging collective expertise of researchers, educators, and organizers within and across the work of the Literacy Task Force and Spanish Literacy Group, the resulting coalition was able to shape policy discussions and policy itself to create space for literacy assessments in students' language of instruction and, after extensive back and forth, abate the pressures of monolingual English normativity.

These relationships remain active in the face of emerging data showing disproportionate classification of emergent bilingual students as having Significant Reading Deficiencies. The persistence of this struggle despite regulatory victories demonstrates the intractable nature of opposition to bilingual students and their speech communities, most often Latinxs (García 2009), within education policy. Thus, the case study of the READ Act in Colorado and lengthy debates about its implementation offers social justice advocates an example of how alliances and formal involvement in the political process can produce change, while also providing a reminder of the linguicism and racism that students continue to encounter as they try to exercise their right to a quality education.

References

Abedi, Jamal and Patricia Gándara. 2006. "Performance of English Language Learners as a Subgroup in Large-Scale Assessment: Interaction of Research and Policy." *Educational Measurement: Issues and Practice* 25(4): 36–46.

Agirdag, Orhan. 2014. "The Long-Term Effects of Bilingualism on Children of Immigration: Student Bilingualism and Future Earnings." *International Journal of Bilingual Education and Bilingualism* 17(4): 449–464.

Cheung, Alan C. K. and Robert E. Slavin. 2012. "Effective Reading Programs for Spanish Dominant English Language Learners (ELLs) in the Elementary Grades: A Synthesis of Research." *Review of Educational Research* 82(4): 351–395.

García, Ofelia. 2009. "Racializing the Language Practices of US Latinos: Impact on their Education." In *How the United States Racializes Latinos: White Gegemony and its Consequences*, edited by José A. Cobas, Jorge Duany, Joe R. Feagin, 101–115. Abingdon: Routledge.

García, Ofelia. 2014. "US Spanish and Education Global and Local Intersections." *Review of Research in Education* 38(1): 58–80.

Garcia, Robert. 2014. Predictors of Success: The Impact of Biliteracy on Post Secondary Education Completion. Doctoral dissertation. Retrieved from Proquest (3621829).

Genesee, Fred, Kathryn Lindholm-Leary, William Saunders, and Donna Christian. 2005. "English Language Learners in U.S. Schools: An Overview of Research Findings." *Journal of Education for Students Placed at Risk* 10(4): 363–385.

Goldenberg, Claude. 2008. "Teaching English Language Learners: What the Research Does-and Does Not-Aay." *American educator* 32(2): 8–44.

Goldenberg, Claude and Rhoda Coleman. 2010. *Promoting Academic Achievement Among English Learners: A Guide to the Research.* Thousand Oaks, CA: Corwin.

Lutz, Amy. 2004. "Dual Language Proficiency and the Educational Attainment of Latinos." *Migraciones Internacionales* 2(4): 95–122.

Mitchell, Kara. 2012. "English is not ALL that Matters in the Education of Secondary Multilingual Learners and their Teachers." *International Journal of Multicultural Education* 14(1): 1–21.

Mitchell, Kara. 2013. "Race, Difference, Meritocracy, and English: Majoritarian Stories in the Education of Secondary Multilingual Learners." *Race Ethnicity and Education* 16(3): 339–364.

Proctor, C Patrick, Diane August, María Carlo, and Chris Barr. 2010. "Language Maintenance Versus Language of Instruction: Spanish Reading Development Among Latino and Latina Bilingual Learners." *Journal of Social Issues* 66(1): 79–94.

READ Act. 2012. "House Bill 12–1238: Reading to Ensure Academic Development Act." Accessed November 28, 2016, at www.cde.state.co.us/sites/default/files/documents/cdesped/download/pdf/sdm2012oct_cooradoreadact.pdf.

Slama, R. B. 2014. "Investigating Whether and When English Learners are Reclassified into Mainstream Classrooms in the United States: A Discrete-Time Survival Analysis." *American Educational Research Journal* 51(2): 220–252.

Slavin, Robert E., Nancy Madden, Margarita Calderon, Anne Chamberlain, and Megan Hennessy. 2011. "Reading and Language Outcomes of a Multiyear Randomized Evaluation of Transitional Bilingual Education." *Educational Evaluation and Policy Analysis* 33(1): 47–58.

Suthers, John W. 2014. "Formal Opinion of John W. Suthers, Attorney General, No. 14–02." Accessed November 28, 2016, at https://coag.gov/sites/default/files/contentuploads/ago/agopinions/johnw-suthers/2014/no-14-02.pdf.

Thompson, Karen D. 2015. "English Learners' Time to Reclassification: An Analysis." *Educational Policy* 31(3): 330–363.

Umansky, Ilana M. and Sean F. Reardon. 2014. "Reclassification Patterns Among Latino EnglishLearner Students in Bilingual, Dual Immersion, and English Immersion Classrooms." *American Educational Research Journal* 51(5): 879–912.

Valentino, Rachel A. and Sean F. Reardon. 2015. "Effectiveness of Four Instructional Programs Designed to serve English Learners: Variation by Ethnicity and Initial English Proficiency." *Educational Evaluation and Policy Analysis* 37(4): 612–637.

Viesca, Kara M., Jeanette Amayo, Lorretta Chávez, and Karla J. Esser. 2015. "Statewide Collaboration in Support of Improved Teaching and Teacher Education Practices for Bilingual Students: When Competitors Don't Compete." Paper presented at the American Educational Researchers Association, Chicago, IL.

8 Dual Language Education as a State Equity Strategy

Kathryn Lindholm-Leary, Martha I. Martinez, and Rosa G. Molina

Beginning in 2013, the State of Oregon devoted considerable resources to better address the needs of students who enter school speaking a language other than English (English learners, or ELs). A committee of state education leaders drafted an EL strategic plan. The Oregon Department of Education responded by adopting the plan, creating an Education Equity unit, and investing in a variety of EL-focused initiatives. These actions were prompted by the rapid growth of ELs in Oregon schools and their relatively low educational outcomes. In the 2010–2011 school year, there were about 65,000 English Learners in Oregon, a 48 percent increase in ten years (Oregon Department of Education 2011a). While more students reached proficiency on the state's English language proficiency test in 2010–2011 than in previous years, educational outcomes for ELs continued to lag far behind those of native English speakers. For example, among third graders in 2010–2011, the percentages of ELs who met the reading and math standards on the state's assessments were more than 20 percent lower than the percentages for all students in Oregon, and, among fifth graders, this gap in achievement between ELs and native English speakers was greater, with ELs scoring about 40 percent lower on both assessments (Oregon Department of Education 2011b). Education leaders from several districts highlighted their concerns with these achievement gaps in the call for a statewide focus on ELs, and educators within the Oregon Department of Education identified several strategic initiatives to improve educational outcomes and promote social justice for English Learners. One initiative expanded dual language programs and prioritized the needs of ELs in their design, delivery, and evaluation. This led to the state's first dual language grant project in 2013, which funded new programs and expanded existing programs in eight Oregon communities over three years. State leaders supported The Dual Language/Two-Way Bilingual grant because a substantial body of research demonstrates the effectiveness of dual language programs in closing achievement gaps for ELs.

What is Dual Language Education?

In dual language programs, instruction occurs through two languages, where the target, or non-English (e.g., Spanish, Chinese, Vietnamese), language is used for at least 50 percent of the students' instructional day. Though there are different types of dual language programs, we focus on *two-way* programs. Two-way programs integrate native speakers of English and native speakers of a target language (e.g., native Spanish speakers) in a single classroom where all academic instruction is provided separately through two languages. One language is the native language of each student group; the other is a second language. Instruction is provided in English and a target language beginning in kindergarten and continuing until the end of elementary school. These programs aim to enable students to (1) become bilingual, (2) read and write at grade level or above in both languages, (3) achieve at grade level or above in content areas like math and science, and (4) establish enhanced socio-cultural competencies (e.g., understand and value the languages, cultures, and people of their own and other groups).

Social Justice Elements of Dual Language Education

Dual language education is connected to social justice in five important ways. First, anti-immigrant sentiment is sometimes reflected in policies directed at bilingual education. Ovando (2003) details a cyclical pattern toward bilingual education since the 19th century that mirrors the political and social events of the times, identifying relatively permissive or restrictive periods with respect to U.S. language policy. As evidence of higher anti-immigrant sentiment in the past twenty years, several state ballot initiatives passed in California, Arizona, and Massachusetts greatly restricting bilingual approaches for English learners. In contrast, concerted efforts in Colorado and Oregon led to the defeat of a similar measure in their states. Dual language programs may promote more equitable and social justice perspectives because the integration and participation of children and families of ELs and English-speakers provide opportunities for community members to develop more meaningful relationships with immigrant children and families. Thus, parents express positive attitudes toward these programs, and administrators experience greater demand for dual language programs in these communities. This may be in part why California voters recently passed Proposition 58, which repealed the previous restrictions on bilingual programs and gave immigrant parents greater power to request bilingual programs for their children.

Second, two-way programs provide greater academic benefits for EL and other at-risk students than English-only instruction. As mentioned previously, the Oregon Department of Education expanded dual language programs because research consistently indicates that dual language participants develop high levels of English proficiency and intermediate to high levels of proficiency in the target language, and they demonstrate academic achievement at levels comparable to or surpassing their non-dual language peers (e.g., Genesee, Lindholm-Leary, Saunders, and Christian 2006; Lindholm-Leary 2001, 2016a; Lindholm-Leary and Genesee 2010; Lindholm-Leary and Howard 2008; National Academies of Sciences, Engineering, and Medicine 2017; Steele, Slater, Zamarro, Miller et al. 2017). These results hold true for students:

- at elementary, middle, and high school levels;
- of various demographic characteristics (e.g., low income, different ethnic backgrounds, students with special education needs);
- in different target languages (e.g., Spanish, Chinese, Korean); and
- in different types of communities (e.g., rural, urban, suburban, inner city).

Third, research demonstrates that high levels of bilingualism are associated with higher levels of social development in young children, and with certain advantages in problem solving and higher levels of academic achievement in children of all ages (National Academies of Sciences, Engineering, and Medicine 2017), as well as greater college and career benefits. This body of research indicates the critical importance of policies that enhance bilingualism for promoting social justice for these students, so they may experience higher levels of social and cognitive development and academic achievement, especially for ELs and other at-risk students.

Fourth, research also shows positive results in the areas of socio-emotional and cultural competencies (Block 2012; Lindholm-Leary 2016a, 2016b; National Academies of Sciences, Engineering, and Medicine 2017) in the following ways:

- Dual language students who speak the target language at home are more likely to be bilingual and communicate with family members than students who do not attend dual language programs, as non-dual language students are likely to lose their ability to speak their home language.
- Students demonstrate positive attitudes toward others who are culturally and linguistically different from them, bilingualism, and the dual language program.
- Dual language students perceive many cognitive, social, and cultural career-related advantages to being bilingual.
- Former EL students perceive that the dual language program kept them from dropping out of school and they are doing better than their non-dual language peers.

These results clearly provide an important argument for dual language programs from a social justice perspective. That is, these programs celebrate students' cultural backgrounds and enable students to further develop their home language in an environment that promotes equity, which leads to positive language, achievement, and socio-emotional and cultural competencies.

Finally, there is reason to believe that dual language programs can serve as a promising desegregation strategy (Orfield 2002). Several studies (Fern 1995; Freeman 1995; Lindholm-Leary and Borsato 2005; Rolstad 1997) provide evidence that two-way dual language programs integrate students who differ by language background, race/ethnicity, and socioeconomic status. Two-way dual language programs provide a promising alternative for Spanish-speaking Latinos who, along with other Latinos and Blacks, are frequently concentrated in high poverty, majority-minority schools that tend to be under-resourced (Ferg-Cadima 2004; Fry 2006).

The Oregon Dual Language Grant Project

The Oregon Department of Education built on this research base with the Dual Language/Two-Way Bilingual grant project in 2013, awarding grants to seven districts and one charter school, and enlisting the support of national experts on dual language program design, implementation, and evaluation to assist the grant sites in launching or improving dual language programs in their communities. Seven of the funded programs include Spanish as the partner language, and the final grant helped establish the first Vietnamese dual language program in the state. The grants also supported the creation and expansion of programs in both urban and rural communities across various regions of the state. As a result of the dual language grant project, four new dual language programs were created in different areas of the state. Over the course of the three-year grant project, seven schools served students in grades K–5 or K–6, and one charter school served students in grades K–8. In addition, all but one of the schools included between 70 and 94 percent low income students.

The schools used one of two different language allocation models, either 90/10 or 50/50. At five of the 90/10 schools, students entered kindergarten and spent 90 percent of their instructional day in Spanish; reading/language arts, math, social studies, and science were taught through Spanish and 10 percent of the day was spent in English language development. Each year, more time was spent in English until grade 4 or 5 when the students spent half their day in English and half their day in Spanish. In the three 50/50 programs, at all grade levels, students received half of their instructional day in Spanish (or Vietnamese) and half in English. Students in both 90/10 and 50/50 models learned to read, write, listen and speak in both languages. They were required to read textbook and other materials at grade level in both languages, and to write grade-level appropriate papers in each language.

Supporting the Work of the Dual Language Grant Sites

The national experts hired as consultants for the grant project provided participating schools with professional training and evaluation assistance to help guide the development of the dual language programs. One type of professional training included site visits to each school. These visits consisted of classroom observations and discussions with school teams and district leadership. After each visit, the consultants sent the schools a *technical assistance report* describing observations from the initial visit, suggestions for implementation when needed, specific recommendations for immediate action, and recommendations for the future. These recommendations became the basis for follow-up discussions with team members at each site and on-going professional support. The consultants also advised school staff to refer to the *Guiding Principles of*

Dual Language handbook (Howard, Sugarman, Christian, Lindholm-Leary, and Rogers 2007), which provides research-based principles and rubrics to help school leaders develop or improve a dual language program.

The most challenging issues facing the grant sites were focused on staffing issues, such as a limited supply of credentialed teachers with advanced academic biliteracy skills. The difficulty of finding qualified and credentialed bilingual teachers was particularly pronounced in small rural communities. To address this staffing challenge, some districts hired visiting teachers from Mexico or Spain while others sought out ideas for how to create a career ladder program for future native-speaking teachers from the ranks of their classified staff.

Preliminary Results

There was a common evaluation design for each school, though the data are limited because most schools were in their first or second year of implementation. Nonetheless, preliminary results provide information about the student populations and an indication of their initial language and academic development.

In the dual language project, the schools varied in terms of their student populations. Overall, students in these mostly rural or small communities were largely Latino (66%) and low-income (88%), and about half were ELs. Most students were in grades K–1 (55%), 10 percent each were in grades 2–4, and about 3 percent each in grades 5–8. In the first year of implementation, there were 593 students and in the second year, 1014 students in the evaluation study. Of the parents who responded to a parent survey, a quarter of parents had not graduated from high school, a quarter had a high school diploma and the remaining half had at least some college. Data collection included: teacher ratings of students' proficiency in the two languages, the state language proficiency test, the state achievement test in English, and a norm-referenced achievement test in Spanish. Unfortunately, there was a change in assessments from year 1 to year 2 due to a state-level change to Common Core-aligned assessments.

Two years of program implementation resulted in three major student outcome findings. First, students showed statistically significant gains on the language assessments in both languages, increasing both in their overall score and in their proficiency levels. Thus, native speakers of the partner languages (Spanish, Vietnamese) made good progress in further developing proficiency in their primary language and in developing language proficiency in English: by sixth through eighth grades, 85–100 percent were rated as proficient in English and in Spanish, and 82–100 percent were scored as Proficient on the state assessment of English language proficiency. Native speakers of English continued to develop in their native language while acquiring proficiency in the partner language; by sixth through eighth grades, 88–100 percent were rated as proficient in English and in Spanish. In fact, of the 71 middle school graduates who had taken the college-level exam for Spanish language credit,

85 percent were able to receive 12 units (34%) or 24 units (51%) of college-level coursework in Spanish.

Second, though there were limited achievement data from two sites (since most of the students were in grades K–2), results showed that students were making good progress as measured by state assessments in reading/language arts and math. By fifth and eighth grades, in assessments in English, Latino and EL students scored similar to or far higher than their peers at the state level in reading/language arts and EL students scored higher than their state peers in math. In reading, half to two thirds of students at most grade levels met or exceeded grade level expectations. Similar achievement was attained on the national Measures of Academic Progress (MAP) assessment. Achievement data in Spanish, which were available from only two sites at grades 2–3, indicated that students were scoring well above grade level (at or above 70th percentile) in Spanish reading and language achievement.

Third, satisfaction with the dual language program was very high. Overall, 93 percent of teachers were satisfied with the program. Parent satisfaction was also very high. Among the parents who responded to the parent survey, almost all (97%) of the English-, and Spanish-, and Vietnamese-speaking parents would recommend the program to other parents and were satisfied that the dual language program was giving their child access to the subject matter s/he needs. Also, most parents felt that studying through the partner language provided a number of benefits, such as enabling their child to be bilingual (95%), making their child a more knowledgeable person (98%), providing the child with a bilingual advantage for his/her career (94%), and allowing him/her to meet and talk with more people from different backgrounds (98%). Furthermore, most parents (90%) believed that students and parents in the program were treated as valuable.

Conclusions

While it is too early to rigorously evaluate the effectiveness of the project (only one participating school had a fully implemented program at the start of the grant), early findings are promising and in line with what we would expect at this stage of program development. Over the course of the two years of this initiative, the dual language schools worked to review, study and implement their program according to research-based practices and student outcomes within a well-defined dual language framework. The data are important in showing that dual language programs designed to promote equity and social justice in students typically at risk (EL, Latino, low-income) can promote bilingualism and biliteracy as well as academic achievement outcomes that are similar to, or higher than, those of their monolingual peers in traditional English classrooms. In addition, social justice perspectives carried over to the parents of EL students, who often feel marginalized at school, but who felt valued at these dual language school sites. Also, perhaps these social justice values of more equal educational opportunities, including bilingualism, for immigrant/EL and other potentially at-risk students is a community by-product of effective dual language programs. That is, more recently, with increasing proliferation of two-way/dual language programs in California and other states, we have witnessed voters in the State of California overturning the restrictive English-only educational policy and replacing it with a law that promotes bilingualism for youth. In addition, in the past few years, the majority of states have adopted the Seal of Biliteracy, which rewards students with a seal on their high school diploma if they pass a language proficiency test in a language other than English.

Achieving equity in education is a long-term goal that requires long-term investments and attention. The Oregon Department of Education recognizes this and is aware that well implemented dual language programs are those that produce the highest educational outcomes for students and significantly reduce achievement gaps for ELs. In addition, when continued through high school, these programs provide students with advanced biliteracy skills that they can parlay into college credit and/or enhanced employment opportunities. Therefore, the state launched the K–12 Biliteracy Pathways grant project in 2015 in order to improve and replicate well-established dual language programs that were operational through at least grade 8. In this way, the Oregon Department of Education is supporting not just the expansion of these programs, but laying the foundation for high quality program implementation and a long-term evaluation of these programs in the state in order to maximize their positive outcomes for all students, and to promote social justice for English Learners and other students in Oregon.

References

Block, Nicholas. 2012. "Perceived Impact of Two-way Dual Immersion Programs on Latino Students' Relationships in their Families and Communities." *International Journal of Bilingual Education and Bilingualism* 15(2): 235–257.

Ferg-Cadima, James. 2004. *Black, White and Brown: Latino school desegregation efforts in the pre- and post- Brown v. Board of Education era.* Washington, DC: Mexican-American Legal Defense and Education Fund.

Fern, Veronica. 1995. "Oyster Stands the Test of Time." *Bilingual Research Journal* 19(3–4): 497–512.

Freeman, Rebecca. 1995. "Equal Educational Opportunity for Language Minority Students: From Policy to Practice at Oyster Bilingual School." *Issues in Applied Linguistics* 6(1): 39–63.

Fry, Richard. 2006. *The Changing Landscape of American Public Education: New Students, New Schools.* Washington, DC: Pew Hispanic Center.

Genesee, Fred, Kathryn J. Lindholm-Leary, William Saunders, and Donna Christian. 2006. *Educating English Language Learners.* New York: Cambridge University Press.

Howard, Elizabeth R., Julie Sugarman, Donna Christian, Kathryn Lindholm-Leary, and David Rogers. 2007. *Guiding Principles for Dual Language Education* (2nd edition). Washington, DC: Center for Applied Linguistics.

Lindholm-Leary, Kathryn J. 2001. *Dual Language Education.* Clevedon: Multilingual Matters.

Lindholm-Leary, Kathryn J. 2016a. "Bilingualism and Academic Achievement in Children in Dual Language Programs." In *Bilingualism across the Lifespan: Factors Moderating Language Proficiency*, edited by Elena Nicoladis and Simona Montanari, 203–223. Washington DC: APA Books.

Lindholm-Leary, Kathryn J. 2016b. "Students' Perceptions of Bilingualism in Spanish and Mandarin Dual Language Programs." *International Multilingual Research Journal* 10(1): 59–70.

Lindholm-Leary, Kathryn J., and Graciela Borsato. 2005. "Hispanic High Schoolers and Mathematics: Follow-Up of Students who had Participated in Two-Way Bilingual Elementary Programs." *Bilingual Research Journal* 29(3), 641–652.

Lindholm-Leary, Kathryn J., and Fred Genesee. 2010. "Alternative Educational Programs for English Language Learners." In *Improving Education for English Learners: Research-Based Approaches*, edited by California Department of Education, 323–382. Sacramento, CA: CDE Press.

Lindholm-Leary, Kathryn J., and Elizabeth Howard. 2008. "Language and Academic Achievement in Two-Way Immersion Programs. In *Pathways to bilingualism: Evolving perspectives on immersion education*, edited by Fortune, Tara and Diane Tedick, 177–200. Clevedon: Multilingual Matters.

National Academies of Sciences, Engineering, and Medicine. 2017. *Promoting the Educational Success of Children and Youth Learning English: Promising Futures*. Washington, DC: The National Academies Press.

Oregon Department of Education. 2011a. "Record Number of English Language Learners Reach Proficiency." Accessed January 20, 2016, at www.ode.state.or.us/news/announcements/announcement.aspx?ID=7782&TypeID=5.

Oregon Department of Education. 2011b. "Statewide Report Card: An Annual Report to the Legislature on Oregon Public Schools." Accessed January 20, 2016, at www.ode.state.or.us/data/annreportcard/rptcard2011.pdf.

Orfield, Gary. 2002. *Schools More Separate: Consequences of a Decade of Resegregation*. Cambridge, MA: The Civil Rights Project, Harvard University.

Ovando, Carlos. J. 2003. "Bilingual Education in the United States: Historical Development and Current Issues." *Bilingual Research Journal* 27(1): 1–24.

Rolstad, Kellie. 1997. "Effects of Two-Way Immersion on the Ethnic Identification of Third Language Students: An Exploratory Study." *Bilingual Research Journal* 21(1): 43–63.

Steele, Jennifer L., Robert O. Slater, Gema Zamarro, Trey Miller, Jennifer Li, Susan Burkhauser, and Michael Bacon. 2017. "Effects of Dual-Language Immersion Programs on Student Achievement: Evidence from Lottery Data." *American Educational Research Journal* 54(1): 282S–306S.

9 Ubuntu Translanguaging and Social Justice

Negotiating Power and Identity through Multilingual Education in Tanzania

Monica Shank Lauwo

The violence of colonial education systems derives, in part, from linguistic and epistemic hegemonies that systematically delegitimize local languages and knowledge systems. While movement has been made towards the decolonization of Tanzania's education system in the 50+ years since independence in 1961, formal schooling still aggressively marginalizes local languages, other than Swahili, and is based on decisively Western epistemological foundations. This paper demonstrates how multilingual interventions can contribute to educational decolonization, through the centring of local languages, epistemologies, and agency in the processes of learning, teaching, and knowledge production.

Cheche Community Library in Northern Tanzania is a multilingual learning centre supporting the education of a predominantly Maasai community. In a context where local languages are muted in formal schooling and local culture is seen as an obstacle to educational success (Shank 2016), centring local languages *alongside* dominant codes challenges the linguistic status quo and destabilizes entrenched power hierarchies between different languages and their speakers. Unlike mainstream schools which are dominated by monolingual ideologies, Cheche welcomes learners to use and expand their entire linguistic repertoires, which in this community include varying degrees of Maa (Maasai language), Swahili (the national language), and English. These languages are used concurrently through a process of translanguaging, a systematic use of multiple languages simultaneously with the aim of asserting the importance of familiar languages, and using them in the learning of additional languages (Garcia and Li Wei 2014).

Multilingual education has important social justice implications. The muting of local languages like Maa in mainstream Tanzanian schooling marginalizes Maa-dominant learners. Challenging this system by incorporating familiar languages allows speakers of non-dominant languages to access school knowledge, assists them in the learning of additional languages, and positions them as knowledgeable and potential knowledge producers. Making space for a given language in the learning process also implies making space for ways of thinking which are idiomatic to that language, as well as knowledge which is not easily translated. The integration of historically marginalized languages in teaching and learning contributes to the dismantling of divisive power hierarchies, through which speakers of dominant languages (like Swahili and especially English) have privileged access to learning, as well as to naming—and thus constructing—reality in school settings and in broader society. As language is central to identity, multilingual education affirms existing (linguistic) identities, while creating opportunities to expand and contest these multivalent identities. Cheche Community Library illustrates the potential transformative power of multilingual education for broader struggles for social justice and decolonization throughout the world.

Multilingual Education and Social Justice

Multilingual education, in its vast variety of iterations, equips learners "both to maintain and develop their cultures and to participate in the wider society" (Skutnabb-Kangas et al. 2009, xvii). Innumerable studies show that students learn most effectively through languages they understand, and that people learn additional languages more successfully when they have developed strong linguistic foundations in their most familiar languages. Schooling through the medium of an unfamiliar language has dire consequences for learners, including that it:

- "Prevents access to education, because of the linguistic, pedagogical and psychological barriers it creates;
- Often curtails the development of the children's capabilities, perpetuates poverty, and causes serious mental harm;
- Is organized against solid research evidence about how best to reach high levels of bilingualism or multilingualism and how to enable [indigenous/minority] children to achieve academically in school" (Skutnabb-Kangas 2009, 40).

The vast majority of children throughout Africa are forced to "learn" through media which they do not speak (mostly ex-colonial languages: English, French, and Portuguese). The result is that schooling is an alien world for many of them, and they encounter significant challenges in understanding, critiquing, applying, and adding to the content they are taught in school.

Language, education, and colonization are inextricably intertwined. Many education systems are more oriented towards enculturation into foreign [colonial] values and a neoliberal world order than towards having direct relevance to, and transformative potential for, local communities. Familiar languages are indispensable tools for naming issues according to local (*not* colonial) epistemologies. They are also an important part of the cultural and political capital with the power to resist domination.

Julius Nyerere, Tanzania's first president and champion of African liberation struggles, acknowledged the colonial tendency for schooling to "divorce its participants from the society it is supposed to be preparing them for," and developed a policy response, *Education for Self-Reliance* (1967), which was to help graduates to "fit into, and to serve, the communities from which they come" (Nyerere 2004, 75, 87). Cheche furthers this quest for local relevance, and enacts a commitment to decolonization and resistance to domination, through its innovative approach to multilingual education.

Specifically, Cheche's approach to multilingual education embraces *translanguaging*, "a purposeful pedagogical alternation of languages in spoken and written, receptive and productive modes" (Hornberger and Link 2012, 262). Translanguaging honours the multilingual reality of Africa (and the majority of the world), where the vast majority of people uses two or more languages on a daily basis. Translanguaging practices are aligned with the African epistemological orientation of *Ubuntu*, characterized by a "communal orientation and continuum of social, linguistic and cultural resources and denotes the interconnectedness of all human existence" (Makalela 2015, 214). Thus, Ubuntu translanguaging (ibid.) entails interdependence and the notion that languages, like people, cannot exist in isolation from each other.

Tanzanian Context

Tanzania is blessed with rich linguistic diversity, with over 130 different local languages spoken by its people. However, these local languages are invisibilized in formal schooling in favour of Swahili and English. Swahili, spoken as a first or additional language by roughly 99 percent of Tanzanians, represents national unity, Tanzanian identity, and decolonization. English, spoken by only 5 percent of Tanzanians, is a language of power and prestige, and is the language of instruction for all post-primary schooling.

In this context, extremely hierarchical relations exist between languages. While government primary schools are in Swahili, there has been a dramatic growth of a lucrative English-medium private school industry, which thrives under the myth of the superiority of English. These English-medium schools grant the wealthy privileged access to English, intensifying the linguistic divide between economic classes. Local languages are relegated to an extremely low status, along with their speakers.

Cheche Community Library

In response to these language hierarchies and the system of language education which marginalizes speakers of local languages, Cheche Community Library offers a space that celebrates and develops all of learners' linguistic and cultural resources. All library activities are carried out using a fluid process of Ubuntu translanguaging, in which participants are free to make contributions in any language/s. Library participants are a combination of Maa-dominant Maasai children and Swahili-dominant children of diverse ethnicities, aged 2–14. Their previous exposure to English is minimal. Those who have been to school attend government primary schools (Swahili-medium), where their Maasai language and culture are left at the door.

Activities at Cheche Community Library (or "Cheche" for short) are facilitated by youth volunteers from the local community. There is a strong emphasis on creativity and critical literacies, with an interest in how learners use language to construct and intervene in the world. In practice, Ubuntu translanguaging enables participants to use their familiar languages for higher order thinking, for accessing prior knowledge, and generating new ideas. Participants simultaneously gain exposure to, and are encouraged to use, less familiar languages (like English) and find great joy and pride in making English language contributions whenever they can. This translanguaging approach enables participants to internalize their learning and to position themselves as experts and knowledge producers (possibilities which are suppressed when schooling is in unfamiliar languages), while simultaneously gaining exposure to languages of strong economic and academic currency.

The following sections detail how this translanguaging approach impacts power relations and the assertion of participants' agency, while opening up space for the affirmation and negotiation of participants' complex identities. The data cited is from an action research study conducted at Cheche Community Library over a year-long period, from October 2015 to October 2016.

Translanguaging and Power

Cheche uses language education to maximize participants' agency and consciousness of their worlds. Its approach is distinctive both in *which* languages are used, and *how* language is used. Acknowledging that "it is largely through language that meaning is mobilized to keep things the way they are" (Janks 2014, 5), Cheche supports the development of language practices which interrupt relations of domination and oppressive social hierarchies. It does this through centring Maa, cultivating authorship, and emphasizing critical literacies, all through practices of translanguaging.

The validation and active encouragement of Maa challenges social hierarchies which require Maa-dominant speakers to compromise themselves to accommodate Swahili-dominant speakers. At Cheche, Maa-dominant children position themselves as experts and share knowledge with fellow participants, knowledge which is inaudible in monolingual Swahili-medium schooling. The case of one participant, Nawassa (all names are pseudonyms), illustrates how the centring of Maa, together with multimodal forms of expression, can release powerful agency, transform repressive hierarchies, and expand the resources and power of the collective.

Nawassa came to Cheche as a timid, socially uncomfortable 10-year-old Maasai girl. Having never been to school, she was extremely self-conscious of her lack of exposure to reading, writing, and Swahili. As she discovered the esteemed position of Maa at Cheche, she began to quietly assert her extensive Maa knowledge through contributions to trilingual games. Her social position started changing as other children began seeing her as an expert and an invaluable team member. Nawassa took the initiative to teach the teacher a traditional Maasai song. She gained the courage to re-tell a story in Swahili in front of her peers. She became a leader in call and response singing, leading a large group in a song and dance performance for visitors. Initially refusing to touch a pen, she became an author of stories, depicted through drawings and oral narrations. Nawassa's blossoming confidence opened her up to both learning and teaching, through her increasing participation in the translanguaging space. Her Swahili improved, she began using some English vocabulary, and she generously shared her Maa expertise with her peers.

In mainstream models of schooling, Nawassa's talents would have been marginalized and she would have been considered a failure. The translanguaging environment allowed Nawassa to use her strong communicative resources, including Maa, to name, draw, sing, and dance the world, allowing her to claim the agency and confidence to expand her communicative repertoire to include Swahili, English, and the beginnings of writing skills.

Cheche emphasizes *productive* literacies, positioning learners as knowledge producers and not only knowledge consumers. Participants discover that written texts have no monopoly over truth, that texts were written by human beings and are thus fallible and alterable, and that students have the power to be authors. Participants learn to "recognise texts as selective versions of the world; they are not subjected to them and they can imagine how texts can be transformed to represent a different set of interests" (Janks 2010, 22).

With this emphasis on productive literacies, participants are encouraged to write their own stories. Books in Maa are extremely rare, as are books which reflect these children's realities. In defiance of this reality, children are actively writing stories of interest to them, some of them inspired by stories narrated to them by community elders.

Jesca, whose dream is to be an illustrator, is the author/illustrator of one such book. Her grandmother told her a story in Maa. Jesca chose to write her version of her grandmother's story in Swahili, as her schooling is in Swahili and she had never before read or written in her own language of Maa. After improving her Swahili version, she wrote a Maa version, and (with significant assistance) another version in English. She illustrated her story, and we printed high quality copies of her trilingual book. Her book is now a popular addition to both Cheche and her school's book collection, and she has become famous in the community as an author/illustrator. Jesca's authorship demonstrates how children can claim the power of language to create texts which reflect their own languages and cultures, thereby asserting that their own languages and worldviews are book-worthy and constitutive of knowledge, despite mainstream schooling implicitly teaching them otherwise.

In addition to authorship, Ubuntu translanguaging contributes significantly to Cheche's critical literacies practices: learners interrogate what language *does* in the world, whose interests are served by particular instances of language use, and how language use could be altered to further a different set of interests. At Cheche, learners engage in practices of re-design (Janks 2010, 2014) to re-write/re-create texts to make them more accessible to their community, and more reflective of their realities and interests. For example, learners collaboratively and creatively re-designed *The Peace Book*, by Todd Parr, a "multicultural" book, located in the Global North, which explores the concept of peace through examples of peace in action. Although the book is written in English, making it inaccessible to most of Cheche's participants, we read the book together through translanguaging. In Swahili and Maa, participants discussed the book's contents, extended the concept of peace with their own ideas and experiences, and deemed some of the book's ideas and illustrations incomprehensible to their context. For example, the notion that "peace" is "pizza for everyone," "watching it snow," or "napping by the fire" makes no sense to children who have no experience of pizza or snow, and know that a fireplace is for cooking. Participants re-designed the book, using languages, concepts, and images which are meaningful and actionable in their own contexts. Cheche participants' conceptions of peace (in Maa, Swahili, and illustrations) involved sharing *ugali*, helping someone fetch water, and making new friends. By writing and drawing "peace" using their own linguistic, cultural and geographical orientations, they challenge Eurocentric constructions and use language and multiple modes of expression to assert alternatives.

Translanguaging and Identity Negotiation

Language is central to identity, thus to deprive someone of the right to use their own language(s) is to suppress central aspects of their identity. At the same time, learning additional languages increases a learner's cultural capital (Bourdieu 1991), leading learners to re-evaluate their "sense of themselves, their identities, and their opportunities for the future" (Norton 2010, 3). This section illustrates ways in which Cheche's multilingual approach offers opportunities to affirm and explore existing identities, while also negotiating and expanding these identities to expand possibilities for the future.

The multilingual space enables community elders, *wazee*, to play an important role in Cheche. Using Maa, sometimes mixed with Swahili, these *wazee* tell traditional Maasai stories and share aspects of their life experiences. The *wazee*'s teachings, facilitated by translanguaging, decentre the hegemony of school languages, the written word, and Western paradigms of knowledge to claim space for local languages and knowledges, while offering a chance for children to engage with traditional knowledge systems and aspects of their identities which are unwelcome in mainstream schools.

Certainly, all people's identities are complex, plural, and constantly in motion, and it is dangerous to essentialize identity according to presumed ethnic, or linguistic, communities. Translanguaging assists learners to use "hybrid language space to identify and ethnify—choosing who they want to become beyond traditional linguistic and exact ethnic affiliations" (Nkadimeng and Makalela 2015, 7). The active learning of and engagement with a variety of languages, including English, also enable learners to imagine a broad range of identities for themselves, including membership in "imagined communities" (Anderson 2006) requiring proficiency in certain languages.

Creating "identity texts," written and drawn representations of who they are (Cummins and Early 2011), is one way Cheche participants explore their identities. Participants use the full range of their linguistic abilities to convey different aspects of themselves. In one example, a boy chose to write and draw about his aspirations to be a teacher, using both Swahili and Maa to explain that he wants to teach people to read and write in Maa—a transformative ambition, as the teachers he observes at school certainly do not teach anyone Maa. He annotated his school-based illustrations in both English and Swahili, and his out-of-school illustrations in both Maa and Swahili, signifying the importance of all of these languages to a range of activities and to his ambition. In another example, a girl wrote a (scripted, school-learned) English paragraph introducing various aspects of her current identity, positioning herself as an English speaker and someone who is educated. She then wrote, in Swahili, that her dream is to be doctor, with the word "doctor" written in both English and Swahili. She wrote Maa and Swahili prayers to God to help her become a doctor, and wrote approximate transcriptions of English words from a church song.

While both of these children used written Maa to express aspects of themselves (courageously, considering their negligible exposure to written Maa), and Swahili to explain their main message, English seemed to play a central role in their imagined future identities as highly educated professionals. Thus, it is clear that while local/familiar languages are essential for grounding learners in a sense of where they come from, international languages also play an important role in unleashing their dreams. Encouraging these languages to develop and thrive alongside each other affirms the compatibility of these identities: one's language and culture can co-exist with a successful professional career.

In these ways, engagement with local languages and knowledges alongside languages and forms of learning associated with schooling, supports learners to strengthen their rootedness in their own language(s) and culture(s), while simultaneously increasing their cultural capital and their access to more diverse potential futures.

Conclusion

This chapter has demonstrated ways in which multilingual education, and Ubuntu translanguaging in particular, can contribute to struggles for social justice and decolonization. The case of Cheche Community Library illustrates how creation of space for familiar languages can allow learners to claim the power to resist dominant interpretations of reality, and to restructure linguistic and epistemological hierarchies which delegitimize their own languages and knowledge systems. The cultivation of authorship, multimodal forms of expression and critical literacies enables learners to use language to re-design texts (as opposed to being subjected to them), to position themselves as experts, and to name the world according to their own worldviews.

The employment of Ubuntu translanguaging, in accordance with African orientations to wholeness and interdependence, honours the complementarity of different languages and knowledge systems. Thus, Ubuntu translanguaging assists learners to negotiate their complex identities, in ways which affirm and reinforce their linguistic and cultural backgrounds while creating space for the expansion of linguistic identities and memberships in diverse imagined communities. English, and the Western epistemologies dominating mainstream schooling, are not inherently colonizing forces in and of themselves. Rather, they are incomplete, and in danger of overpowering local languages and knowledges, when taught in isolation, shrouded by the myth of their superiority. Ubuntu translanguaging supports learners to delve into new linguistic and epistemological spaces without alienating them from the linguistic and cultural communities from which they come.

Cheche Community Library reveals the power of Ubuntu translanguaging to make learning more accessible, to unleash the agency of learners, and to support multidimensional identity affirmation and negotiation. Indeed, the adoption of Ubuntu translanguaging in more multilingual contexts in Africa and beyond is a critical aspect of the ongoing struggles for social justice and decolonization in the twenty-first century.

References

Anderson, Benedict. 2006. *Imagined Communities: Reflections on the Origin and Spread of Nationalism*. London: Verso. First published 1983.

Bourdieu, Pierre. 1991. *Language and Symbolic Power*. Cambridge: Polity Press.

Cummins, Jim, and Margaret Early, ed. 2011. *Identity Texts: The Collaborative Creation of Power in Multilingual Schools*. Stoke on Trent: Trentham Books.

Garcia, Ofelia, and Li Wei. 2014. *Translanguaging: Language, Bilingualism and Education*. Basingstoke: Palgrave Macmillan.

Hornberger, Nancy, and Holly Link. 2012. "Translanguaging in Today's Classrooms: A Biliteracy Lens." *Theory into Practice* 51: 239–247.

Janks, Hilary. 2010. *Literacy and Power*. New York: Routledge.

Janks, Hilary. 2014. *Doing Critical Literacy: Texts and Activities for Students and Teachers*. New York: Routledge.

Makalela, Leketi. 2015. "Moving out of Linguistic Boxes: The Effects of Translanguaging Strategies for Multilingual Classrooms." *Language and Education* 29(3): 200–217.

Nkadimeng, Shilela, and Leketi Makalela. 2015. "Identity Negotiation in a Super-Diverse Community: The Fuzzy Languaging Logic of High School Students in Soweto." *International Journal of the Sociology of Language* 234: 7–26.

Norton, Bonny. 2010. "Identity, Literacy, and English Language Teaching." *TESL Canada Journal* 28(1): 1–13.

Nyerere, Julius. 2004. "Education for Self Reliance." In *Nyerere on Education/Nyerere Kuhusu Elimu*, edited by E. Lema, M. Mbilinyi and R. Rajani, 67–88. Dar es Salaam: E. & D. First published 1967.

Shank, Monica. 2016. "Language Education in Maasai Land, Tanzania: Parental Voices and School Realities." Master's thesis, OISE, University of Toronto.

Skutnabb-Kangas, Tove. 2009. "Multilingual Education for Global Justice: Issues, Approaches, Opportunities." In *Social Justice through Multilingual Education*, edited by T. Skutnabb-Kangas, R. Phillipson, A. K. Mohanty, and M. Panda, 36–62. Bristol: Multilingual Matters.

Skutnabb-Kangas, Tove, Robert Phillipson, Ajit K. Mohanty, and Minati Panda. 2009. "Editors' Forward." In *Social Justice through Multilingual Education*, edited by T. Skutnabb-Kangas, R. Phillipson, A. K. Mohanty, and M. Panda, xvii–xviii. Bristol: Multilingual Matters.

10 A Critical Interrogation of the "Language Gap"

Eric J. Johnson

Whose Gap?

The common use of the term "gap" to describe disparities in academic achievement between different economic and ethnic communities has essentially normalized the notion of "at risk" groups within educational contexts (see McCarty in Avineri et al. 2015). It is important to point out that the "gap" concept is based on measuring social norms from a dominant group perspective (Blum 2017). While striving to expose factors that contribute to academic disparities is a worthwhile social justice endeavor, casting blame on economically challenged communities for being linguistically diverse is misguided and socio-academically counterproductive.

In this discussion, I scrutinize the deficit-oriented perception framing the communication patterns of families living in poverty as producing a "language gap" that predetermines academic failure and stymies cognitive development. I interrogate the "language gap" from an anthropological stance that emphasizes power inequities to shed light on underlying ideological assumptions that make such an insidious concept so widely accepted. This type of approach "unmasks the focus on language as the source of the problem, pointing to how little educators and policymakers actually know about different ways of speaking and raising children, and underscoring the decisive role of the gatekeepers who control access to success" (Johnson and Zentella 2017, 2).

Mapping Gaps

Since the 1960s, the communication patterns of children from disadvantaged socioeconomic groups have been disparaged in terms of "verbal deprivation" (Bereiter and Engelmann 1966), "restricted codes" (Bernstein 1971), and "word gaps" (Hart and Risley 1995). These types of characterizations are based on a *deficit orientation* that views cultural features that differ from those of dominant groups as defective and in need of remediation (Hadjistassou 2008). The "language gap" portrays linguistic features that do not align with middle- and upper-class communication patterns as factors that impede academic and cognitive development. These ideas have been widely adopted within educational contexts to blame low academic performance on family language patterns. Unfortunately, these views often hinder policymakers and educators from promoting more effective teaching methods that build on community funds of knowledge (González et al. 2005) and engage in culturally sustaining pedagogical practices (Paris and Alim 2014).

The idea of a "language gap" stems from Hart and Risley's (1995) publication *Meaningful Differences in the Everyday Experience of Young American Children*. These authors (Hart and Risley 1995, 2003) claimed that by age 3, children from more economically affluent households were exposed to approximately 30 million more words than children from low socioeconomic backgrounds. They conclude this "word gap" is responsible for inferior cognitive development and eventual lower academic achievement. Despite serious theoretical and methodological deficiencies in Hart and Risley's study (Baugh 2017; Johnson 2015), their work has been cited over 5,000 times in scholarly literature (Rothschild 2016) and is widely embraced by policymakers and educators. Furthermore, current research premised on the "word gap" spans multiple linguistic dimensions (Johnson et al. 2017)—including quality of communication (Hoff 2003), language processing (Fernald et al. 2013), and health related issues stemming from language use (Crow and O'Leary 2015).

The proliferation of "language gap" research has produced a swell of programs and policies aimed at remediating so called linguistic "deficiencies" of families from low socioeconomic status backgrounds (e.g., Suskind 2015). Large-scale initiatives like Providence Talks, the Thirty Million Words Initiative, and Too Small to Fail are examples of programmatic efforts designed to close the "language gap" by attempting to change the ways parents from minoritized cultural groups communicate with their children. Moreover, the increase of "language gap" programs and research has received widespread publicity in the public media, further reinforcing deficit orientations towards minority communities and promoting dominant group norms of language use (Johnson et al. 2017). Although some media articles that problematize the "language gap" exist (e.g., Rothschild 2016), the vast majority are based on the misguided assumption that language patterns found in school-contexts are inherently superior to those of groups from low-income communities. Research conducted within linguistic anthropology and sociolinguistics shows that this is false.

Sociolinguistic and Anthropological Perspectives

A strong tradition of sociolinguistic and anthropological scholarship demonstrates that individuals acquire specific language patterns to achieve communicative competence within a given community. Hymes's (1972) application of communicative competence explains how the linguistic norms of interaction established by members of a community shape the way individuals acquire language to meet the cultural expectations of interaction within that community. Additional fields of linguistic inquiry demonstrate that language features like pronunciation, turn-taking, register, gestures, questioning strategies, and vocabulary (among others) vary among groups from diverse cultural backgrounds (Labov 1966; Pinker 1994). Anthropological research on language socialization further illuminates the processes through which children develop culturally appropriate linguistic abilities.

Ochs (1986, 2–3) explains that language socialization entails "both socialization through language and socialization to use language," such that "children and other novices in society acquire tacit knowledge of principles of social order and systems of belief (ethnotheories) through exposure to and participation in language-mediated interaction." Ochs's description underscores the inextricable link between language development and an individual's cultural identity and worldview. The field of language socialization provides important insight into children's language acquisition, as demonstrated by research within diverse cultural groups (Duranti et al. 2014). Thus, to evaluate appropriate language use, it is necessary to focus on the communicative norms established within a specific cultural context. Proponents of the "language gap" ignore this view by overly prioritizing the dominant language patterns found in schools.

I am not suggesting that linguistic diversity should be ignored in classrooms. The issue is how the proposed "language gap" concept shapes the way educators view their students' language abilities and, to a greater extent, how diverse language abilities are excluded and/or targeted for remediation instead of being used as valuable resources to help make meaningful connections to academic language forms. Applying a language socialization lens for examining academic struggles helps unveil the underlying economic, linguistic, and racial biases that are reflected in the "language gap." Heath's (1983) ethnographic work on language and literacy patterns of families from different economic groups demonstrated that the oral interactions and literacy practices common in affluent homes (e.g., features like questioning strategies and the structure of literacy events involved in reading books) paralleled the language patterns promoted in schools. She also found that students from less affluent backgrounds struggled with literacy and language expectations in schools because they were different from those used in their home and community settings, not because they are linguistically or cognitively inferior.

Heath's seminal work gave rise to a range of scholarly research that validates the sophisticated nature of language and literacy within culturally diverse communities (e.g., Pérez 2004; Zentella 2005). These studies clearly demonstrate that the linguistic hierarchies that position school-based language and literacy forms as inherently superior are based on dominant-class "language ideologies" (Woolard and Schieffelin 1994). Applying the idea of a linguistic hierarchy based on dominant-class interests is especially relevant to the "language gap" research since many of the families targeted for remediation come from culturally diverse backgrounds with well documented linguistic strengths (Baugh 2017; García and Otheguy 2017).

Social Manifestations of Gap Discourses

In their critical discourse analysis of the rhetoric used by researchers, institutions, and in the media to describe the "language gap," Johnson et al. (2017)

describe how communities from low economic backgrounds are portrayed from a deficit perspective. Echoing the critical approach employed by Johnson et al. (ibid.), I examine below how deficit orientations based on the "language gap" emerge by providing examples of rhetoric from: (1) influential organizations that support programs to modify language use in low-income families; (2) media coverage of "language gap" issues; and (3) commentaries from classroom teachers about students who live in poverty. My discussion of these examples draws attention to the subtle ways the "language gap" permeates a variety of social contexts to reinforce the opinion that low-income communities are linguistically inadequate.

Organizations

Too Small to Fail (2017), backed by the Clinton Foundation, is a large public awareness organization that claims "to promote the importance of early brain and language development and to empower parents with tools to talk, read, and sing with their young children from birth" (para. 1). In its "strategic roadmap" publication, Too Small to Fail (n.d., 2) outlines the organization's focus on "[i]mproving the health and well-being of America's youngest children." Based on Hart and Risley's "word gap" research, academic achievement gaps are described in terms of a "troubling difference in children's early vocabularies" (Too Small to Fail n.d., 4). The publication then makes a call for action to combat academic inequities by focusing on language:

> When a child is deprived of food, there is public outrage. And this is because child hunger is correctly identified as a moral and economic issue that moves people to action. We believe that the poverty of vocabulary should be discussed with the same passion as child hunger.
>
> (Too Small to Fail n.d., 11)

Here, the language patterns of families from low economic backgrounds are equated to starvation. In other words, the language that parents use is metaphorically described as insufficient and harmful to their children. The LANGUAGE AS FOOD metaphor is a common rhetorical strategy that depicts dominant class vocabulary patterns as nutritionally (i.e., linguistically) superior (see Johnson et al. 2017). This example illuminates how linguistic hierarchies are reproduced by openly denigrating the inherent value of language forms used in economically underprivileged communities.

Media

Media stories about the "language gap" publicize broad sweeping statements that describe the linguistic skills of families from low-income backgrounds as flawed. In this *Washington Post* article citing a speech by President Obama, the "language gap" is framed as if it were common knowledge:

> You have probably heard about what is called the "word gap" found in many low-income children, who were found in a famous 1995 research study to be exposed to 30 million fewer words than their more fortunate peers by age 3, and that this deficit affects literacy development.
>
> (Strauss 2015)

Not only is the language of low-income families depicted as a "deficit," framing it with "you have probably heard" makes the "language gap" seem as a taken for granted fact, which then makes the claim about literacy development appear credible. Absent in public media stories like this is any mention of multicultural approaches that can be applied in schools to build on diverse students' background experiences and skills as educational assets (Delpit 2006).

Schools

The "language gap" concept frequently surfaces in the views that educators hold towards their students from low socioeconomic backgrounds. In schooling contexts, "language gap" perspectives range from explicit and egregious to implicit and assumed. In previous research on language policies in high-poverty schools in Arizona, I have demonstrated educators' outright negative portrayals of students' language abilities that reflect a "language gap" orientation:

- "I try to tell these kids that they're extremely lucky that they're bilingual, [but] I tell these guys you can know street Spanish, but you're not going to get a decent job" (Johnson 2011, 15).
- "When you don't have a language, which many of our kids that are coming into us, they don't have a language, so there is nothing to build on" (Johnson 2014, 169).

Whereas the first educator describes the "gap" in his students' bilingual abilities in terms of colloquial (i.e., street) vs. prescriptive/academic linguistic forms, the second educator depicts her Spanish speaking students as lacking language altogether (i.e., English is the only language that really counts). While disturbing perspectives like these are easy to identify, just as harmful are deficit orientations that are tacitly portrayed as common knowledge.

During an interview with a teacher in a high poverty school in Washington state, home language patterns and poverty were openly mentioned:

Teacher: Personally, I'm just obsessed with research involving poverty, low achieving students, at risk students, and I apply that a lot ... Poor homes are noisy. They're noisy. There's a lot of people. There's a lot of things going on, and nobody is bothered by it. Me, I would go to his house and be like, "I can't even stand it. I feel like I need to wear ear plugs."

Interviewer: Where's that idea from?
Teacher: Oh gosh, I don't know. (laughs)

Most teachers receive extensive and ongoing professional training, especially in school districts with high numbers of students from a low-income background. The educator interviewed here has been exposed to ample "research" on poverty that colors her view of what takes place in low-income homes (e.g., a lot of noise)—without being able to identify the actual research. Although the teacher does not explicitly mention language in the previous passage, her subsequent comment describes interactional and communicative patterns that she imagines to be typical of many students she teaches:

Teacher: When they come to school and their homework is not finished, or it looks really messy, I have an idea that they were probably sitting at a table where one person was eating dinner, and one person was on the on their phone, and one person was over here watching the game and yelling at the TV, and mom was in the kitchen and things were hot and loud. And so, that child, I'm not going to expect perfection from their homework. The fact that they got it done in the first place was amazing, you know.

Here, the teacher paints a picture of communicative patterns that are constructed as obstructive and academically counterproductive. Although the teacher's comments may seem to be sympathetic to her students' experiences, they reflect a significant effect of the "language gap" research: ingrained low academic expectations towards low-income students based on family communication patterns.

The teacher's comments demonstrate a dominant class perception of what constitutes a constructive communicative environment. Regardless of the culturally insensitive and linguistically inaccurate assumptions involved in judging linguistic interactions, the focus on "quality" of communication patterns is a major focus in "language gap" research literature (see Johnson et al. 2017). Furthermore, this particular teacher had recently attended a school district workshop on helping students in poverty. The training was facilitated by Eric Jensen, a popular "brain-based teaching" author who points to language deficits as impeding cognitive development in children from low-income families. Jensen frames his discussion about language by citing both Hart and Risley's (1995) and Hoff's (2003) deficit-orientation research mentioned above, claiming that "[t]here is considerable evidence that children from poverty are more likely to have impaired exposure to critical enrichment factors resulting in substandard cognitive skills" (Jensen n.d., 3).

I am not intending to undermine the professionalism of the teachers in this example, nor to vilify education workshop presenters like Jensen. My point here is to stress how easily the larger concept of a "language gap" directly seeps into the daily interactions between students and teachers. School districts should be applauded for seeking professional development to support teachers who work with low-income students, but when the training is based on a foundation of "language gap" research, deficit orientations are exacerbated and not ameliorated, causing educators to have substandard expectations of their students. Regrettably, topics related to the "language gap" remain a popular feature of professional trainings in public education and continue to overshadow an emphasis on building upon student strengths to support academic progress.

Moving Forward

The objective of this chapter has been twofold. First, I outlined the underlying deficit orientation of the "language gap" and demonstrated the linguistic flaws in the research that supports it. Next, I illustrated how "language gap" research is publicly promoted and eventually manifests in social and academic settings. I conclude my discussion by encouraging strategies of public awareness that are driven by a social justice impetus to improve academic opportunities. Instead of perpetuating a view of low-income families as inferior, we must acknowledge that most schools are ill-equipped to support students from culturally, linguistically, and economically diverse backgrounds. To remedy this situation, scholars, policymakers, educators, and other community stakeholders must back programs that are grounded in socially just pedagogies.

Recognizing that linguistic differences are determined by community context (instead of judging them hierarchically) is a positive step towards honoring the actual language abilities that economically disadvantaged children have. We can all heighten awareness of linguistic strengths on a broader social level by starting with small acts that promote a language and social justice stance. Such acts can be accomplished in many ways, for example: confronting language deficits in discussions with peers and colleagues, publishing editorial articles, conducting original research, mentoring students from low-income backgrounds, or teaching with a focus on students' strengths—not weaknesses. Regardless of how it happens, every time notions of linguistic deficits are challenged, we all move forward.

References

Avineri, Netta, et al. 2015. "Invited Forum: Bridging the 'Language Gap.'" *Journal of Linguistic Anthropology* 25(1): 66–86.

Baugh, John. 2017. "Meaning-less Differences: Exposing Fallacies and Flaws in 'the Word Gap' Hypothesis that Conceal a Dangerous 'Language Trap' for Low-Income American Families and Their Children." *International Multilingual Research Journal* 11(1): 39–51.

Bereiter, Carl, and Siegfried Engelmann. 1966. *Teaching Disadvantaged Children in the Preschool.* Englewood Cliffs, NJ: Prentice Hall.

Bernstein, Basil. 1971. *Class, Codes and Control: Theoretical Studies Towards a Sociology of Language.* New York: Schocken Books.

Blum, Susan D. 2017. "Unseen WEIRD Assumptions: The So-Called Language Gap Discourse and Ideologies of Language, Childhood, and Learning." *International Multilingual Research Journal* 11(1): 23–38.

Crow, Sarah, and Ann O'Leary. 2015. "Word Health: Addressing the Word Gap as a Public Health Crisis." Accessed August 18, 2017, at thenextgeneration.org/files/Word_Health_v3.pdf.

Delpit, Lisa. 2006. *Other People's Children: Cultural Conflict in the Classroom.* New York: The New Press.

Druanti, Alessandro, Elinor Ochs, Bambi B. Schieffelin. 2014. *The Handbook of Language Socialization.* Malden, MA: Wiley Blackwell.

Fernald, Anne, Virginia A. Marchman, and Adriana Weisleder. 2013. "SES Differences in Language Processing Skill and Vocabulary Are Evident at 18 Months." *Developmental Science* 16(2): 234–248.

García, Ofelia, and Ricardo Otheguy. 2017. "Interrogating the Language Gap of Young Bilingual and Bidialectal Students." *International Multilingual Research Journal* 11(1): 52–65.

González, Norma, Luis C. Moll, and Cathy Amanti. 2005. *Funds of Knowledge: Theorizing Practices in Households, Communities, and Classrooms.* New York: Routledge.

Hadjistassou, Stella K. 2008. "Deficit-Based Education Theory." In *Encyclopedia of Bilingual Education, Vol. 2*, edited by Josue González, 218–222. Los Angeles, CA: Sage.

Hart, Betty, and Todd R. Risley. 1995. *Meaningful Differences in the Everyday Experience of Young American Children.* Baltimore, MD: Brookes Publishing.

Hart, Betty, and Todd R. Risley. 2003. "The Early Catastrophe: The 30 Million Word Gap by Age 3." *American Educator*, Spring: 4–9.

Heath, Shirley Brice. 1983. *Ways with Words: Language, Life, and Work in Communities and Classrooms.* New York: Cambridge University Press.

Hoff, Erika. 2003. "The Specificity of Environmental Influence: Socioeconomic Status Affects Early Vocabulary Development Via Maternal Speech." *Child Development* 74(5): 1368–1378.

Hymes, Dell. 1972. "On Communicative Competence." In *Sociolinguistics*, edited by J. B. Pride and J. Holmes, 269–285. London: Penguin.

Jensen, Eric. n.d. "The Effects of Poverty on the Brain." *The Science Network* website. Accessed on August 29, 2017, at thesciencenetwork.org/docs/BrainsRUs/Effetcs%20of%20Poverty_Jensen.pdf.

Jensen, Eric. 2013. *Teaching with Poverty in Mind: What Being Poor Does to Kids' Brains and What Schools Can Do about It.* Baltimore, MD: ASCD.

Johnson, Eric J. 2011. "(Re)producing Linguistic Hierarchies in the United States: Language Ideologies of Function and Form in Public Schools." *International Journal of Linguistics* 3(1): E12.

Johnson, Eric J. 2014. "(Re)Categorizing Language-Minority Literacies in Restrictive Educational Contexts." *International Multilingual Research Journal* 8(3): 167–188.

Johnson, Eric J. 2015. "Debunking the 'Language Gap.'" *Journal for Multicultural Education* 9(1): 42–50.

Johnson, Eric J., Netta Avineri, and David Cassels Johnson. 2017. "Exposing Gaps in/between Discourses of Linguistic Deficits." *International Multilingual Research Journal* 11(1): 5–22.

Johnson, Eric J., and Ana Celia Zentella. 2017. "Introducing the Language Gap." *International Multilingual Research Journal* 11(1): 1–4.

Labov, William. 1966. *The Social Stratification of English in New York City*. Arlington, VA: Center for Applied Linguistics.

Ochs, Elinor. 1986. "Introduction." In *Language Socialization across Cultures*, edited by B. B. Schieffelin and E. Ochs, 1–13. New York: Cambridge University Press.

Paris, Django, and H. Samy Alim. 2014. "What Are We Seeking to Sustain through Culturally Sustaining Pedagogy? A Loving Critique Forward." *Harvard Educational Review* 84(1): 85–100.

Pérez, Bertha, ed. 2004. *Sociocultural Contexts of Language and Literacy*. Mahwah, NJ: Lawrence Erlbaum Associates.

Pinker, Steven. 1994. *The Language Instinct: How the Mind Creates Language*. New York: William Morrow & Company.

Rothschild, Amy. 2016. "Beyond the Word Gap." *The Atlantic*, April 22. Accessed August 28, 2017, at www.theatlantic.com/education/archive/2016/04/beyond-the-word-gap/479448.

Strauss, Valerie. 2015. "The Famous 'Word Gap' Doesn't Hurt Only the Young. It Affects Many Educators, Too." *The Washington Post*, February 16. Accessed August 28, 2017, at www.washingtonpost.com/blogs/answer-sheet/wp/2015/02/16/the-famous-word-gap-doesnt-hurt-only-the-young-it-affects-many-educators-too.

Suskind, Dana. 2015. *Thirty Million Words: Building a Child's Brain*. New York: Dutton.

Too Small to Fail. n.d. "Preparing America's Children for Success in the 21st Century: Too Small to Fail Strategic Roadmap." Accessed August 28, 2017, at www.clinton foundation.org/files/2s2f_framingreport_v2r3.pdf.

Too Small to Fail. 2017. "Our Mission." Accessed on August 28, 2017, at http://toosmall.org/mission.

Woolard, Kathryn A., and Bambi B. Schieffelin. 1994. "Language Ideology." *Annual Review of Anthropology* 23: 55–82.

Zentella, Ana Celia, ed. 2005. *Building on Strength: Language and Literacy in Latino Families and Communities*. New York: Teachers College Press.

Part III

Language and Health

Introduction

The chapters in this section consider the various intersections between language use and health in diverse communities. In each case, there is an exploration of the ways that persons, experiences, and bodies are constructed through language. In addition, there is a consideration of the ways that languages of particular communities are valued or devalued, acknowledged or disregarded. These cases highlight how languages become associated with particular persons, and the ways that those persons can become constructed and marginalized by dominant groups. The case studies included in this section span foci including global health efforts in South Africa, language and healthcare in indigenous communities in Guatemala, Deaf AIDS activism in the US, and the treatment of epidemics in indigenous communities in Venezuela. Issues including community, equity, access, participation, power, privilege, and marginalization are all relevant across the different cases. Collectively, these chapters challenge us to think about the ways that language connects to individual, community, and public health and to broader issues of social change.

Critical Questions

As you read these cases, we encourage you to consider the following questions:

1 In each of the chapters, how is language used as a mode to provide or deny access to community and individual health needs?
2 Why is language so central to equity in health care?
3 How can language effectively be used in health care contexts to enact social change?

11 Language, Justice, and Rabies

Notes from a Fatal Crossroads

Charles L. Briggs

I reflect here on an apprenticeship in language in social justice, reporting lessons learned after being invited to participate in an innovative effort to challenge social injustices in eastern Venezuela's Delta Amacuro rainforest. Since these efforts unfolded in the middle of an epidemic, they might seem to have more to say about health and social justice, but my goal is to use them in suggesting innovative ways that linguistic anthropologists can contribute to social justice debates.

I think it important to think through how linguistic anthropologists enter into discussions of social justice which, as Amaryta Sen (2011) and others suggest, are complex. In a short essay, I can only briefly outline my theoretical approach. The need for critical analytic work here springs from a foundational separation between how scholars have defined notions of language and politics. In a text that helped shape the foundations of modernity, seventeenth-century writer John Locke constructed language as an autonomous "province of knowledge" that had to be carefully separated from politics (Bauman and Briggs 2003). Locke similarly marginalized considerations of embodiment, affect, poetics, and rhetoric, and he carefully bounded language from scientific research. The lingering impact of this opposition is reflected to this day in a common failure by linguistic anthropologists and critical medical anthropologists to recognize important parallels between their work, respectively, on language ideologies and constructions of medicine, disease, and health. Given that patterns of injustice involve multiple loci of ideology and practice, failing to challenge such foundational binaries can limit the scope and depth of work on language and social justice.

Secondly, I emphasize inequities rather than inequalities. Focusing on *inequalities* involves identifying two phenomena and projecting their relationship through an expectation of sameness; difference thus seems exceptional and ipso facto problematic. Frameworks for identification and comparison, often statistical, pose as preexisting, standing outside engagement with social justice. Identifying inequalities involves a process of decontextualization, meaning isolating particular phenomena to make them visible, and it contains debates within the contours of what is projected as an existing social order, restricting questions of justice to potential redistributions of existing forms of power, resources, and recognition. By focusing on *inequities*, I draw attention to ways that imbalances in power and wellbeing are produced. Analyzing connections between forms of inequity and injustice obscured by dominant frameworks, it points to the possibility for fundamental social change.

As work on indigenous methodologies would suggest (Smith 1999), starting with received scholarly approaches and using them to explore social justice issues fails to grasp how scholarly tools and approaches enter into the production of inequities. Claims to provide scholarly analyses of folk understandings of language project scientific authority and essentialize particular ideological positions. The situation I describe rather called for what I will refer to as *ethnographic humility*, for viewing myself as part of broader knowledge-making processes and my role as documenting innovations without claiming credit for producing them. A related principle that I stress is *critical ethnographic openness*. When I was asked to join efforts to end a mysterious epidemic that had been killing children and young adults, I saw it initially as an issue of health and social justice. Parents and local leaders rather pointed to ways that health- and language-related inequities were fatally entangled. The need to challenge established disciplinary boundaries thus led me to see how what I call health/communicative inequities had thwarted efforts to diagnose the disease.

The mysterious epidemic

Venezuela's second-largest indigenous population, referred to as "the Warao," lives primarily in the Orinoco delta. Most scholars classify Warao as a linguistic isolate (Campbell 2012: 70).[1] An ethno-racial binary between "indigenous members of the Warao ethnic group" and "non-indigenous" residents structures the region's political economy, and pro-indigenous and poor-policies of President Hugo Chávez's socialist revolution failed to displace these inequities. Health conditions are abysmal. Access to potable water and sewage facilities is virtually nil. Child mortality is a staggering 26 percent (Villalba et al. 2013). Respiratory and diarrheal diseases, tuberculosis, and HIV/AIDS are common. Cholera—a preventable and treatable bacterial infection—killed approximately 500 in 1992–1993 (Briggs and Mantini-Briggs 2003).

Then in July 2007 children began to die from a mysterious disease in Mukoboina, a small community whose health-related services consisted of female herbal specialists and a healer who uses music, touch, and tobacco smoke (see Figure 11.1).[2] Odilia and Romer Torres's son Yordi developed a strange fever in August. Odilia remembers, "He was really hot." Yordi's grandmother, an herbal medicine specialist, tried to lower the fever. The parents approached healer Inocencio Torres, telling him anxiously that it was "the same fever" that had already killed two cousins. Inocencio used new songs to lure *hebu* pathogens into his own larynx and force them to reveal why they

Figure 11.1 Houses in Mukoboina, Delta Amacuro, Venezuela, 2010.
Photograph by Charles L. Briggs

were killing Mukoboina's children. Giving up, he stated, "The doctors have medicines. We should take patients to them."

At the Nabasanuka clinic, Dr. Ricardo Cáceres hospitalized Yordi. Having failed in his efforts to diagnose other children with the strange fever, he proposed sending Yordi to an urban hospital. Yordi had heard how his cousin died in an ICU. Demanding a role in shaping his treatment, Yordi refused: "Mommy, I don't want to go. If I go, I'll die." Released "against medical advice," in Cáceres's words,[3] the couple took him to another healer, but his fever grew worse. "When he saw a glass of water, he couldn't look at it, he was afraid. And saliva kept coming." The parents agreed to doctor's plan, but Yordi died before they left.

Two days later, Yordi's little brother came down with "the same fever." The parents took Henry to the doctor, who treated and released him, then to healers. Henry died on September 14. After seven Mukoboinan children died, the disease mysteriously disappeared. Two months later, Odilia gave birth to a girl (see Figure 11.2). But in January, a new wave of cases began with four-year-old Yomelis. The couple had not lost faith in Cáceres, who proposed hospitalization. After trying to multiply chances of finding a cure by taking Yomelis to two healers, they left.

Hospital doctors diagnosed some kind of neurological disorder. Yomelis's breathing produced crackling noises, and she salivated profusely. Romer and

112   *C. L. Briggs*

Figure 11.2 Odilila Torres and Her Daughter Yunelis, 2008.
Photograph by Charles L. Briggs

Odilia lacked money and food. They tried to comfort Yomelis, restless and in acute pain. Romer recalls when physicians first spoke to them, in Spanish:

> The doctor called us into the hallway. Yomelis was holding my arm tightly ... "Your daughter is not going to recover. Your daughter is dying. Sit down here, next to me." We sat down next to her. "You can't go near her right now." I didn't say anything. We went back inside ... She was already dead. The non-indigenous doctor called us again, "Come here, sit down next to me." We sat next to her. "Your daughter has died."

Arriving home two days later, they opened Yomelis's coffin: "it looked as if they had split her head open from front to back, and she was cut from her neck down." Romer slid his finger around the crown of his head and from neck to navel. Seeing the signs of an autopsy—performed without notice, explanation, or consent—led them to retrospectively construct care provided by hospital physicians as torture.

This second wave of deaths ended in February. A third, June–August, killed sixteen. In all, thirty-two children and six young adults died.

Health/Communicative Inequities and Social Injustice

If, as residents suggested, the epidemic embodied social injustice, where should we look for the factors that produced it? Paul Farmer (2003) famously called attention to inequities in access to healthcare as a social justice issue.

Here, however, no one was denied care or received a bill. Listening to the parents' stories suggests what they identified as social justice issues.

When their child fell ill, parents attempted to access all available forms of diagnosis and treatment. The failure of all of them increased the complexity and precarity of their decision-making. Beyond transporting, holding, and comforting their children, they compiled archives containing details obtained from other parents, their own perceptions, and experiences with each new caregiver. Nevertheless, no caregivers considered the parents to be knowledge producers; few were interested in the narratives they used to share their observations.

Local nurses listened to the parents' narratives, but they mainly looked for details to correlate with what they heard with their stethoscopes and medicines neatly arranged in cabinets. Things were different at the clinic. Nurses quickly called the doctor, who asked, with nurses translating, questions designed to elicit fill-in-the-blank answers. Nurses recorded names, dates of birth, places of residence, symptoms, and dates on which symptoms emerged in the clinic logbook. No space enabled parents to offer their observations. Many parents reported feeling frustrated, angry as the doctor projected himself as the only producer of knowledge about their children's illnesses, reducing them to suppliers of details that only became knowledge when he elicited and interpreted them. When parents widened the scope of diagnosis and treatment by visiting healers, Cáceres responded angrily; he wrote of one patient that "the treating physician decided to refer her [to the hospital], but the parents refused and proceeded to discharge the patient against medical advice" in order to visit a healer. The indigenous/nonindigenous ethno-racial binary and its recoding as a multilingual hierarchy—in which doctors spoke only Spanish and patients mostly Warao—is important here. The parents' experience was similar with healers, however, all Warao speakers, who similarly extracted details but failed to consider parents as knowledge producers.

The parents' grief was thus compounded by what I call *health/communicative inequities* that confined their health/communicative labor to minute spaces that were conferred, structured, and constrained by caregivers. Each increase in the level of care brought a significant *increase* in health/communicative inequities, culminated by stays in metropolitan hospitals in which parents were not asked questions and procedures were not explained to them. Undisclosed autopsies were the last straw.

In what Judith Irvine and Susan Gal (2000, 38) refer to as fractal recursivity, which they characterize as "the projection of an opposition, salient at some level of relationship, onto some other level." Here hierarchical relations between the physician and his patients—projected as knowledge producers versus passive (and possible defective) recipients—was reproduced upwards in biomedical and institutional terms through Cáceres's interactions with officials and urban physicians. After sending patients to the hospital, Cáceres asked by radio, letter, and visits to town for results of tests and treatment; the regional director warned that further inquiries could cost him his career. When parents demanded to know what killed their children and what the autopsies had shown, Cáceres had no answers; anger and distrust led many parents to stop bringing their children to him for any illness.

Health/communicative inequities emerged in other sites. Local leaders tried to hold events in which parents could tell their stories. They framed their stories as acts of witnessing, demanding forms of listening that signaled recognition that their children's lives were grievable (Butler 2009). Parents wanted their stories to become mobile, to reach distant audiences and move them to action. When the state epidemiologist came to investigate the deaths, the parents excitedly gathered. The visitors did not grant Mukoboinans control over the encounter, but rather "interviewed community leaders," asked parents for the children's names and ages, dates of death, and symptoms, and took water and blood samples. The epidemiologists denied residents a chance to share their observations or ask questions. Other epidemiological commissions followed, but each encounter was pervasively structured by health/communicative inequities. The epidemiologists' lack of interest in more extensive dialogue was often signaled by using motorboat operators—not bilingual nurses—as interpreters. Mukoboinans asked the visitors to share their observations and hypotheses, but none bothered to do so. Language entered multiply into reproducing fatal forms of inequity here, as Spanish was fashioned as the language of medicine and Warao as simply a vehicle for acquiring "facts" from a subordinate population and in terms of which ways of speaking were deemed to constitute knowledge and which seemed to embody forms of ignorance that seemingly produced these fatal health conditions.

Inequities got stacked upon inequities. One language, Spanish, was cast as the voice of science, medicine, and modernity, just as Warao seemed to doctors, epidemiologists, health officials, and journalists as only suitable for conveying ignorance and superstition. Words spoken in Warao could not become mobile, could not leave delta communities and enter public health offices or newsrooms. Speakers of the two languages ipso facto became respectively knowledge producers and individuals beyond the pale of medical reason. What was projected as linguistic and cultural difference seemed to turn Warao bodies into natural repositories of infectious illness. Thus, the failure to diagnose a disease for more than a year called more for political containment than an all-out effort to stop it.

Challenging Health/Communicative Inequities

Parents and local leaders increasingly came to see the health/communicative inequities that were woven into the discursive background of interactions focused on diagnosis and treatment as the major impediment to collective efforts to stop the mysterious disease. Accordingly, they increasingly tried to challenge them. Parents sometimes rejected Cáceres's recommendation to transport patients, at least initially. One father wanted more control over his daughter's treatment, so he took her directly to Tucupita, the state capital. Yordi, as noted, objected to being sent to the hospital. Elbia Torres Rivas (see Figure 11.3) had accompanied her dying husband to a metropolitan ICU. After witnessing the failure of treatments he received and feeling the painful effects of health/communicative inequities, she rejected her parents' plan to take her

Figure 11.3 Elbia Torres Rivas, an hour before her death, with her mother, Anita
        Rivas, 2008.

Photograph by Charles L. Briggs

to the clinic when she developed the same symptoms: "No," she replied, "I'm
not going to any clinic. I'm going to die in my home." Mukoboinans grew
increasingly angry when epidemiologists deemed them to have no health/com-
municative rights, even in their own community. They accordingly grew less
willing to participate in each subsequent investigation. Epidemiologists read
these responses as evidence of "the community's closed nature" rather than as
indicators of health/communicative inequities, and they blamed Mukoboinans
for their own diagnostic failure. The parents were shocked to see newspaper
articles reporting that health officials thought they might have killed their own
children by feeding them garbage or poisonous fruit or fish.

I noted above that analyzing inequities, the underlying factors that produce
inequalities, can produce new imaginaries and foster efforts to transform existing social (dis)orders. Pushed by the parents to find a way to challenge health/
communicative as much as the successive waves of death, two local leaders,
brothers Conrado and Enrique Moraleda, decided to launch their own investigation. Their broader goal was to turn the stereotype of "the Warao" as being
unable to understand what doctors told them on its head by becoming producers
of knowledge about the epidemic. Venezuelan physician Clara Mantini-Briggs
and I happened to be in the delta, and they recruited us, along with healer Tirso
Gómez and nurse/EMT Norbelys Gómez. We began by honoring the parents'
demands to tell their narratives; our six-person team became their audience.
We listened to the laments they sang over their children's bodies. When not

limited to filling in blanks, the parents' narratives provided rich details that suggested a recurrent pattern: fever, headache, body ache, strange tingling and paralysis, hallucinations, convulsions, dysphagia (difficulty in swallowing), excessive salivation, hydrophobia (fear of water), and, in every case death. Examining dying patient Elbia Rivas Torres confirmed Clara's presumptive hypothesis of rabies. The parents reported that most of the dead children had been bitten nocturnally by vampire bats 1–2 months prior to developing symptoms, suggesting a mode of transmission. Easily prevented by vaccination, rabies is untreatable and nearly always fatal once symptoms appear. In delivering a report to national health officials and making articulate statements to national and international journalists, Conrado, Enrique, Norbelys, and Tirso shattered health/communicative stereotypes and demanded an end to health/communicative inequities. Their efforts can offer important insights into language and social justice issues and how anthropologists and other scholars enter into them.

Lessons Learned about Language and Social Justice

Franz Boas framed anthropology as the key for achieving social justice. He argued that all of us are duped by culture, taking particular ways of seeing the world as natural and necessary; racism and imperialism spring, he argued, from efforts to impose one set of cultural beliefs and practices on others.[4] By revealing hidden assumptions and documenting other cultural perspectives, anthropology could free individuals from "the fetters of tradition" (Boas [1911]1965, 201), promoting the rationality, scientific outlook, and cosmopolitanism that would prevent discrimination, xenophobia, and war. Writing in the United States in 2017, Boas's goals resonate strongly. Nevertheless, my experience in the epidemic prompts me to challenge Boas's understanding of the relationship between scholarship and social justice and to suggest two guiding principles.

The first is *ethnographic humility*. Multiple mysteries emerged in the epidemic: what was the disease, why it had it not been diagnosed, and what could sustain such a pervasive regime of injustice. Coming to recognize that health/communicative inequities were playing a key role in obstructing the exchanges of knowledge that could have led much earlier to diagnosing and stopping the epidemic did not spring directly from Boasian anthropological clairvoyance, from an ability to see what was invisible to everyone else. Delta residents are painfully aware of health/communicative inequities. Like deaths from cholera in 1992–1993, the mysterious epidemic sparked intense debates in the area regarding how these inequities moved across sites and scales (Carr and Lempert 2015)—clinical medicine, epidemiology, health education, health policy, and journalism. The children's deaths rendered the way that health/communicative inequities produce, not simply reflect, health inequities extraordinarily visible. Reproducing stereotypes and enforcing forms of discrimination that are simultaneously linguistic and medical provided the central ideological basis for the region's ethno-racial economy. Claiming analytic work that was well under-way when I arrived in July 2008 as my own would reproduce these very health/communicative inequities.

A second lesson that emerged could be termed a spirit of *critical ethnographic openness*. When Conrado recruited me, the cause of the disease was a mystery but the social justice issue seemed obvious: health inequities were to blame. Focusing on health and social justice alone would, however, have pre-cluded grasping the crucial role of the parents' failed efforts to be recognized as collaborators in solving the mystery. Rather than helping to illuminate these connections, received scholarly practices imposed constraints. The organiza-tion of anthropological practice teaches us to follow particular subdisciplinary paths. Although some anthropologists have contributed greatly to health and social justice debates and others to language and social justice issues, these discussions have existed largely in complementary distribution—adopting mutually intelligible scholarly languages, citing non-overlapping bodies of literature, and seldom entering into the same texts. Social justice issues, how-ever, do not respect scholarly boundaries. In the delta's ethno-racial economy, language and social justice will never be achieved without health and social justice—and vice versa. What is required here goes beyond combining schol-arly approaches to do the hard theoretical work of challenging their premises and boundaries.

To circumvent the tendency of case studies to circumscribe issues, I suggest two broader implications. First, health/communicative inequities are hardly confined to Delta Amacuro. Decades of research have identified systemic factors that produce health inequities, both between wealthy and low-income countries and within each. In the United States, studies suggest that African Americans and Latinos/as get poorer healthcare; clinicians' racialized stereo-types of patients as worse communicators—as less able to understand their doctors and less capable of turning discourse into behavioral changes—shape less desirable treatment outcomes. Projections of racialized patients as defec-tive medical communicators—and therefore as partially responsible for health problems—is a leitmotif in news stories (Briggs and Hallin 2016). Extensive research on "doctor-patient interaction" is generally geared toward producing better techniques to enhance biomedical outcomes;[5] linking what happens in clinical settings to other health/communicative inequities would suggest that we should rather ask how existing social orders must be transformed in order to achieve *communicative justice in health*.

Second, although ideological constructions of language and health struc-ture social relations in Delta Amacuro, connections between ideological constructions of language and other social fields—such as legal and car-ceral arenas—might be more important elsewhere. Adopting the principles of ethnographic humility and critical ethnographic openness and challenging theoretical assumptions and (sub)disciplinary boundaries provides, I suggest, a crucial point of departure for locating the particular ways that issues of language and social justice are enmeshed in other social worlds.

118   *C. L. Briggs*

Notes

1 Greenberg (1987: 106) lists Warao as Chibchan-Paezan.
2 The epidemic is recounted in greater detail in Briggs and Mantini-Briggs (2016).
3 From the report of Delta Amacuro's regional epidemiologist, dated February 6, 2008.
4 See Bauman and Briggs (2003) on the place of language in Boas's construction of anthropology and social justice.
5 For an important exception, see Waitzkin (1991).

References

Bauman, Richard, and Charles L. Briggs. 2003. *Voices of Modernity: Language Ideologies and the Politics of Inequality*. Cambridge: Cambridge University Press.
Boas, Franz. [1911]1965. *The Mind of Primitive Man*. New York: Free Press.
Briggs, Charles L., and Daniel C. Hallin. 2016. *Making Health Public: How News Coverage is Remaking Media, Medicine, and Contemporary Life*. Abingdon: Routledge.
Briggs, Charles L., and Clara Mantini-Briggs. 2003. *Stories in the Time of Cholera: Racial Profiling during a Medical Nightmare*. Berkeley, CA: University of California Press.
Briggs, Charles L., and Clara Mantini-Briggs. 2016. *Tell Me Why My Children Died: Rabies, Indigenous Knowledge, and Communicative Justice*. Durham, NC: Duke University Press.
Butler, Judith. 2009. *Frames of War: When Is Life Grievable?* London: Verso.
Campbell, Lyle. 2012. Classification of the Indigenous Languages of South America. In *The Indigenous Languages of South America: A Comprehensive Guide*, edited by Lyle Campbell and Verónica Grondona, 59–166. Berlin: De Gruyter Mouton.
Carr, E. Summerson, and Michael Lempert. 2015. *Scale: Discourse and Dimensions of Social Life*. Oakland, CA: University of California Press.
Farmer, Paul. 2003. *Pathologies of Power: Health, Human Rights, and the New War on the Poor*. Berkeley, CA: University of California Press.
Irvine, Judith T., and Susan Gal. 2000. Language Ideology and Linguistic Differentiation. In *Regimes of Language: Ideologies, Polities, and Identities*, edited by Paul V. Kroskrity, 35–84. Santa Fe, NM: School of American Research Press.
Greenberg, Joseph. 1987. *Language in the Americas*. Stanford, CA: Stanford University Press.
Sen, Amaryta. 2011. *The Idea of Justice*. Cambridge, MA: Harvard University Press.
Smith, Linda Tuhiwai. 1999. *Decolonizing Methodologies: Research and Indigenous Peoples*. London: Zed Books.
Villalba, Julian A., Yushi Liu, Mauyuri K. Alvarez, et al. 2013. Low Child Survival Index in a Multi-dimensionally Poor Amerindian Population in Venezuela. *PLoS One* 8(12): 1–13.
Waitzkin, Howard. 1991. *The Politics of Medical Encounters: How Patients and Doctors Deal with Social Problems*. New Haven, CT: Yale University Press.

12 Ethics, Expertise, and Inequities in Global Health Discourses

The Case of Non-Profit HIV/AIDS Research in South Africa

Steven P. Black

Introduction

This chapter discusses inequities in global health discourses, focusing on implicit assumptions (discussed later as "indexical presuppositions") about the communicative roles of medical professionals and patient–activists. The discussion is rooted in ethnographic fieldwork with people living with HIV/AIDS in Durban, South Africa, based on my participation on a community outreach board of a non-profit biomedical research organization. This chapter examines a top-down model of medical communication that is prevalent in global health (Briggs and Hallin 2016). In this model, patients are sources of medical data for doctors and epidemiologists. Health professionals analyze this data and patients then receive the results of these studies, often in prescriptions for behavior and treatment. Even in efforts described by global health professionals as "collaborative," the perceived scientific objectivity of the top down model in conjunction with entrenched relationships of inequity may yield a "biopower" (Foucault 1965) that is difficult, if not impossible, to counteract. This chapter argues that the persistence of a top down model of scientific knowledge creation and health communication hinders social justice efforts in global health (see also Briggs and Mantini-Briggs 2016). The case study highlights how marginalized patient–activists contributed to the creation of medical knowledge, detailing how these contributions were ignored or minimized. In response, this chapter advocates what has been theorized as accompaniment (Bucholtz et al. 2016)—inverting or mitigating expert-activist communicative hierarchies—as one way to enact social justice in global health contexts. The dominance of scientific medicine (biopower) may make this language and social justice case study distinct. Still, inequities embedded in the roles of expert and aid recipient may apply more broadly, and advocates of social justice should closely attend to implicit assumptions about similar communicative role hierarchies in other contexts.

Biocommunicability and Indexical Presupposition

This chapter utilizes two key theories about language and culture: biocommunicability and indexical presupposition (Briggs 2011; Silverstein 2003).

The theory of biocommunicability explains cultural models of health communication. Not only patients but also medical practitioners use cultural models (including dominant biomedical models) to understand illness and engage in healing (Garro 2000; Kleinman 1978). Circulation—how pathogens, medicine, resources, discourses, and people move through the world (see Hörbst and Gerrits 2016)—is an important component of cultural models of health, and communication is central to this circulation. The term *biocommunicable models* refers to cultural models about health communication, especially models of how health discourse (e.g. medical terms, phrases, ways of speaking about illness, epidemiological data) could or should circulate (Briggs 2011). In reality, health discourse circulates among patients, doctors, epidemiologists, and others in ways that are complex and non-linear. However, some biocommunicable models simplify or obscure this complexity in ways that may shape the course of epidemics, as is discussed below (Briggs and Hallin 2016, 7).

This chapter also utilizes the concept of indexical presupposition. A presupposition is an unspoken idea that is necessary to understand the meaning of a phrase or sentence. For instance, the statement "the king of France is bald" only makes sense if there is a king of France. However, this idea (that there *is* a king of France) is not stated explicitly. It is a presupposition of the sentence (Russell 1905). Power relationships between conversational participants may also be presumed but unstated (Silverstein 2003, 199). For instance, the roles of professor and student (or doctor and patient) can shape a conversation between two individuals without either party explicitly mentioning those roles. Power relationships are often assumed based on past interactions, institutional configurations, and human social spaces (e.g. classrooms, medical offices). These are *indexical* presuppositions because they presuppose and create social contexts for communication. When presumed social roles and hierarchies are connected to the circulation of medical discourses, indexical presupposition becomes a part of biocommunicability. Both biocommunicability and indexical presupposition are aspects of language use that run like a current or undertow beneath the river of spoken discourse. A careful analysis of social encounters can reveal some of the ways that these hidden undertows impact speakers as they engage in collaborative social action.

The Biocommunicable Model of Collaboration in Global Health

Global health is a relatively young discipline that includes a complex array of actors, including doctors, public health specialists, patient–activists, government and international institutions (e.g. the US Centers for Disease Control and Prevention, the World Health Organization, the South African National AIDS Council), non-profit organizations (e.g. the Bill and Melinda Gates Foundation), and corporations (e.g. drug companies that donate a portion of their medications). The consolidation of the field in the 1980s and 1990s was catalyzed in part by the growing HIV/AIDS pandemic. At that time, global health professionals worked to distance themselves from predecessors in such fields as colonial medicine, missionary medicine, and tropical medicine by emphasizing health as a human right and compassionate (though objectively motivated) care (Greene et al. 2013).

After the 9/11 US terrorist attacks of 2001, especially, global health was increasingly divided into two regimes: global health security and humanitarian biomedicine (Lakoff 2010; see also Fassin 2011). Humanitarian approaches have sometimes emphasized how structural violence and illness are interconnected (Farmer 1999). This has become a moral call to action to effect social justice: "As wealthy individuals learn to perceive that the privileges they enjoy on a daily basis are mediated by the same structures that deny the poor a fair shake, many will be compelled to try to change the system" (Suri et al. 2013, 255). Humanitarian biomedical professionals comment on the power imbalances inherent when doctors and researchers of the global North intervene in health challenges of the global South (ibid.). In response, global health professionals have emphasized their intention to work with and benefit "partners" in host countries through an ethics of "collaboration." In some cases, different modes of collaboration have been specified to correspond to distinct types of interventions (e.g. loose collaboration for an urgent response to an Ebola outbreak versus close collaboration in HIV/AIDS interventions). Collaboration is now a well-developed global health cultural model of how different global health actors should communicate across social, economic, cultural, and national borders to plan and implement health interventions (Rosenberg et al. 2010). In other words, collaboration is a key biocommunicable model employed by global health professionals. The discussion below focuses on one example of this sort of collaboration.

In 2008, I conducted nine months of ethnographic fieldwork in Durban, South Africa, with an HIV support group and activist organization. The fieldwork was complemented by my earlier study of Zulu language and culture, pilot research, and follow up fieldwork in the summer of 2013. The HIV support group members with whom I worked were black South Africans who were bilingual isiZulu/ English speakers, and all were living with HIV. Most were impoverished or working class. Many were unemployed or underemployed. Individually, a number of group members had completed lay care and counseling courses. They saw HIV counseling as a possible career path, though most opportunities were part-time and low paying. Several group members worked and volunteered with treatment and counseling organizations in the metropolitan Durban area.

Indexical Presuppositions of Collaboration

During my fieldwork, I was fortunate to learn about a fairly radical approach in a TB/HIV treatment organization that was co-run by a Harvard-trained doctor and a research participant. That organization hired people with HIV, who then received intensive training on biomedical understandings of HIV and TB.

Several research participants worked for the organization in this capacity. These worker-patient–activists became experts at communicating about biomedicine to other South Africans, translating/ interpreting between languages (English and isiZulu), and navigating multiple cultural models of illness (biomedicine, Christian faith, and traditional medicine). Such an approach also employed people with HIV and provided marketable job training. It implicitly rejected the presupposition that patients were endpoints of top-down biocommunicable models and reconfigured hierarchies to value the contributions of people living with HIV as individuals with expert knowledge and skills. Unfortunately, the doctor–leader of this program saw ethnography as, at best, a potential distraction, and did not allow me access to audio-video record or conduct participant observation with the group.

Four research participants were part of another effort, a community outreach board for a Durban-based global health NPO, the AIDS Research Center (the ARC—all names of people and South African organizations used in this chapter are pseudonyms). The ARC was an excellent example of the complex interconnections of global health "collaboration." It was linked to UNAIDS (the United Nations AIDS program), funded by the US President's Emergency Plan for AIDS Relief (PEPFAR) and CARE (an Atlanta, Georgia-based NPO), and aided by doctors and researchers from ivy league universities. The ARC's collaborative approach included an outreach board, called the Community Research Support Group (CRSG), which was comprised of twelve community leaders and patient–activists. One research participant in my project, who was a leader of the CRSG, invited me to attend. I participated in group meetings about once a month from June through September 2008.

Ethically Participating in Collaboration

CRSG meetings were held at the ARC's two-story downtown office, where medical services for ARC study participants were provided. Meetings were upstairs in a small board room with a conference table and projector screen. Discussion was held primarily in English, as was common in South African contexts where speakers came from different linguistic backgrounds. Many Indian and White South Africans did not speak African languages. The institutional preference for English was sometimes difficult for isiZulu-speaking research participants, who occasionally apologized and switched into isiZulu to be able to fully express themselves when topics relating to community engagement were raised. English was presupposed, a correlate and reinforcement of the unstated favored position of the doctors and researchers.

Research participants attended the meetings both because they were contributing to the fight against AIDS and because they were offered lunch and 50 Rand (approximately 7 dollars) for transportation. When I drove them to the meeting and donated my transportation money, each earned about 8 dollars and a free meal. Donating my funds and offering rides might be interpreted as coercing the participation of research "subjects." However, in attending the

CRSG I had entered into a social activity that was already regularly occurring at the invitation of people who were already both participants in my research project and CRSG members. In this context, I think the extra funds were an added benefit but not a coercive motivation for participation. Furthermore, I was in a position of relative wealth. I would also be taking the results of field-work with me back to the United States to write a dissertation and get a job. I was materially benefiting from my involvement. I suggest that to *not* offer available resources to participants would be unethical and would be counter to the ethos of social justice that informed my research.

I did not audio-record CRSG meetings. This group met only occasionally and thus did not have time to become accustomed the presence of an audio-recorder, where issues of HIV stigma and confidential medical issues would arise (for more on this topic, see Black 2017). Instead, I took detailed notes, writing down words, phrases, and exchanges to the best of my ability that I found significant during the course of the meetings.

Enacting Participant Roles: Doctors and Patients, or Researchers and Activists?

My notes from a September 2008 CRSG discussion of a medical study examining simultaneous treatment of tuberculosis (TV) and HIV revealed differences in models of biocommunicability between doctor-researchers and patient–activists. In South Africa, tuberculosis was closely correlated with HIV infection. At the meeting, the ARC director, Dr. Naidoo, visited the CRSG. Dr. Naidoo explained to us that there was little medical research on TB/ HIV co-treatment because "TB is not a big problem in the West" other than among Haitians in New York. He said that the South African government guidelines were based on World Health Organization guidelines, which were in turn based on the "opinions of experts." One purpose of the ARC study was to provide some measurable data on the impact and efficacy of co-treating TB and HIV. Dr. Naidoo stated that the study's main concern was "pill burn"—whether patients' livers would be able to handle both the TB and HIV medication at the same time.

One CRSG member and HIV patient–activist, Sbu, asked Dr. Naidoo about how the recommended TB/HIV pill regimen might change as a result of the findings of the ARC's co-treatment study. Naidoo responded, "we can't answer that yet."

Sbu followed up with another question: "was the study successful?"

"Yes," Naidoo answered. "We have answered the study question, but specific recommendations will come out next year." Naidoo then suggested that patients continue to follow the WHO guidelines for pill regimens and noted that he thought those guidelines would be changed soon. Sbu was unsatisfied. He said, "We appreciate it [the guideline] if it is evidence-based" (emphasizing these last two words). Notably, "data-driven" and "evidence-based" are two buzz terms in contemporary global health media. Sbu was unhappy that the current WHO guidelines were not evidence based. He wanted preliminary recommendations rooted in the current ARC study. Naidoo did not respond and the meeting continued, ending with Naidoo asking us to keep this information private until after PEPFAR and the WHO were notified.

In his role as ARC director and researcher, Dr. Naidoo did his best to enable collaboration throughout the research and treatment process—the CRSG was a prime example of these efforts. Despite his emphasis on collaboration, though, patient perspectives were still sometimes marginalized. The above encounter involved a conflict of two biocommunicable models. Naidoo enacted a dominant global health model in which patients were presumed to be passive recipients of medical knowledge/ care and sources of raw medical data. PEPFAR and the WHO were the relevant institutions that would provide new recommendations to patients after studying the ARC findings, which were in turn based on input data from patients. He urged Sbu and others to wait (patiently) until the findings from the study were fully vetted, sent to the highest levels of global health administration, and returned to people living with HIV in the form of bureaucratized recommendations. Sbu, on the other hand, was not content to wait and passively receive recommendations. He responded not just as a patient but also as an HIV activist with expertise in the subject matter and a stake in the outcome of the research project.

Presuppositions of Patient Passivity versus Activist Ethical Intercorporeality

One reason that this conflict of models was noticeable was that the dominant top-down global health model did not fit with the ARC's espoused model of collaboration. Many patient–activists such as Sbu felt that their participation in medical trials—and in documentary films and ethnographic research—was a donation of their time and efforts to a cause they felt strongly about. Medical anthropologists have described patients' intent engagement with medical research as "ethical intercorporeality" (Wentzell 2016). Thinking of himself as an active, ethically engaged participant in the world of global health, Sbu was critical of previous recommendations that were not "evidence based." He was also likely suspicious of the notion that people whose lives depended on their treatment decisions should simply wait another year until official recommendations were produced.

The dominant biocommunicable model of patient passivity shaped this communicative encounter but was never stated. In other words, the hierarchical patient-doctor relationship was presupposed. If Sbu had directly confronted Naidoo, a person who controlled his access to life-saving treatment, what word or phrase of Dr. Naidoo's would he have countered? There was little recourse for him or others to confront this social relationship because it was not explicitly articulated. In its broader context, this encounter demonstrates how health inequities and communicative inequities are co-produced (Briggs and Mantini-Briggs 2016). Dr. Naidoo and others at the ARC enjoyed notable benefits as a result of their work and expertise. For instance, in 2016, Dr. Naidoo was inducted as a Fellow for a prestigious academic organization in South Africa. Even in the midst of a collaborative approach to global health research, patient–activists' agency and contributions to the research process were minimized due to presuppositions embedded in global health biocommunicable models.

Conclusion

This case study demonstrates how presupposed participant role hierarchies in dominant biocommunicable models of global health may shape patient–activist involvement in global health collaboration. Dr. Naidoo was a relatively privileged Indian South African doctor working with South African health institutions, American doctors, American aid groups, American governmental initiatives, and international institutions. Sbu was a relatively impoverished black South African HIV patient. The web of global health collaboration interfaced with overlapping dichotomizations of inequity: resource rich vs. resource poor countries, privileged vs. marginalized racial groups, and doctors vs. patients. Such dichotomizations also intersected with other societal inequities patterned by gender, sexuality, and class, molded by centuries of colonialism and imperialism. The result was that Sbu was encouraged to collaborate and participate, but his participation was shaped by Dr. Naidoo's assumptions about how the creation and distribution of authoritative biomedical knowledge should unfold.

Top-down biocommunicable models that are dominant in global health privilege doctors and researchers as sources of authoritative discourse and medical knowledge. In reality, "knowledge about health is coproduced by health and communication professionals and laypersons in a broad range of sites" (Briggs and Mantini-Briggs 2016, 8). However, patient–activist input and analysis may be devalued or dismissed by doctors due to social role hierarchies. This results in communicative inequities in patient-expert encounters during collaboration. Such communicative inequities reinforce already existing inequities in access to health care (ibid.).

Patient–activists' words may be constrained by not only the power imbalances of inequity but also the need to maintain access to treatment. They may feel unable to voice strong criticism. As a result, change must be initiated by the relatively powerful—by global health professionals, researchers, and scholars. My fieldwork has led me to reject top-down biocommunicable models and to emphasize the high value of patient–activists as experts at translating between languages and navigating multiple cultural models of illness. A broader application of this approach might help to alleviate communicative inequities in global health and, in so doing, positively impact health inequities.

Acknowledgements

Thank you to Elizabeth Falconi and Lynette Arnold for comments on previous versions of this paper. Funding for this project was provided by the National

Science Foundation, a Fulbright-Hays Zulu Group Project Abroad, a Foreign Language and Area Studies grant, UCLA, and Georgia State University. Thank you to Netta Avineri for her excellent editorial guidance, to the editors of this volume for their inclusion of the chapter, and to the anonymous reviewers whose patient commentary greatly improved the chapter.

References

Black, Steven. 2017. "Anthropological Ethics and the Communicative Affordances of Audio-Video Recorders in Ethnographic Fieldwork: Transduction as Theory." *American Anthropologist* 119(1): 46–57.

Briggs, Charles L. 2011. "Biocommunicability." In *A Companion to Medical Anthropology*, edited by Merrill Singer and Pamela I. Erickson, 459–476. Malden, MA: Wiley-Blackwell.

Briggs, Charles L., and Daniel C. Hallin. 2016. *Making Health Public: How News Coverage is Remaking Media, Medicine, and Contemporary Life*. New York: Routledge.

Briggs, Charles L., and Clara Mantini-Briggs. 2016. *Tell Me Why My Children Died: Rabies, Indigenous Knowledge, and Communicative Justice*. Durham, NC: Duke University.

Bucholtz, Mary, Dolores Inés Casillas, and Jin Sook Lee (2016). Beyond Empowerment: Accompaniment and Sociolinguistic Justice in a Youth Research Program. In *Sociolinguistic Research: Application and Impact*, edited by Robert Lawson and David Sayers, 25–44. New York: Routledge.

Farmer, Paul. 1999. *Infections and Inequalities: The Modern Plagues*. Los Angeles, CA: University of California Press.

Fassin, Didier. 2011. *Humanitarian Reason: A Moral History of the Present*. Los Angeles, CA: University of California Press.

Foucault, Michel. 1965. *The Birth of the Clinic: An Archaeology of Medical Perception*. New York: Vintage.

Garro, Linda. 2000. "Cultural Knowledge as Resource in Illness Narratives: Remembering Through Accounts of Illness." In *Narrative and the Cultural Construction of Illness and Healing*, edited by Cheryl Mattingly and Linda Garro, 70–87. Los Angeles, CA: University of California Press.

Greene, Jeremy, Marguerite Thorp Basilico, Heidi Kim, and Paul Farmer. 2013. "Colonial Medicine and Its Legacies." In *Reimagining Global Health: An Introduction*, edited by Paul Farmer, Jim Yong Kim, Arthur Kleinman, and Matthew Basilico, 33–73. Los Angeles, CA: University of California Press.

Hörbst, Viola, and Trudie Gerrits. 2016. "Transnational Connections of Health Professionals: Medicoscapes and Assisted Reproduction in Ghana and Uganda." *Ethnicity and Health* 21(4): 357–374.

Kleinman, Arthur. 1978. "Concepts and a Model for the Comparison of Medical Systems as Cultural Systems." *Social Science and Medicine* 12: 85–93.

Lakoff, Andrew. 2010. "Two Regimes of Global Health." *Humanity: An International Journal of Human Rights, Humanitarianism, and Development* 1: 59–79.

Rosenberg, Mark L., Elisabeth S. Hayes, Margaret H. McIntyre, and Nancy Neill. 2010. *Real Collaboration: What it Takes for Global Health to Succeed*. Los Angeles, CA: University of California Press.

Russell, Bertrand. 1905. "On Denoting." *Mind* 14(56): 479–493.

Silverstein, Michael. 2003. "Indexical Order and the Dialectics of Sociolinguistic Life." *Language and Communication* 23(3–4): 193–229.

Suri, Arjun, et al. 2013. "Values and Global Health." In *Reimagining Global Health: An Introduction*, edited by Paul Farmer, Jim Yong Kim, Arthur Kleinman, and Matthew Basilico, 245–286. Berkeley, CA: University of California Press.

Wentzell, Emily A. 2016. "Medical Research Participation as 'Ethical Intercorporeality': Caring for Bio-Social Bodies in a Mexican Human Papillomavirus (HPV) Study." *Medical Anthropology Quarterly* 31(1): 115–132.

13 Interpreting Deaf HIV/AIDS

A Dialogue

Mark Byrd and Leila Monaghan

HIV/AIDS in Deaf communities is a social justice and language issue, part of a larger problem of Deaf access to all kinds of healthcare (Kuenberg, Fellinger, and Fellinger 2016). Differences between the communication norms of most medical establishments and those of Deaf communities have led to systematic disenfranchisement in medical settings. Communication gaps "reinforce ableism, demand extra social labor from disabled people, or pressure people into silence," (Jarman, Monaghan, and Harkin 2017, 97). Since the passage of the Americans with Disabilities Act (the ADA) in 1990, Deaf people have had the right to professional ASL interpreting in public spaces including medical settings (Shapiro 1994). Despite this right, however, Deaf people still have trouble getting access to the information they need to protect themselves and to stay healthy. The National Association of the Deaf regularly sues medical organizations to ensure appropriate services for Deaf people (NAD 2017).

This chapter is a conversation between Mark Byrd and Leila Monaghan. Together we will present a macro (large scale) and micro (small scale) ethnography and history of the impact of AIDS on the US Deaf community, and the barriers that Mark has faced when he has tried to receive medical care. Linguistic anthropologists often look at specific interactions to understand their implications (e.g., Duranti 1997). Combining linguistic anthropological and Deaf and disability studies theory and methods provides a way to understand the "extra social labor" Mark has had to perform to get the treatment he needs. Mark is a Deaf man living with HIV. Leila Monaghan is a hearing HIV-negative woman who has been conducting research on HIV/AIDS in Deaf communities for over 15 years. Together we want to link Mark's specific story to the widespread epidemic of HIV/AIDS in the United States Deaf community.

* * *

Leila: I first became aware of the Deaf AIDS crisis in 1989 when I was taking American Sign Language classes at Gallaudet University. One of my classmates, Gene Bourquin, was part of the network of volunteers as known buddies, organized by the Gay Men's Health

Crisis in New York. There was a vibrant New York Gay Deaf community in the 1980s including a bustling theater scene. AIDS devastated the community. It affected everyone from well-known figures like actor, dancer and activist Sam Edwards, and the first Deaf actor on Broadway Bruce Hlibok, to lesser known individuals such as Constante DeValle, Jr., Bourquin's first buddy who died in 1987 (Monaghan and Schmaling 2010).

Deborah Karp, former director of the Deaf AIDS Project, remembered that even after the death of two close friends from AIDS in the late 1980s, "I didn't know how you got AIDS. There were rumors, but I had no accurate information on how AIDS was actually transmitted" (Monaghan and Karp 2010). This lack of information meant that HIV spread rapidly through the US Deaf community and reflects linguistic barriers between the hearing and Deaf communities. Deaf people often did not have access to prevention materials in ASL or even information in simple written English with illustrations that many people prefer. For example, the word POSITIVE[1] in ASL can be problematic because the sign has connotations of goodness. Experienced signers will often use the sign HAVE-HIV to avoid this confusion.

In 1992 and 1993, the height of the AIDS epidemic, over 75,000 people a year were diagnosed with HIV/AIDS in the United States (MMWR 2011). Despite waning public attention to the disease, HIV is still widespread, with 39,513 US people newly diagnosed as having HIV in 2015 (CDC 2016). Mark has lived with HIV since the worst part of the epidemic. Between 2000 and 2008, Maryland HIV-infection figures showed a Deaf infection rate often double that of hearing people. Recorded Deaf infection rates and number of Deaf people tested have dropped in more recent figures (Monaghan and Schmaling 2010; MDHMH 2018).

Mark: I was diagnosed with HIV in 1993, and received an AIDS diagnosis in 2002. When I was first diagnosed with HIV, I was living in rural Ohio. I saw a sign that the American Red Cross was collecting blood donations. I went ahead and donated a pint of blood. A month later, I received a letter from them to get into contact with them. I had to travel to Columbus, the nearest big city, to receive my diagnosis. The day before, I contacted the American Red Cross and was informed that an interpreter would be there for the appointment.

The next day I was nervous. I got into my car and stopped at the Drive Thru to purchase a Mountain Dew and cigarettes. That midmorning drive, the farmers were out in the fields, getting things ready for planting season. I arrived at the office only to be ushered into a formal office with plush carpeting, stately oak cabinetry, and a large desk. I was alone in the office and wandered to the window to look out and see the gardeners outside planting spring flowers.

I felt a tap on my shoulder. I turned around and came eye to eye with an elegant woman with brown shoulder length hair and a navy suit. I noticed her lips were moving and realized that she was not the interpreter. As I could not hear her introduce herself, I was not sure who she was. I smiled and pointed to my ears. She smiled back with warmth and motioned me to a chair in front of the desk. She pointed to her wrist and tapped it, stating, "time." I nodded my head, "yes."

I sat in the chair and looked around the room and thought, "Where is the interpreter? The interpreter better show up. This is going to be awkward . . ." My train of thoughts were interrupted by the return of the woman. She looked at me half smiling, half apologetically while pointing to her wrist as of indication of "TIME." I smiled, nodded and motioned my hand "COME-ON" for her to tell me what the diagnosis is. She hesitated and opened up her file and pulled out a paper. It was a computer printout with bold letters across it: "HIV."

I was stunned beyond belief.

"HIV."

I chuckled and stared at the words, "HIV." I looked up at her and she had sad expression on her face. I knew that I had to leave. I smiled at her and pointed to my wrist, "TIME." I got up and she motioned me to wait. I stood there, looking at her while she was writing notes asking if I was okay and to call her if I needed to talk. She gave a list of resources as well as information about a local support group with stars around it. I looked at the list and the paper with "HIV" on it, I looked back to her and she opened her arms.

I smiled and fell into her arms.

Leila: There was no known cure for AIDS in 1993. The peak death period of the epidemic was 1995, when 50,628 people died in the US alone. Deaths did not start dropping until the widespread introduction of antiretroviral therapies in 1996 (MMWR 2011).

Mark: It was a cold dreary October morning in 2002, and traffic was backed up on Interstate 5 for miles causing up to 45 minute delays into Seattle. The rains had arrived for the season and were beginning to settle in. I arrived with five minutes to spare for my second visit to my new doctor.

The doctor had no hair on the top of his head but what he lacked on top, he made up for it by having the bushiest beard a man can grow. He was very personable and accommodating but it was impossible to lip read what he was saying. The ASL interpreter arrived, making an announcement to both the doctor and me that, due to time constraints he had to leave ten minutes early to get to the next appointment, meaning that my appointment with the doctor was now 20 minutes not 30 minutes. The doctor and I were going to be discussing HIV and antidepressant medications as eight months prior, I had lost my boyfriend of three years to AIDS.

"Oh! Your lab work came back. Let me look for it," said the doctor as he fiddled with my bulging medical folder.

I nodded and looked at him and the interpreter.

The clock kept on ticking while the doctor was still looking for the lab results. "I'm sorry. We got a new employee who hasn't quite mastered our filing system in our files. Give me a second . . . Ooh! Found it!"

I was relieved that the doctor had found the documents before time completely ran out with the interpreter. Deaf people's time and needs too often get squeezed out by other people's requirements.

"Okay your numbers came back and I know that you been depressed for a while. That had an impact on your t-cell count and so forth. Depression can bring your immune system down and with Ambien and medication refill, you will get a sense of yourself back. Your liver enzymes are alright, cholesterol is good, T-cell count is 190. You crossed the threshold," he said,

"THRESHOLD? WHAT THRESHOLD?" I asked.

"The CDC has determined that anything below the t-cell count of 200 is a diagnosis of AIDS . . ."

The interpreter stopped the conversation and then signed and said, "I'm sorry. I have to go. Best of luck. Sorry doctor." The interpreter opened the door and walked out.

The doctor and I stood there, looked at one another dumbfounded. He took his hand to his chest and was apologetic. I stood with my mouth agape with a questionable look on my face while shaking my head "no."

He reached out and touched me, I looked up and met his eyes. He reached over and gave me a hug. I held onto him for the longest time. We parted and he looked at me over his wired rimmed glasses. Our eyes connected and I knew that I would be in good hands with this doctor.

Leila: Mark was lucky to find a doctor he liked, but his struggle with interpreters and communication in general is typical. Mark's more recent interactions with the medical system show how variable interpreting services can be.

Mark: In the fall of 2015, I felt tightness in my chest and I knew that I was in trouble. Heart disease runs in my family and I had experienced this before and had needed hospitalization and a stent procedure. The problem was that I was far from home. Far, far from home. I had relocated from Washington state to Washington, DC to attend Gallaudet University.

I went to the health clinic on campus. The receptionist looked up at me and signed, "WHAT'S WRONG?"

"ME THINK ME HAVE HEART ATTACK," I replied.

The receptionist flew out of her chair, grabbed me into the back office, and screamed for the nurse and doctor to attend me. The nurse put me on the EKG machine as I recounted my heart health history. In a flurry of activity, campus police visited along with other university health clinic personnel. An ASL interpreter arrived and was able to interpret all my conversations everywhere from the health clinic room until I was put in the back of a Washington DC ambulance.

The ride in the back of the ambulance with the EMT sitting next to me was a little daunting as he was continually asking, "Can you read my lips? Can you read my lips? Can you read my lips?"

I sat there clueless until my arrival at the emergency room. I was put in the trauma room along with the VRI machine. A VRI machine is a video-remote interpreting which an ASL interpreter is called from a remote location and translates the conversation via video. The program does have its pitfalls as it is not entirely reliable. A dark-haired lady showed up on the screen and started to interpret.

Before she could complete the translation, a man showed up into the room, and said, "Thanks for your help. We won't be needing you. Thanks." Then he turned to me, introduced himself and started signing what the doctor was saying.

Once the interpreter arrived, the communication between me, the doctor, and the nurse was flawless. With every person that I met in the hospital while the interpreter was there, I was able to understand 100 percent of what was going on with my heart problems, what the procedures were going to be, and what to expect. Luckily, I only stayed in the hospital for two nights but the experience of having an ASL interpreter with me at every step of the way at the hospital made me feel like a human. I was able to communicate and had full understanding of what was transpiring around me.

Since then, nothing has compared to that experience.

In fall of 2016, I walked into another medical appointment and checked in with another receptionist. She wrote me a note to let me know that my interpreter had not shown up yet. It had taken me four months to get into the medical practice and to this appointment. There were delays because of my insurance coverage as well as getting a sign language interpreter. After several minutes, a man in a kelly green shirt with a grease spot tapped my arm to get my attention.

"I AM YOUR ASL INTERPRETER FOR THIS MEDICAL APPOINTMENT. THEY ARE CALLING YOU," he signed.

"OKAY." I replied. I wasn't sure about this ASL interpreter. Something did not seem right.

We got into the room and met with the infectious disease doctor. After sharing my medical and social history of being Deaf, Gay, and HIV+ for 23 years, the rapport that I was getting from the doctor via the sign language interpreter was a little strained. After discussing prescription and immunology history, it was decided that I needed to have a PCP shot to prevent pneumonia. The doctor excused herself while the interpreter stayed in the room. I struck up a conversation.

"WHERE STUDY INTERP?" I asked.

"GALLAUDET UNIVERSITY," he replied.

"OHH ... HEARD GOOD PROGRAM. YOU FINISH? CERTIFIED?"

"I NEVER GRADUATED FROM GALLAUDET. I WAS ONLY THERE FOR THREE YEARS AND DROPPED OUT. I BEEN FREELANCE INTERPRETING EVER SINCE. AND NO CERTIFICATION."

When he told me that he never graduated from the interpreting program, I felt assaulted. This medical practice hired an interpreting agency for their sign language needs and I get an interpreter that never graduated from an interpreting program to interpret my medical appointment?! My feelings were not new. For years, I have experienced various hearing individuals deciding what my communication needs are without asking me.

"YOU NEVER FINISH INTERP PROGRAM? YOU PLAN SOON?" I asked.

"OH YES, NEXT YEAR," was his response.

The doctor came back in and picked up our conversation by asking me what arm she should give me my vaccination in. While she was giving me my immunization, I continued to look at this interpreter with the grease spot on his kelly green shirt and thought, "What gives you the right to come into my personal and private life? Especially to a medical appointment knowing you're not qualified and certified to discuss my medical issues? Why is this still happening to us Deaf people?"

After the appointment, I emailed Quality Assurance of the medical practice to voice my concerns. It was hard not to get emotional but I stuck with the facts and relayed my concerns to the manager. Their reply was that they did not know as they contracted their sign language services out to independent agencies. I reiterated that as a Deaf consumer this is not acceptable to be having individuals that know sign language sitting in on one's medical appointments without proper education, training and certification.

A couple days later, I received an email from Quality Assurance informing me that they clarified their contract with the interpreting agency that they want certified sign language interpreters at all their medical appointments with Deaf clients.

I should be elated and happy, but sadly I'm not. I'm just tired.

* * *

Three of the four of these examples show how a Deaf patient's needs were disregarded during medical interactions. The standard Registry of Interpreters for the Deaf "Code of Professional Conduct" includes the provision that "Interpreters possess the professional skills and knowledge required for the specific interpreting situation" (Registry of Interpreters for the Deaf 2015).

Even beginning ASL students learn to present themselves in simple, tidy clothing without patterns or complex jewelry. The uncertified interpreter's stained kelly green shirt broke basic professional norms of the community, leading Mark to worry about privacy issues, a common and appropriate concern. The wider South African Deaf community learned of John Meletse's HIV status because a signing social worker had gossiped with colleagues (Meletse and Morgan 2006). Since the passage of the ADA in 1990, ideas about professional interpreting standards have had the force of law. However, resource issues and "cultural differentiations," mean that these laws are not always enforced leaving Deaf people like Mark to do extra social and communicative labor. It should not be necessary to contact Quality Assurance just to get appropriate interpreting services. In the 1990s, programs like Maryland-based Deaf AIDS Project and Washington DC's Deaf Reach had funds for community outreach, testing, and interpreter training. Today support has dried up and these organizations have had close their doors or stop their AIDS programs.

The Centers for Disease Control identified all major transmission routes for AIDS by 1983 (Avert 2017) but as Deborah Karp's comments reflect, many in the Deaf community did not have this basic information even in the late 1980s. Despite the advocacy done on the issue of Deaf HIV/AIDS by small groups over the years, there is still little recognition of the injustices Deaf people have to face to gain information about HIV/AIDS or to receive medical treatments in an appropriate manner (Hanass-Hancock and Satande 2010).

The fight against Deaf AIDS is a place where linguistic anthropology and Deaf and disability activism need to meet to understand how confront linguistic and social injustice. The institutional prejudices documented here reflect similar struggles faced by marginalized communities in South Africa, Guatemala and Venezuela (see Chapters 11, 12 and 14 of this volume). Linguistic anthropology has tools that can be used to analyze unequal communicative labor. In turn, Deaf and disability studies offer a rich source of language in action, demonstrating how scholarship and activism can go hand in hand. Stopping Deaf AIDS is a fight that needs many partners.

Note

1 CAPITAL LETTERS indicate signed conversations.

References

Avert. 2017. "History of HIV and AIDS Overview." Accessed July 15, 2017 at www. avert.org/professionals/history-hiv-aids/overview.

CDC. 2016. "HIV in the United States: At a Glance." Accessed July 15, 2017 at www. cdc.gov/hiv/statistics/overview/ataglance.html.

Duranti, Alessandro. 1997. *Linguistic Anthropology*. Cambridge: Cambridge University Press.

Hanass-Hancock, Jill and Loveness Satande. 2010. "Deafness and HIV/AIDS: A Systematic Review of the Literature." *African Journal of AIDS Research* 9(2): 187–192.

Jarman, Michelle, Leila Monaghan, and Alison Quaggin Harkin, eds. 2017. *Barriers and Belonging: Personal Narratives of Disability*. Philadelphia, PA: Temple University Press.

Kuenberg, Alexa, Paul Fellinger, and Johannes Fellinger. 2016. "Health Care Access Among Deaf People." *Journal of Deaf Studies and Deaf Education* 21(1): 1–10.

MDHMH. 2018. Maryland Public HIV Testing Results by Hearing Status 2008 to 2014. Personal communication from Maryland Department of Health and Mental Hygiene.

Meletse, John with Ruth Morgan. 2006. "'I Have Two!': Personal Reflections of a Deaf HIV Positive Gay Man in South Africa." In *HIV/AIDS and Deaf Communities*, edited by Constanze Schmaling and Leila Monaghan, S14–S26. Coleford: Douglas McLean.

MMWR. 2011. "HIV Surveillance: United States, 1981–2008." *Morbidity and Mortality Weekly Report*, Centers for Disease Control. Accessed July 14, 2017 at www.cdc.gov/mmwr/preview/mmwrhtml/mm6021a2.htm.

Monaghan, Leila and Deborah Karp. 2010. "HIV/AIDS in the Deaf Community: A Conversation." In *Deaf around the World: The Impact of Language*, edited by Gaurav Mathur and Donna Jo Napoli, 297–306. Oxford: Oxford University Press.

Monaghan, Leila and Constanze Schmaling, 2010. "Deaf Community Approaches to HIV/AIDS." In *At the Intersections: Deaf and Disability Studies*, edited by Susan Burch and Alison Kafer, 120–143. Washington, DC: Gallaudet University Press.

NAD. 2017. "Law and Advocacy Center." Accessed October 28, 2017 at www.nad.org/about-us/law-advocacy-center.

Registry of Interpreters for the Deaf. 2015. "Code of Professional Conduct." Accessed June 15, 2017 at http://rid.org/ethics/code-of-professional-conduct/.

Shapiro, Joseph. 1994. *No Pity*. New York: Three Rivers Press.

14 Language as Health

Healing in Indigenous Communities in Guatemala through the Revitalization of Mayan Languages

David Flood, Anita Chary, Peter Rohloff, and Brent Henderson

Introduction

UNESCO estimates that as many of 50 percent of the world's languages will disappear within the next several generations (Matsuura 2007). Nearly all of these languages are spoken by marginalized communities who are shifting to larger regional or colonial languages in order to access goods and services that are closed off to them by social, political and linguistic barriers (Duchêne and Heller, 2013; Henderson, Rohloff, and Henderson 2014).

Many efforts exist to address linguistic marginalization and language endangerment, though in somewhat disconnected ways. These two justice issues are typically addressed by language activists and scholars who work to document and develop the language, often with education-focused outcomes such as pedagogical materials and texts for teaching and indigenous literacy (Hinton and Hale 2001). While these activities are important and highly valued by communities, they have little to no impact on the drivers of language loss, which, as Tsunoda remarks are "[l]argely political, social, and/or economic. . . in the main neither sociolinguistic nor linguistic" (Tsunoda 2004, 57).

Health disparities, on the other hand, are addressed by local and global efforts—both governmental and non-governmental—to expand health care to marginalized, poor, and rural communities through health promotion, clean water infrastructure, and other health initiatives. These efforts, however, rarely include any consideration of the local language situation (Summer Institute of Linguistics 2014; United Nations 2009). Rather, they tend to take language barriers as minor implementation problems, easily overcome with interpretation services or by assuming beneficiaries' fluency in the colonial language(s). The perception among health policymakers that indigenous languages are merely an implementation barrier not only leads to low-quality health service delivery, but also contributes to linguistic marginalization and language loss (Henderson et al. 2014).

Here, we describe an approach that prioritizes the use of indigenous languages in the context of the delivery of meaningful social and health-related services. In other words, rather than advocating for the use of indigenous languages as an end in itself, we instead aim for the strategic deployment of minority language planning practices within high-quality, community-based social and health programs. We provide a case study from our multidisciplinary collaborative work with Wuqu' Kawoq | Maya Health Alliance, a ten-year-old non-governmental health organization (NGO) in rural Guatemala whose programs include child nutrition, health promoter and midwife training, primary care, and complex medical care. Recognizing that lack of access to health care in Mayan languages is both a driver of language loss and a key determinant of poor health, Wuqu' Kawoq has developed explicit protocols for Maya language-based health care programming.

In the next section, we provide more detail on the specifics of linguistic and health disparities in Guatemala as they affect indigenous Maya people. We then describe Wuqu' Kawoq's diabetes program as a case study. We show how careful attention to language use and linguistic identity in this program has led not only to more effective health outcomes, but also increasing vitality in Mayan language use. We conclude by making a final case for taking local languages seriously when designing development and health programs.

Language and Health Disparities in Guatemala

Guatemala is a Central American country of approximately 16 million people. Twenty-three distinct indigenous languages are spoken in addition to Spanish, the colonial and national language. According to official statistics, the most commonly spoken Mayan languages are Q'eqchi', K'iche', Mam, and Kaqchikel, each with 500,000 or more speakers (Richards 2003). The precise numbers of speakers is a highly politicized issue, however, with most Mayan language activists criticizing official census procedures for systematically undercounting the number of speakers (Tzian 1994).

The Maya population in Guatemala has been politically and economically marginalized due to a history of Spanish colonialism and a civil war and state-sponsored genocide against Maya peoples from 1960–1996. Longstanding economic disparities exist for indigenous groups in Guatemala: While the overall national poverty rate is 59 percent (World Bank 2016), this number climbs to 79 percent among the indigenous population (Central Intelligence Agency 2016). In Guatemala, Maya people are also more likely than their non-indigenous *ladino* counterparts of mixed descent to suffer from poor health. To provide two important examples, the maternal mortality rate among Maya women is two to three times higher than for Guatemalan women overall and rates of chronic malnutrition are approximately twice as high among Maya children as in non-Maya children (Ministerio de Salud Pública y Asistencia Social 2015).

These health disparities are rooted in poverty, historical oppression, and lack of health infrastructure. The Guatemalan constitution in theory guarantees free health care to all citizens through a public health system of hospitals and clinics. However, in reality, the health system is severely under-resourced and does not adequately service the rural areas where half the population lives (World Bank 2016). Costs of public transportation to health facilities, as well as laboratory exams, supplies, and medications, are other important barriers (Chary and Rohloff 2015). Ethnic discrimination and biomedical practitioners' dismissal of indigenous models of health and illness are also important to consider (Berry 2008; Eder and García Pú 2003).

Finally, although Guatemala's 2003 Language Law grants the right to use public health services in a person's preferred language, in practice government health care facilities offer care almost exclusively in Spanish (Government of Guatemala 2003). Most medical practitioners in Guatemala do not speak an indigenous language. Interpreter services for patients who speak indigenous languages are not publically available. While some health care providers recognize this lack of access as a problem, others view indigenous patients' inability to speak Spanish as the real problem. As a result, clinical encounters tend to be unintelligible for monolingual indigenous health seekers, unless they bring a friend or family member with some Spanish knowledge. Of note, while Maya people increasingly engage the growing NGO sector to obtain biomedical health care, only a handful of the thousands of NGOs operating health programs in Guatemala provide care in Mayan languages (Chary and Rohloff 2015).

Wuqu' Kawoq | Maya Health Alliance Diabetes Program: A Case Study

In this section, we focus on Wuqu' Kawoq's diabetes program as a case study on implementation of a social development program informed by the local indigenous language context. Although diabetes is a chronic disease commonly perceived as an illness of wealth and urbanity, it increasingly affects poor and rural populations worldwide. In Guatemala, approximately 760,000 people have diabetes, and the prevalence rate may meet or even exceed that in the U.S (International Diabetes Federation 2015). There are limited data on the epidemic in Mayan-speaking communities, but diabetes increasingly affects this population given rapid shifts away from traditional diets, changes in work and lifestyle patterns, and limited access to quality medical care (Flood et al. 2016).

Our organization began delivering clinical diabetes care in 2007 in the form of home visits with elderly, monolingual Kaqchikel-speaking patients in a primarily indigenous municipality west of Guatemala City with a population of 30,000 people. In 2011, our general medical clinics became increasingly inundated with requests for diabetes services, and we created a diabetes program with dedicated staff, protocols, and clinic days. At that time, our diabetic patients exhibited a strong Mayan language preference with approximately 80 percent speaking Kaqchikel or K'iche' (Chary et al. 2012). In recent years, our program has continued to grow as we have entered new communities, received referral cases from other institutions, and increased our clinical volume in our established primary care sites. Overall, our program has served over 200 diabetes patients with favorable clinical outcomes (Flood et al. 2016).

A central tenet of our diabetes program is the prioritization of Mayan languages. The first page of our clinical diabetes protocol explicitly states that Mayan languages should always be spoken if preferred by patients. Our diabetes staff, including physicians, case managers, nurses, and community health workers, all speak Kaqchikel, and we often conduct routine administrative meetings in this language. On the ground level, where our clinicians interact with patients and families, our language policy is premised on the pragmatic issues of patient comfort and clinical effectiveness. At a broader level, we believe that delivering medical care in Mayan languages has important spillover effects for language maintenance and revitalization. Our language policy was relatively easy to implement since all our staff spoke Mayan Kaqchikel; however, our practices were challenged when we expanded our diabetes program into K'iche' speaking areas, which necessitated hiring new ground-level nurses and social workers who spoke both K'iche' and Kaqchikel.

Mayan Languages in the Clinical Space

Although Guatemala's language rights legislation enshrines access to health services in indigenous languages (Government of Guatemala 2003), most Mayan-speaking people with diabetes who enroll in our program have never spoken to a doctor or nurse in their primary language. In this context, delivering quality care in Mayan languages generates patient trust and improves health outcomes.

In acute health situations in Guatemala, the language one speaks can be an issue of life or death. Our diabetes patients commonly call us with life-threatening complications, but resist our recommendation of immediate transfer to a hospital where providers do not speak Mayan languages and interpreter services are absent. In one case, a patient with a severely infected foot who speaks only K'iche' Maya refused to go to a public hospital for antibiotics and surgical debridement despite our recommendation. His son told us, "He doesn't want to go. He is scared because he doesn't speak Spanish; he would rather stay home and die." In this case, the patient and his family ultimately accepted hospital care with accompaniment from our Mayan-speaking case workers; he returned home alive and happy three weeks later.

The role of language is also salient in routine diabetes care, an area chiefly concerned with motivating behavior change around diet and exercise, fostering solidarity about the illness experience, and offering psychosocial support. We believe that "non-compliance" in diabetes care (often noted by health care providers) in rural Guatemala is frequently due to a lack of understanding generated by language barriers and low health literacy. In our program, we invest heavily in home-based diabetes education delivered in Mayan languages. In home visits, patients frequently tell us that despite having had diabetes for many years, no one had ever explained to them in their own language the meaning of their diagnosis, listened to them about their daily struggles, or educated them about diabetes control strategies. We have learned that patients do best when they can have culturally and linguistically rich discussions about the challenges of living with diabetes and the practical ways to overcome them—conversations that can only take place in their primary Mayan language.

For example, a conversation in Mayan Kaqchikel about a diabetic diet is imbued with enormous cultural expectations around what constitutes food, healthy eating, gender roles, an individual's place in a family-prepared meal, and the role of corn. Linguistically, the word for "food" (wa'im) denotes an entirely separate category from the words for corn-based "tortillas" (wäy) or "tamalito" (sub'an). Culturally, a Maya lifestyle premised on the production and uses of corn comes into tension with a disease for which corn must necessarily be limited. "Yes, we are people of corn," one of our nurses frequently tells patients, echoing a famous phrase about Maya people, "but it's okay to eat fewer tortillas." Discussions invoking such complex themes and cultural perspectives are best conducted in a patient's primary Mayan language.

One challenge of carrying out diabetes education with Kaqchikel-speaking patients is a lack of precise yet easily intelligible medical terminology. Even monolingual Kaqchikel speakers generally use opaque Spanish loan words when describing terms such as "diabetes," "glucose," or "glucometer." In 2010, we undertook a collaboration with Kaqchikel Cholchi', the Kaqchikel arm of the Guatemalan Academy of Mayan Languages, to produce a set of new medical neologisms—newly invented words—in Kaqchikel, including terminology relating to diabetes. One success was the term "kab'kïk'el," or literally "sweet blood," to replace the Spanish term "diabetes." The new word was not only intuitive and immediately memorable to native speakers, but also suggested something about what diabetes treatment or control might entail, an underlying idea we refer to as "neologisms as medical education" (Tummons, Henderson, and Rohloff 2008). Equipped with this word, practitioners could converse with patients about what is making their blood so sweet, how to make it less sweet, etc., leading to much higher levels of patient comprehension of pathology and treatment. We had similar success with terminology for high blood pressure, a common and serious comorbidity for our patients with diabetes, coining the term "Rujotolem ruchuq'a' kïk'," or "elevated blood energy," to engage individuals in discussions about life-style and dietary changes appropriate for lowering blood pressure.

Language Revitalization

This discussion of neologisms brings us to another core argument behind our institution's use of Mayan languages: that the delivery of high-quality medical care in Kaqchikel is not only a health care activity, but also a *language revitalization* activity. We begin this argument by reiterating that indigenous language shift in Guatemala is not driven by linguistic factors but rather by profound economic, political, and social power gradients between indigenous and non-indigenous groups. Successful language revitalization strategies must therefore contend with these power gradients; classic language development strategies that emphasize linguistic solutions like school-based education are important but insufficient.

In our clinics, we have attempted to reverse these power gradients to create space where Mayan language use is respected, accepted, and normalized. The development and health sectors in Guatemala are fertile domains in which to perform this kind of linguistic re-orientation since access to valuable services like diabetes care is often premised on the ability to speak Spanish. The pro-liferation of NGOs in Guatemala in recent years has only reinforced existing language pressures since few organizations meaningfully utilize Mayan lan-guages within their institution or with beneficiaries (Henderson et al. 2014). In our experience, the NGOs delivering diabetes care tend to be thoughtful about implementing Mayan-friendly health programming, but even these institutions marginalize indigenous languages somewhat through limited interpreter avail-ability, assumptions of Spanish fluency, and bias toward Mayan speakers.

In its ten years of existence, however, Wuqu' Kawoq has shown that thoughtfully designed health and social projects can serve as a powerful force to catalyze Mayan language use and remove the underlying structural forces behind language shift—that is, by making services available in Mayan. Consider the following exchange captured in one of our busy clinics:

Petrona is next in line. She is a 50-something [year-old] long-standing patient of the clinic with severe diabetes. However, today she is not here for herself; rather, she has brought her teenage grandchild Jose to the clinic for advice on how to treat his acne. The doctor exits the consultation room and greets Petrona and her husband Florencio, who doesn't have a medical complaint today and has come along just to socialize. He jokes at the doctor, "*Nintz'ët chi at más ti'oj wakamin!*" (You look fatter than the last time I saw you!). The other patients enjoy a collective chuckle. Together Petrona and Jose enter the medical consultation room. The doctor begins, addressing her grandson, "*Achike ab'i'?*" (What is your name?). He replies without hesitation, "*Mi nombre es Jose*" (My name is Jose). Petrona jabs him hard in the ribs with her elbow, "*Ke re yach'o'n!*" (Talk in Kaqchikel!).

(Tummons, Henderson, and Rohloff 2011, 5)

As this vignette illustrates, use of Mayan languages in our clinics is ubiqui-tous. In addition to enriching the patient-provider interaction and improving care quality, this ubiquity serves to showcase the use of Mayan in a profes-sional setting, generates prestige as doctors and nurses are observed speaking Mayan, and creates an environment where elders model language to younger speakers. Cultural norms and modes of authority are also renegotiated through these practices.

We think of a model of language revitalization that emphasizes a lan-guage focus within the collaborative pursuit of other community-defined social and health programs as more bottom-up, organic, and sustainable (Rohloff and Henderson 2015). This approach can be complementary to traditional revitalization activities such as language documentation, child education, and publishing. However, it views improved access to economic, health and social welfare resources and services as the fundamental terrain for expanding and normalizing the use of indigenous languages.

Important corollaries to our model are that linguists must collaborate with a wider range of individuals and groups in their revitalization activities, and that community-based social welfare organizations must build capacity to intentionally re-orient language as more than an "implementation barrier" in their programs. The alternative—continuing to ignore the centrality of language to the development of social welfare programs—is not a "neutral stance" since the work can itself contributes to language loss, if it gives the impression that highly desirable social services are only available if one speaks a colonial language.

Conclusion

Health disparities among indigenous Maya Guatemalans are due to long histories of social, political, and economic marginalization as well as outright prejudice and persecution. Unfortunately, many of the actors seeking to address these disparities—from government agencies to foreign-based NGOs—do so in ways which do not address relevant cultural and linguistic factors. In this article, we have highlighted how our linguistically and culturally informed approach to diabetes care has led to several desirable results, including: (i) better practitioner-patient trust and relationships; (ii) better acute care outcomes; (iii) lower "non-compliance" to treatment; (iv) higher prestige for indigenous language use; and (v) the creation of new and useful indigenous language vocabulary. These last two results are arguably the outcomes that most directly address the basic problems of social marginalization and injustice that foster health disparities among indigenous communities, given that they affect both individuals and the linguistic community as a whole.

References

Berry, Nicole. 2008. "Who's Judging the Quality of Care? Indigenous Maya and the Problem of 'Not Being Attended'." *Medical Anthropology* 27(2): 164–189.

Central Intelligence Agency. 2016. "The World Factbook." Accessed July 13, 2017 at www.cia.gov/library/publications/the-world-factbook/geos/gt.html.

Chary, Anita, Miranda Greiner, Cody Bowers, and Peter Rohloff. 2012. "Determining Adult Type 2 Diabetes-related Health Care Needs in an Indigenous Population from Rural Guatemala: a Mixed-methods Preliminary Study." *BMC Health Services Research* 12: 476.

Chary, Anita, and Peter Rohloff, eds. 2015. *Privatization and the New Medical Pluralism: Shifting Health Care Landscapes in Maya Guatemala*: Lanham, NJ: Lexington Books.

Duchêne, Alexandre and Monica Heller, eds. 2013. *Language in Late Capitalism: Pride and Profit*. New York: Routledge.

Eder, Karin, and María Manueala García Pú. 2003. *Modelo de la Medicina Indígena Maya en Guatemala : Investigación Participativa en Sipacapa, San Marcos; San*

Martín Jilotepeque, Chimaltenango y San Juan Ixcoy, Huehuetenango. Guatemala City: Asociación de Servicios Comunitarios de Salud.

Flood, David, Sandy Mux, Boris Martínez, Pablo Garcia, Kate Douglas, Vera Goldberg, Waleska Lopez, and Peter Rohloff. 2016. "Implementation and Outcomes of a Comprehensive Type 2 Diabetes Program in Rural Guatemala." *PLoS One* 11(9): e0161152.

Government of Guatemala. 2003. "Decreto Numero 19–2003." Guatemala City, Guatemala: Government of Guatemala. Accessed July 13, 2017 at www.unicef.org/guatemala/spanish/LeyIdiomasNacionales.pdf.

Henderson, Brent, Peter Rohloff, and Robert Henderson. 2014. "More Than Words: Towards a Development-Based Approach to Language Revitalization." *Language Documentation & Conservation* 8: 75–91.

Hinton, Leanne, and Ken Hale, eds. 2001. *The Green Book of Language Revitalization in Practice*. San Diego, CA: Academic Press.

International Diabetes Federation. 2015. *Diabetes Atlas*. Brussels: International Diabetes Foundation.

Matsuura, Koïchiro. 2007. *Languages Matter! Message from the Director-General of UNESCO on the Celebration of 2008, International Year of Languages*. Geneva: UNESCO.

Ministerio de Salud Pública y Asistencia Social. 2009. *V Encuesta Nacional de Salud Materno Infantil*. Guatemala City: Ministerio de Salud Pública y Asistencia Social.

Ministerio de Salud Pública y Asistencia Social. 2015. *VI Encuesta Nacional de Salud Materno Infantil*. Guatemala City: Ministerio de Salud Pública y Asistencia Social.

Richards, Michael. 2003. *Atlas Lingüístico de Guatemala*. Guatemala City: Editorial Serviprensa.

Rohloff, Peter, and Brent Henderson. 2015. "Development, Language Revitalization, and Culture: The Case of the Mayan Languages of Guatemala, and Their Relevance for African Languages." In *Language Documentation and Endangerment in Africa*, edited by James Essegbey, Brent Henderson, and Fiona McLaughlin, 177–194. Amsterdam: John Benjamins Publishing Company.

Summer Institute of Linguistics. 2014. *Why Languages Matter: Meeting Millennium Development Goals through Local Languages*. Dallas, TX: Summer Institute of Linguistics.

Tsunoda, Tasaku. 2004. *Language Endangerment and Language Revitalization*. New York: Mouton de Gruyter.

Tummons Emily, Robert Henderson, and Peter Rohloff. 2008. "So that We Don't Lose Words: Reconstructing a Kaqchikel Medical Lexicon." Paper presented at the First Biennial Symposium on Teaching Indigenous Languages in Latin America, Bloomington, Indiana, August 14–16.

Tummons Emily, Robert Henderson, and Peter Rohloff. 2011. "Language Revitalization and the Problem of Development in Guatemala: Case Studies from Health Care." Paper presented at the Second Biennial Symposium on Teaching and Learning Languages of Latin America, Notre Dame, Indiana, October 30–November 2.

Tzian, Leopoldo. 1994. *Mayas y Ladinos en Cifras: el Caso de Guatemala*. Guatemala City: Cholsamaj.

United Nations. 2009. *The State of the World's Indigenous Peoples: Indigenous Peoples' Access to Health Services*. New York: United Nations.

World Bank. 2016. "Guatemala." Accessed July 13, 2017 at http://data.worldbank.org/country/guatemala.

Part IV

Language and Social Activism

Introduction

Activism is taking action to bring about political or social change. An activist is a person who uses or supports strong actions to endorse or oppose an issue. Chapters in this section draw attention to ways that people explicitly and consciously use language as a means, or instrument, to change society. In some cases, people seek to modify language itself as a way to bring about social change. Each case underscores human agency and the use of language and speech as social action. Authors emphasize specific ways that social actors (agents) use language to bring attention to injustice—discrimination, racism, homophobia, social and linguistic exclusion, political and economic inequities—and various ways people use language to effect social change. Authors in this section, as well as others in this book, are activist scholars. Several take explicitly activist positions through their writing. Some *perform* activism in their essays by consciously choosing to use specific language forms, such as certain lexical items (words), pronouns or spelling to draw attention to language itself and thus take explicit political positions, pragmatically as well as referentially. Ultimately these cases demonstrate change *in* language, *through* language and *beyond* language.

Critical Questions

As you read these cases, we encourage you to consider the following questions:

1 What distinct ways of using language to effect social change, or sociolinguistic activism, can you identify in these cases?
2 How do these cases encourage you to think about ways that language and speech interact with other communicative modalities to raise awareness of social inequities?
3 How do you use language in ways that may perpetuate or transform the status quo?

15 Mascots, Name Calling, and Racial Slurs

Seeking Social Justice through Audience Coalescence

Netta Avineri and Bernard C. Perley

White Racist Symbols of Hatred against Native Americans

In these United States there are four seasons of white racism and hatred directed toward Native Americans. It is an insidious form of racism that is exercised as an everyday symbolic hatred toward Native Americans through mascots, name calling, and racial slurs. These everyday practices are direct harmful speech acts that may be viewed as harmless and perhaps jocular, but they also enact indirect historical racism and inflict real and personal harm to Native Americans. The American Psychological Association in 2005 issued a resolution recommending "the immediate retirement of American Indian mascots, symbols, images, and personalities by schools, colleges, universities, athletic teams and organizations," citing a "growing body of social science literature that shows the harmful effects of racial stereotyping and inaccurate racial portrayals, including the particularly damaging effects of American Indian sports mascots on the social identity development and self-esteem of American Indian young people" (American Psychological Association 2018).

Sadly, these harmful effects occur throughout the entire year. Starting with spring and rolling through summer, baseball fans begin to wear team jerseys and caps that depict gross caricatures of supposed Native Americans (Cleveland) and perform the tomahawk chop (Atlanta) to Hollywood style "Indian" music. Baseball starts in spring, rolls through summer, and ends in the fall while Cleveland and Atlanta fans display gross caricatures and play Indian (Deloria 1998). Baseball overlaps with football season as football fans proclaim homage and honor to the fighting spirit of Native Americans by wearing jerseys for the professional sports teams of Kansas City and Washington DC. While some fans wear jerseys emblazoned with egregious racist monikers (Washington) other fans wear stereotypical costumes of faux buckskin and dayglow feathers.

The National Hockey League begins its season in the fall, skates through winter, and finishes in the spring. Hockey fans have three seasons to celebrate the prowess of the Chicago Blackhawks while wearing the jerseys adorned with a stereotypical Indian head profile. The entire year becomes a social and symbolic platform of exercising and displaying American racism against Native Americans. The social and cultural effect of these words and images is the perpetuation of the injustices directed against Native Americans through a

Figure 15.1 "What Honor?"
Courtesy of Bernard C. Perley.

naturalized form of racism. Naturalized racism is a practice through which individuals do not consciously realize that these seemingly innocent yet harmful representations of others are socially constructed and learned. In this country whose founding ideology is equality and everyone's right to happiness, it is time to correct centuries of racism against Native Americans and usher in a new era of respect and redress. Such a change requires the concerted efforts of all Americans to work together to achieve social justice for Native Americans. Current socialization and cultural reproduction practices of naturalized racism against Native Americans must be redirected away from the harmful practices of mascot use, name calling, and racial slurs. Expanding supportive coalitions will support the important work of advocating for and achieving social justice.

Name calling, racial slurs, and mascots are everyday acts of white racism (Hill 2008) against Native Americans that fundamentally contradict the best ideals of American society. Since 2014, the authors, Avineri and Perley, have collaborated with one another, a range of scholars, and American Anthropological Association (AAA) representatives, in building partnerships focused on the issue of sports team mascots and names. As an intervention to these racist attitudes and actions, we use the concept "audience coalescence" to describe an emergent coalition building process that identifies and promotes predispositions and stances toward redressing social injustices. We thank many friends, colleagues, and unknown allies who have supported our efforts to create coalitions through audience coalescence to rectify the ongoing oppression and subordination of the Native Peoples of North America through everyday uses of mascots, name calling, and racial slurs against Native Americans. We present here a program for practical action through coalition building and social justice activism that is possible when white racism is contextualized as ideological socialization through which the symbolism and language of hate are grounded and reinforced in the experience of everyday white racism toward Native American peoples, their cultures, and their sovereignty. We promote audience coalescence as a promising approach that foregrounds interaction and change to achieve the social justice that Native Americans have been denied since October 12, 1492. Hurtful language acts and displays of social injustice against Native Americans must cease if the people of the United States hope to achieve the ideals of a "more perfect Union."

Recognizing and Socializing the Symbols and Language of Hate

The daily reminders of American symbols and language of hatred toward Native Americans in the opening decades of the twenty-first century are seldom recognized as expressions of hate. This may be because of the centuries-long socializing processes that first vilified Native Americans, then marginalized them, and finally naturalized symbols and language of hate by obscuring colonial oppression of North America's original peoples. The proliferation of symbols (e.g., egregious sports mascots and monikers throughout the year, statements defending the use of those mascots and monikers, holiday celebrations that present images of Native Americans as foils for American ideals of nationalism) become a pervasive symbolic landscape of colonial hatred and racism toward Native Americans that reflects a foundational aspect of American culture. Daily practices by often unwitting citizens have a long history that is selectively remembered and celebrated in popular media, national and state holidays, and mascots and monikers (see King and Fruehling Springwood 2001).

The writings, ruminations, and remarks from commentators, beginning with Columbus to today's Washington professional football team owner Daniel Snyder, represent a long history of expressions of colonial hatred of the native peoples of the Americas. These practices have significantly contributed to the socialization and reproduction of hatred toward Native Americans today. American popular history and culture are the incubators of colonial fantasies of conquest and the disappearance of Native Americans from their ancestral homelands (see Strong 2013). Popular representations have reproduced the Manifest Destiny narrative (framing Westward expansion and Native American removal as divinely ordained) since John O'Sullivan coined the phrase in the mid-nineteenth century. The idea was popularized in paintings, newspaper articles and public speeches.

The ideology of divine providence making the ascent and prominence of the United States a foregone conclusion made the removal and eradication of Native Americans an unfortunate but inevitable consequence of progress. Just as Columbus imagined the native islanders of Hispañola to be unworthy of sovereignty so, too, did nineteenth-century Americans regard Native Americans as obstructions to their manifest destiny. Those ideologies justified forced removal, assimilation, eradication, and confinement thereby leading to the popularization of the image of the vanishing Indian in the late nineteenth and early twentieth centuries. There was good reason to imagine the disappearance of any tribe, as one by one they were forced to succumb to the national narrative and ideology of extinction. This narrative gained popular and visual support through Buffalo Bill's Wild West Shows, Edward Curtis photographs, and novels romanticizing America's "winning the west."

Celebrations of manifest destiny would feed the American popular imagination through the image machine of Hollywood with narratives of the vanishing Indian and courageous cowboys taming the Wild West. Elementary schools have continually performed thanksgiving pageants across the country and celebrated Columbus Day with the assertion that he discovered America. The weight and inertia of popular media and their embrace of American ideologies of conquest, divine providence, and willful ignorance of Native Americans is the result of broad socialization and reproduction of the insidious stealth hate practiced today.

Identifying the Prospects for Social Justice

The American public can no longer ignore the injustice that Native American mascots and monikers inflict upon Native Americans and their communities (see Calloway 2010; Guiliano 2015). The seasonal calls from Native American activists and the broad support from advocates pressing sports organizations to "change the mascot" (see www.changethemascot.org) make it impossible to ignore the openly practiced racism that supports the continued use of mascots and monikers.

We recognize that the possibility of achieving social justice for Native Americans and their communities requires ongoing conversations through as many forms of communication as possible. In order to redress the wrongs of white racism against Native Americans, we have presented our appeals to the public at professional/disciplinary conferences, and through various media such as op-ed pieces, cartoons, and essays (described in further detail below). Though these may be powerful venues for facilitating social change, words are just one aspect of taking action. What we have learned through these various forms of communication and outreach is that *identifying the problem is not a solution*. We recognize the efficacy of communication as a means of bringing coalitions of individuals supporting social justice together to coalesce into a broader movement toward actions that would finally end the use of mascots and monikers.

Audience Coalescence as Social Action

Recipient Design and Epistemic Ecologies

The racist use of Native American mascots and monikers involves a damaging lack of empathy and understanding of Native American perspectives and experiences. In addition, by their very nature mascots and sports team names take on a life of their own, as they are often thought to be based in tradition (and therefore immutable) and symbolic of a deep commitment to a team. Audience coalescence, on the other hand, provides a framework for engaging in social justice issues that is flexible based on the participants involved, values diverse perspectives, and has the potential to counteract oppressive institutional structures. Audience coalescence has an intellectual history in linguistics, conversation analysis, and linguistic anthropology. Over the past forty years, there has been a sustained interest in examining the ways that speakers shape their language for their interlocutors. Notions including "recipient design" (Sacks, Schegloff, and Jefferson 1974), footing and "participation frameworks" (Goffman 1981), "audience design" (Bell 1984), "responsive audience design" (Bell 2001), "participation" (Goodwin and Goodwin 2004), and "interactive footing" (Goodwin 2010) highlight the relevance of including a focus on audience in any consideration of language and interaction. These recent trends set the groundwork for our concept of audience coalescence, an interactive, interpersonal, and critically empathetic process for social justice. Audience coalescence is a process that involves recognizing the knowledges and histories of everyone in a given ecology or dynamic system, or "epistemic ecologies" (Goodwin 2013) in which "distributed cognition" (Hutchins 1995) exists across multiple individuals in a given context. All interpersonal relations in shared knowledge production are dependent on subjects being in the world together. All knowledge depends on the willingness of other subjects to maintain strategies to share that knowledge between them, a central tenet of audience coalescence.

Social Relations

"Epistemic ecologies" (Goodwin 2013) and "distributed cognition" (Hutchins 1995) are shared knowledge practices that require the participation of other persons, groups, and any human collective engaged in discursive interactions. A field of knowledge is articulated and identified according to a group's agreed upon definitions. That knowledge is then distributed and shared, creating the necessary conditions for social/cultural action. In our shared epistemic and cognitive worlds, we must recognize the necessity to disseminate and communicate our knowledge and experience to fulfill the promise of social justice for all citizens. The hatred toward Native Americans is not just a Native American problem. It is a social injustice that harms every one of us. The cherished American ideals of equality and justice for all will be revealed as deep-rooted hypocrisy if racism against Native Americans is neither recognized nor resolved. Once we recognize that injustice toward Native Americans is an injustice to all, then we can share our knowledge through interpersonal relations to redress this colonial wrong. Coordinating our conversations and sharing epistemic ecologies and experiences will help redress white racism against Native Americans. Epistemic ecologies and distributed cognition emphasize the production of knowledge and cognition in the discourses of our everyday lives. However, it is social and cultural shared empathy through interpersonal relations that will be instrumental in redressing the injustice of Native American mascots and monikers.

Social Action as Social Justice

Knowledge about the problem of mascots and monikers alone is powerless to change the hurt, confusion, and feelings of diminished self-worth that Native American children endure when taunted by others using egregious monikers or when they are exposed to displays of gross stereotypes and caricatures. Knowledge must accompany critical empathy (DeStigter 1999; Palmer and Menard-Warwick 2012) in order to acknowledge the limits of our ability to see the world from someone else's eyes. The pain experienced by Native American children can only be understood when it is shared through empathy and affect in interpersonal relations. The knowledge gained through epistemic ecologies and distributed cognition contribute to *knowing* the pain associated with name-calling and stereotypes, but *understanding* the pain is where audience coalescence starts. Interpersonal emotional sharing through strategies of audience coalescence has great potential for taking knowledge and applying it toward social action.

Using critical empathy to shape an approach to social justice in relation to sports team mascot names would involve consciousness of the symbolic systems of hate, racism, and colonial legacies indexed, as well as agency and resistance to counteract what have become nationally recognizable forms of naturalized hate and racism. Social action as social justice would need to acknowledge physical and psychological safety and security for Native

Americans that foregrounds their self-determination and interdependence with those working toward social justice.

Coalition Building

Coalition Building in Professional Organizations

In recent years, we have sought to embody audience coalescence and coalition building through various collaborative efforts focused on sports team mascots and monikers. In June 2014, the Society for Linguistic Anthropology's (SLA) Task Force on Language & Social Justice (subcommittee on mascots) initiated a resolution on mascot names. The subcommittee included the two authors of this chapter as well as two additional members (Patricia Baquedano-Lopez and Laura R. Graham). The subcommittee collaboratively created a draft over several months. It was then sent to the SLA Task Force, the AAA Committee for Human Rights, and the AAA Association of Indigenous Anthropologists. After discussion of wording, concepts, and stances, the statement was endorsed by all the committees. It was then sent to the Society for Linguistic Anthropology Executive Committee, which provided feedback and ultimately endorsed the statement. The AAA Executive Committee reviewed the statement, made further revisions, and approved it on March 20, 2015. The resolution can be found at the AAA website (American Anthropological Association 2017).

In December 2014, we collaborated to publish another op-ed piece about this topic, highlighting the perspectives of anthropologists on the issue and intended for a wide readership. This involved collaboration with AAA staff, as well as coalescence with audiences who would engage with it (Avineri & Perley, 2014). One of us also wrote a piece for linguistic anthropologists focused on naturalized racism in relation to Indian mascots, in which he focused on ways that anthropologists can counteract overt and covert racism (Perley 2015). Together we presented at the Society for Linguistic Anthropology's Presidential Conversation on Language & Social Justice about the topic, providing another forum in which to coalesce with diverse audiences with their own perspectives and agendas.

Audience Coalescence and Interdisciplinarity

These forms of coalition building can move us toward audience coalescence, including interactions and collaboration across disciplines. In 2016, Netta Avineri and Jonathan Rosa organized an interdisciplinary forum at the American Association for Applied Linguistics, to explore various ways that linguistic anthropologists and applied linguists can come together around issues of social justice (Rosa and Avineri 2016). This interdisciplinary approach provided opportunities to engage with other's "epistemological universes" (Liddicoat 2017) and communities of practice (Lave and Wenger 1991), therefore leading to diverse ways to conceptualize similar issues. While presenting on this topic, we encountered distinct understandings of the issues. This challenged all participants to engage in critical empathy (DeStigter 1999; Palmer

Figure 15.2 Installation Art as Audience Coalescence through Empathetic Sharing.

and Menard-Warwick 2012) by recognizing other perspectives as well as the limits of taking on others' perspectives.

Bernard Perley coordinated an art installation piece that brought together University of Wisconsin-Milwaukee faculty from the departments of English, History, Education, and Anthropology as well as Native American language teachers from the Milwaukee Indian Community School to address the themes of social injustices against Native Americans featuring sports mascots and monikers. The installation was displayed at a variety of conferences as well as school and university campuses.[1] The installation encouraged participants to empathize with Native Americans by creating the emotive environment for sharing the joy of Native American languages while experiencing the trauma associated with colonial history. Conversations generated by the audiences who experienced the installation led to requests for the installation to be displayed in other venues and has served as a catalyst for innovative Native American language pedagogies.

Conclusion: From "Making a Difference" to "Being the Difference"

To combat centuries of colonialism and racism, it is essential to turn audiences into networks of social justice. This means that audiences are no longer passive recipients of language, imagery, and symbolic systems, but are active participants in envisioning a socially just present and future. This involves imagining a symbolism of social justice—in which signs and symbols are not taken-for-granted but are reimagined. This critical approach involves a reorientation towards recognizing language, embodiment, and symbolism such that analysis and advocacy occur simultaneously. We continue to wonder: what are the prospects of coalescence in a time of divisiveness?

Audience coalescence involves engagement with diverse texts and genres, as well as potential discomfort, misunderstanding, or ironic recognition. Social action includes interpersonal practice and experiential participation. We can recognize these troubling symbols as well as reframe this naturalized hate, engaging in "epistemic slippage" (Perley 2013). There is some hope: Adidas has offered financial support to high schools that change their logos or mascots "from potentially harmful Native American imagery or symbolism" (Woodrow Cox 2015); and in California all public schools are banned from using the R-word as a team name or mascot; and most recently, the Cleveland Indians owner has agreed to discontinue displaying the Chief Wahoo logo in their ballpark and uniforms starting in the 2019 season. However, there is much more work to do—and this involves creating new genres that invite audience coalescence as an interactive, interpersonal, and critically empathetic process.

Note

1 Wisconsin Indian Educators Association (2015, 2016), Educators Network for Social Justice (2015), Native American Literatures Symposium (2017), UWM C21 LandBody Conference (2106), Milwaukee Indian Community School (2015), and UWM Art Department's KSE Teacher Workshop, Milwaukee (2018).

References

American Anthropological Association. 2017. "AAA Statement on Sports Team Mascot Names." Accessed February 22, 2018 at www.americananthro.org/ConnectWithAAA/Content.aspx?ItemNumber=13107&RDtoken=41455&userID.

American Psychological Association. 2018. "Summary of the APA Resolution Recommending Retirement of American Indian Mascots." Accessed February 22, 2018 at www.apa.org/pi/oema/resources/indian-mascots.aspx.

Avineri, Netta & Perley, Bernard C. 2014. "This Holiday Season Let's Replace Disparaging Slurs." *The Huffington Post*, December 4. Accessed at www.huffingtonpost.com/american-anthropological-association/in-this-holiday-season-le_b_6262672.html.

Bell, Alan. 1984. "Language Style as Audience Design." *Language in Society* 13(2): 145–204.

Bell, Alan. 2001. "Back in Style: Reworking Audience Design." In *Style and Sociolinguistic Variation*, edited by Penelope Eckert and John R. Rickford, 139–169. Cambridge: Cambridge University Press.

Calloway, Colin G. 2010. *The Indian History of an American Institution: Native Americans at Dartmouth*. Hanover: Dartmouth College Press.

Deloria, Philip J. 1998. *Playing Indian*. New Haven: Yale University Press.

DeStigter, Todd. 1999. "Public Displays of Affection: Political Community through Critical Empathy." *Research in the Teaching of English* 33(3): 235–244.

Goffman, Erving. 1981. *Forms of Talk*. Philadelphia, PA: University of Pennsylvania Press.

Goodwin, Charles. 2010. "Interactive Footing." In *Reporting Talk: Reported Speech in Interaction*, edited by Elizabeth Holt and Rebecca Clift, 16–46. Cambridge: Cambridge University Press.

Goodwin, Charles. 2013. "The Co-operative, Transformative Organization of Human Action and Knowledge." *Journal of Pragmatics* 46(1): 8–23.

Goodwin, Marjorie and Charles Goodwin. 2004. "Participation." In *A Companion to Linguistic Anthropology*, edited by Alessandro Duranti, 222–244. Oxford: Basil Blackwell.

Guiliano, Jennifer. 2015. *Indian Spectacle: College Mascots and the Anxiety of Modern America*. New Brunswick, NJ: Rutgers University Press.

Hill, Jane H. 2008. *The Everyday Language of White Racism*. Malden, MA: Wiley-Blackwell.

Hutchins, Edwin. 1995. *Cognition in the Wild*. Cambridge, MA: MIT Press.

King, Richard and Charles Fruehling Springwood. 2001. *Team Spirits: The Native American Mascots Controversy*. Lincoln, NE: University of Nebraska Press.

Lave, Jean and Etienne Wenger. 1991. *Situated Learning: Legitimate Peripheral Participation*. Cambridge: Cambridge University Press.

Liddicoat, Anthony. 2017. "Language Teaching and Learning as a Transdisciplinary Endeavour." Paper presented at the American Association for Applied Linguistics Conference, Portland, OR, March 2017.

Palmer, Deborah K., and Julia Menard-Warwick. 2012. "Short-Term Study Abroad for Texas Preservice Teachers: On the Road from Empathy to Critical Awareness." *Multicultural Education* 19(3): 17–26.

Perley, Bernard C. 2013. "Gone Anthropologist": Epistemic Slippage, Native Anthropology, and the Dilemmas of Representation." In *Anthropology and the Politics of Representation*, edited by Gabriela Vargas-Cetina, 101–118. Tuscaloosa, AL: University of Alabama Press.

Perley, Bernard C. 2015. "Indian Mascots: Naturalized Racism and Anthropology." November 5. Accessed June 4, 2018 at http://linguisticanthropology.org/blog/2015/11/05/an-news-indian-mascots-naturalized-racism-and-anthropology-by-bernard-c-perley-university-of-wisconsin-milwaukee.

Rosa, Jonathan, and Netta Avineri. 2016. "Interdisciplinary Collaborations around Language and Social Justice." Accessed at http://linguisticanthropology.org/blog/2016/07/27/an-news-interdisciplinary-collaborations-around-language-and-social-justice-by-jonathan-rosa-stanford-university-and-netta-avineri-middlebury-institute-of-international-studies-at-monterey.

Sacks, Harvey, Emmanuel A. Schegloff, and Gail Jefferson. 1974. "A Simplest Systematics for the Organization of Turn-Taking for Conversation." *Language* 50: 696–735.

Strong, Pauline Turner. 2013. *American Indians and the American Imaginary: Cultural Representation Across the Centuries*. Boulder, CO: Paradigm Publishers.

Woodrow Cox, John. 2015. "Adidas stand against Native American high school mascots praised by Obama, condemned by Redskins." November 5. Accessed June 4, 2018 at www.washingtonpost.com/news/local/wp/2015/11/05/rgiii-sponsor-adidas-announces-support-for-high-schools-that-want-to-drop-native-american-mascots/?noredirect=on&utm_term=.236d9317f1c8.

16 The Language of Activism

Representations of Social Justice in a University Space in Argentina

Suriati Abas and James S. Damico

Introduction

On March 24, 1976 the military took over Argentina's government in a coup, which led to military control of the country through 1983, a time period (1976–1983) of severe state repression and violence as thousands of Argentines were disappeared, tortured, and killed. In 2016, during the week leading up to the 40th anniversary of the March 24 coup, now a public holiday called El *El Día de la Memoria por la Verdad y la Justicia* (The Day of Remembrance for Truth and Justice), a range of signs including posters, flyers, and placards filled public spaces in the city of Buenos Aires. We define these signs that convey specific messages to viewers, who bring in their own knowledge and understanding of the world, as the linguistic landscape (LL, hereafter).

We had the fortune to be in Buenos Aires on the days leading up to several commemorative events on March 24, 2016. During our visits at two public universities, and the most popular community gathering place for protest, the Plaza de Mayo, we were struck by the ways signs in the LL engaged with social justice issues. We focus here on two signs in a public university space in Buenos Aires to explore the intersections of language, social justice, and activism. In this chapter, we view language as a combination of texts and images since both can be utilized as tools for activism. By activism, we mean "the active participation of individuals in group behavior for the purpose of creating change" (Chambers and Phelps 1993, 20). Hence, to interpret the language of activism, we began by asking a set of questions about the LL:

- What is communicated on the sign?
- Who created it and for what purposes?
- How do the signs connect with the surroundings?

As we do our best to answer these questions we keep three core responsibilities in mind: (1) engaging and understanding the perspectives communicated through the signs; (2) posing critical questions about purposes and goals; and (3) seeking to stand together in a participatory community (Damico and Lybarger 2016). In order to engage the ideas and perspectives communicated in a sign, we need to strive to understand what is being communicated and why. This can be challenging, especially when one is not familiar with the area and has limited knowledge of the historical and contemporary context in which a sign resides. This was the case for the two of us, outsiders to the Argentine context.

Social Justice and Activism in the Linguistic Landscape

The work of Brazilian educator and theorist Paulo Freire helps situate and frame the social justice commitments and activism we witnessed in Buenos Aires in March 2016. A core concept that cuts across much of Freire's wide body of work is *conscientização*, often translated as "critical consciousness" (Freire [1970]2005). The process of *conscientização* entails learning to cultivate deeper understandings of the world by identifying the causes and consequences of injustices (social, economic, and political) such as economic policies that reap significant benefits for the rich at the expense of the poor or programs that discriminate against or restrict basic freedoms to groups of people. Freire described the process of *conscientização* as learning to "read the word and read the world." In his work with illiterate peasants in Brazil, "reading the word" corresponded to learning how to decode the alphabet and comprehend words and "generative themes" which connected deeply to the lives of the adult peasants. "Reading the world" entailed making sense of local and larger social, economic, and political issues and injustices, which occurred at the same time as learning to read and comprehend words. For example, the word "well" served as a generative theme and led to provocative questions like: Who owns and who doesn't own the wells in this town and why? What unjust conditions exist here and what can we do about them (Cervetti, Pardales and Damico 2001)?

Some essential research in LL exemplifies the ways people use language to address injustices (e.gs. Waksman and Shohamy 2016; Shohamy and Waksman 2012; Hanauer 2015). In a study about social protests in Israel, Waksman and Shohamy (2016) analyzed displays, poetry and photographic exhibits within the precincts of a teacher training college and found the LL echoed the topics of the protests in public spaces outside of the institution (costly housing, discrimination against women and deprivation of foreign workers). The ways the LL was repositioned by either the teachers or students to advocate for basic human rights embodies the essence of *conscientização*. In another significant LL study, Hanauer (2015) examined handmade signs, banners, clothing, flags, tents and leaflets in public spaces that were part of the Occupy Wall Street movement. At three demonstration sites in Baltimore, Maryland, there was clear evidence of *conscientização* as people communicated broader societal inequalities, especially about the economic system. As these two research studies that explore the intersections of language, social justice, and activism illustrate, the work of *conscientização* does not occur in a vacuum; it is always tied to specific contexts.

The University Space

At the university space we visited, the entire walkways were filled with messages criticizing the US. The target for much of this criticism was then US President Barack Obama who was in Buenos Aires the days leading up to the March 24 commemorative events. Obama was there for an official state visit to meet the new Argentine President, Mauricio Macri, a political conservative whose right leaning views were in sharp contrast to the strong politically left leaning faculty and students at this university. Through our conversations with students in this university space, we learned that many students identified as activists or "*militantes*" and that the signs displayed throughout the hallways and in many classrooms were artistic expressions of their political activism that strongly opposed the Macri administration and President Obama for his apparent alliance with Macri.

Methodology

To help us understand the language of activism in the LL, we employed qualitative approaches, drawing from our observations, interpretations as non-Argentines, informal conversations with university faculty and students and by collecting related newspaper articles. Although the LL can be examined quantitatively (e.g, Backhaus 2007; Spolsky and Cooper 1991), or by using a combination of quantitative and qualitative methods (e.g, Malinowski 2009; Rubdy 2015), adopting a qualitative stance similar to Hanauer (2015) and Shohamy and Waksman (2012) enabled us to explore in greater detail social justice commitments in a university space.

Selection of Signs

We selected two signs (Figures 16.1 and 16.2) for closer analysis based on two primary reasons: their content was representative of the attempts to make issues of social justice visible to the public; and these signs were placed at the main walkway areas, accessible to all passers-by. Figure 16.1 contains two parts, a hand-painted section and a poster (bottom right of sign) that was mass-produced and placed in various spaces within and outside the university. The other sign (Figure 16.2) was handwritten by student(s). While we were not able to speak directly with the creators of these posters, other students we interacted with confirmed that the signs in this LL were created by students who identified as social justice activists (they called themselves *militantes*) who strongly opposed social and economic policies of President Macri and President Obama.

Contending the Past into the Present: Argentina and US

Both parts of Figure 16.1 represent a call to fight for social justice and to connect events of the past to the present. The first two lines of the hand-painted section establish the 40-year time period for commemoration—the March 24

date flanked by the years 1976 and 2016. The next three lines present a call
to action "Seguimos luchando contra la impunidad de ayer y hoy" ("We continue fighting against the impunity of yesterday and today"). The next two
lines, "Fuera Obama de Argentina" ("Obama, [get] out of Argentina"), target then U.S president, Barack Obama, not only for the timing of his visit
to Argentina during that week, but presumably also for being a symbol of
US power and influence in the region in ways that have not helped many
Argentines. The poster ended with "29 de Mayo" (May 29) to seemingly
remind viewers about the "Cordobazo" which was a civil revolt in 1969 led
by students and workers in Còrdoba, Argentina against the military government. The other section of this sign, the mass-produced poster at the bottom
right, echoes the content of the hand-painted section and extends its critique
by naming the military coup a "genocida" (genocide) and by more directly
linking Obama and Macri with an explicit call to reject Macri's policies of
"el saqueo y la represion" ("pillage and repression").

Figure 16.1 A Poster along the Hallway Leading to the Cafeteria.
Photo courtesy of Suriati Abas, 2016.

The activists who created this sign exercised critical consciousness by identifying impunities that track from the past to the present. The idea of impunity links to specific historical events where those directly involved with the severe state repression and violence were granted impunity for the crimes they committed. According to one of the students:

> My mum and people over fifty or sixty years old still remember those horrible days; too much violence. In the eighties there was a trial against the *represores*, those responsible for the horrible thing that happened [people killed and still missing]. Most of them were found guilty. However, it was a controversial trial because the highest ranks were condemned but the rest [the simple soldiers] had *obediencia debida* [see below] as an excuse for killing and kidnapping people. That's why the poster claims that the struggle still continues.

(Interview, March 18, 2016)

A brief chronology of events that reflect impunities from the past include:

> 1986—The Ley de Punto Final (or the "full stop law") was mandated to end investigations and prosecutions of people accused of excessive political violence during the dictatorship.

> 1987—The Ley de Obediencia Debida ("Law of Due obedience") was passed, exempting all military personnel except top commanders from legal punishment for crimes carried out during the dictatorship because they were just obeying orders from their superiors.

> 1990—Top military officers who had committed crimes were pardoned.

While present-day impunities are not named specifically in this sign, they were in other signs in this university space, such as in Figure 16.2.

Figure 16.2 addresses similar issues but the link between Argentina and the US and Obama is more explicit. There are nine lines of text with one central provocative image: Obama with a big smile sitting on the back of a vulture and holding the reins to control it. The first two lines correspond with this image: "Abajo el pacto buitres" ("Down with the agreement with the vultures") and "Fuera Obama" ("Obama, get out"). Some understanding of history is necessary to understand why Obama is depicted smiling atop a vulture.

At the end of 2001, during the economic collapse in Argentina, more than half of Argentines were living in poverty, unemployment rose to more than 20 percent, and there were riots. During this time, Argentina defaulted on roughly $100 billion in loans and needed to restructure its debt, so it discounted bonds. The Argentine economy stabilized and more than 90 percent of Argentina's creditors accepted a deal to take a discounted payment. Several prominent hedge funds in the US, however, held out for better repayment terms. The result was a heated, protracted 15-year legal battle between Argentina and these US hedge funds who sued Argentina for repayment. This kept Argentina from

Figure 16.2 A Poster by the Staircase Leading up to the Second Level.
Photo courtesy of Suriati Abas, 2016.

selling bonds on the international market and, in turn, crippled the nation's economy. The hedge funds also attempted to seize Argentine holdings around the world (Guzman and Stiglitz 2016). Previous Argentine President Christina Kirchner refused to settle with these hedge funds on their terms, calling them "vultures" because they buy bonds cheaply, sue countries for full repayment, and reap enormous profits when they are paid. University students whom we talked to viewed this as an issue of concern. Here is an example of one student's response to this sign:

> We have a problem because we have to pay to FMI [International Monetary Fund] and to other banks because, like 20 years ago, they nationalized, they have rates. So, we have to pay but we don't agree with them because

we didn't spend the money. You know like, spend the money one day, take up credit with United States. So we use the word, *buitres*. It's an expression to say that the promise and that people, that businessman from International Capital, they want our money as Argentinians and they have not good intentions with our country. Because they are like *buitres*, like they want to eat everything they can. It's an expression that we use here.

(Interview; March 16, 2016)

Conclusively, the text and image about the vultures and Obama can be understood as activists' expressing their concerns about what they perceive to be injustices: It is politically unjust to allow private citizens (hedge fund investors) to negotiate with Argentina as a sovereign nation. Obama is implicated for not taking a position on the legal dispute between the U.S. hedge funds and the Argentine government.

Another social justice issue is addressed in the third line, "No Al Protocolo Represivo" ("No to the repressive protocols"). This statement refers to a new set of rules (or protocols) about use of public space laid out by the Minister of Security in February 2016 in the early days of Macri's administration. This policy instituted a series of new guidelines to deal with street protests. The rules provided a legal justification for the use of security personnel to forcibly remove people who are blocking streets. This contemporary example (*de hoy* or from today) calls to mind historical injustices when the dictatorship suppressed, stamped out, and eliminated any forms of protest, or even basic rights to assemble freely in public spaces.

A similar social justice issue and one of the most direct concerns about "impunities of today" is expressed in Figure 16.2 with the phrase "Carcel comun a Pedraza" (common jail for Pedraza). Josè Pedraza, former head of the Railway Union, was convicted and sentenced in 2013 to 15 years in prison for his role in the murder of Mariana Ferreyra, a member of the Workers' Party. Pedraza's sentence, however, was commuted to house arrest, ostensibly for health reasons and his age, being older than 70 (La Nacion 2016). This case makes a clear link to the past when leaders during the dictatorship were found guilty of crimes but did not need to fulfill sentences.

Finally, the final text in Figure 16.2 (lower right hand corner) calls viewers to take action and join the March 24 march scheduled to take place at the famed gathering place, the Plaza de Mayo.

Conclusion

The Argentinian university that we described above is one example of a space that functions as a site of critical reflection. While student activism is not a new phenomenon, the uniqueness of this site contributes to the dynamism of the LL. The university space changes frequently in response to any form of perceived systemic injustice within Argentina or other world events that resonate with the students' shared experiences of experiencing violence and injustices, as a nation (e.g., several LL items were constructed on September 14, 2014 at the university, in solidarity with the 2014 Israel–Gaza conflict; many signs and posters were created expressing their views on the 2017 Catalonia referendum violence in Barcelona, Spain). Besides shaping learning experiences, the work of activism enables students to engage in "deeper self-understanding of the historical and social contexts that have made them who they are" (Burawoy 2004, 9; see also Freire [1970]2005). Through conscientização, students learn to look closely at their own realities and attempted to see how the world can be altered into a more just society. The work of cultivating a LL specific for the commemoration also provided opportunities for activists to use language creatively (such as using an image of a vulture in Figure 16.2) for authentic purposes. What these posters share is a committed effort that draws attention to, mobilizes action towards or attempts to intervene in, systems of recurring inequality. On the whole, analysis of the two posters above, is based on posing and pursuing a set of basic questions:

- What is on the sign?
- Who created it?
- How do the signs connect with the surroundings?

Answering these questions helps elucidate the ways student activists in a university space used language to cultivate *conscientização* and promote social justice by creating linkages between the past and present to communicate their ideas publicly for a general audience.

Acknowledgement

We would like to thank students at the university for participating in our research.

References

Backhaus, Peter. 2007. *Linguistic Landscapes: A Comparative Study of Urban Multilingualism in Tokyo*. Clevedon: Multilingual Matters.

Burawoy, Michael. 2004. "Public Sociologies: Contradictions, Dilemmas, and Possibilities." *Social Forces* 82(4): 1603–1618.

Cervetti, Gina, Michael Pardales, and James Damico. 2001. "A Tale of Differences: Comparing the Traditions, Perspectives, and Educational Goals of Critical Reading and Critical Literacy." *Reading Online* 4(9).

Chambers, Tony, and Christine Phelps. 1993. "Student Activism as a Form of Leadership and Student Development." *NASPA Journal* 31(1): 19–29.

Damico, James and Loren Lybarger. 2016. "Commemoration, Testimony, and Protest in Argentina: An Exploration of Response and Responsibilities." *Ubiquity: The Journal of Literature, Literacy and the Arts* 3(1). Accessed October 20, 2017 at https://ed-ubiquity.gsu.edu/wordpress/damico-and-lybarger-multimodal-3-1.

Freire, Paulo. [1970]2005. *Pedagogy of the Oppressed*. New York: Continuum Publishing Company.

Guzman, Martin and Joseph Stiglitz. 2016. "How Hedge Funds Held Argentina for Ransom." *New York Times*, April 1. Accessed October 20, 2016 at www.nytimes. com/2016/04/01/opinion/how-hedge-funds-held-argentina-for-ransom.html.

Hanauer, David. 2015. "Occupy Baltimore: A Linguistic Landscape Analysis of Participatory Social Contestation in an American City." In *Conflict, Exclusion and Dissent in the Linguistic Landscape*, edited by Rani Rubdy and Ben Selim, 207–222. New York: Palgrave Macmillian.

La Nacion. 2016. "Concedieron prisión domiciliaria a José Pedraza, condenado por el crimen de Mariano Ferreyra" ["José Pedraza, Was Granted House Arrest, Sentenced for the Crime of Mariano Ferreyra"]. *La Nacion*, February 25. Accessed October 20, 2016 at http://www.lanacion.com.ar/1874218-concedieron-prision-domiciliaria-a-jose-pedraza-condenado-por-el-crimen-de-mariano-ferreyra.

Malinowski, David. 2009. "Authorship in the Linguistic Landscape: A Multimodal-Performance View." In *Linguistic Landscapes: Expanding the Scenery*, edited by Elana Shohamy and Dork Gorter, 107–125. New York: Routledge.

Rubdy, Rani. 2015. "A Multimodal Analysis of the Graffiti Commemorating the 26/11 Mumbai Terror Attacks: Constructing Self-Understandings of a Senseless Violence." In *Conflict, Exclusion and Dissent in the Linguistic Landscape*, edited by Rani Rubdy and Ben Selim, 207–222. New York: Palgrave Macmillian.

Shohamy, Elana, and Shoshi Waksman. 2012. "Talking Back to the Tel Aviv Centennial: LL Responses to Top-Down Agendas." In *Linguistic Landscapes, Multilingualism and Social Change, LL: Multiple Perspectives*, edited by Christine Hélot, Monica Barni, Rudi Janssens and Carla Bagna, 109–126. Frankfurt am Main: Peter Lang.

Spolsky, Bernard, and Robert Cooper. 1991. *The Languages of Jerusalem*. Oxford: Clarendon Press.

Waksman, Shoshi and Elana Shohamy. 2016. "Linguistic Landscape of Social Protests: Moving from 'Open' to 'Institutional' Spaces". In *Negotiating and Contesting Identities in Linguistic Landscapes*, edited by Robert Blackwood, Elizabeth Lanza and Hirut Woldermariam, 85–98. London: Bloomsbury Academic.

17 California Latinx Youth as Agents of Sociolinguistic Justice

Mary Bucholtz, Dolores Inés Casillas, and Jin Sook Lee

Introduction

Over the past twenty years, young Californians from minoritized groups, especially Latinxs, have been subjected to legalized bigotry via the banning of their language from the classroom. This cruel policy took effect in a climate of anti-immigrant hysteria that began in the 1980s and 1990s. In 1986, California voters passed Proposition 63, which made English the state's official language (even though the United States itself does not have an official language). This was followed in 1994 by the openly xenophobic Proposition 187, or the "Save Our State" initiative, which aimed to deprive unauthorized immigrants of education and health care services.[1] Thus, by 1998, the groundwork was in place for California voters to approve Proposition 227, a ballot initiative ending nearly all bilingual education in public schools. Instead, it required students classified as English learners to be taught exclusively in that language and for them to be moved into mainstream classes after only a year. Despite its campaign's feel-good slogan "English for the Children," Proposition 227, along with similar measures in Arizona and Massachusetts, has had deeply harmful effects on the language and education of an entire generation of students, particularly young Latinxs (Gutiérrez, Baquedano-López, and Asato 2000). Proposition 227 was not rescinded until November 2016, when California voters passed Proposition 58, which gives local communities control over decisions about how best to educate English learners in their schools (the effects of this measure are not yet clear).

Four months before Proposition 227 passed, a similar policy was enacted in the city of Santa Barbara, where the three of us teach at the University of California. The all-white school board unanimously approved a measure to immediately place all English learners in mainstream classrooms, ignoring the powerful arguments of researchers, educators, and Latinx parents in favor of bilingual education. The racism and xenophobia that often motivate such policies were evident in the comments of many white residents; in one notorious—and paradoxical—remark, a board member explained that the policy reflected the preferences of white parents: "They don't want their kids to go to a school where half the kids speak Spanish. People want their children to have a happy, open learning experience" (Bruni 1998).

Some states went even further: After rendering students' languages illegal, Arizona lawmakers began to target their cultures and histories (Cammarota and Aguilera 2012). Chicanx studies classes were banned from Arizona's public schools in 2010, even though such classes result in greater academic success for Latinx students (Cabrera, Milem, Ozan, and Marx 2014). Justifications for the ban included blatantly racist assertions that such courses foment "ethnic solidarity," racism (against whites), and even the overthrow of the U.S. government.

Due to these political developments, many Americans of Latinx heritage have experienced their entire education under draconian and discriminatory policies that ban both their language and their culture. Young people's languages of heritage have been devalued and ignored, despite the established importance of students' home languages for future academic success and social well-being (Wiley et al. 2014). In the face of such marginalization, Latinx youth in California have been demanding sociolinguistic justice, or "self-determination for linguistically subordinated individuals and groups in sociopolitical struggles over language" (Bucholtz et al. 2014, 145).

These acts of sociolinguistic justice are also acts of agency—that is, directed action that affects the self, others, and/or the larger world. Yet adults often fail to recognize the considerable social agency of youth, especially in institutional settings such as schools, which impose structural constraints on what counts as legitimate knowledge and action. As the three examples below demonstrate, such agency is the basis of social activism by challenging and potentially changing conditions of injustice.

The SKILLS Program

We focus on the social agency of youth participants in an academic partnership program with a social justice focus, School Kids Investigating Language in Life and Society (SKILLS), which was established in 2010 to address linguistic, educational, socioeconomic, and racial inequities in our region (skills.ucsb.edu). SKILLS creates collaborations between teams of graduate student instructors and undergraduate mentors on the one hand and youth from area high schools and youth-serving organizations on the other. Most participants are from low-income Mexican American families and are the first generation in their families to have the opportunity to pursue higher education. Within the SKILLS partnership, our goal is not youth empowerment, which presupposes an asymmetrical distribution of power and knowledge, but rather accompaniment, which involves joint activity and mutual learning among all participants (Bucholtz, Casillas, and Lee 2016).

The SKILLS program supports young people's linguistic and cultural identities as well as their development of academic skills and knowledge. Together, participants work through a five-month-long college-level curriculum on language and race; whenever possible, students receive college credit at no cost thanks to a partnership with a local community college. Activism within SKILLS draws on the model of youth participatory action research, in which young people carry out original research to challenge inequitable conditions in their lives and communities (Cammarota and Fine 2008). The student researcher-activists combine their linguistic and cultural expertise with the conceptual and methodological tools they encounter in SKILLS to critically examine issues of language, race, identity, and power in their everyday lives. They develop original projects about these issues and share the results in public presentations at the end of the program. Through their work, SKILLS students contribute to the advancement of sociolinguistic justice both locally and more widely.

Youth Agency and Sociolinguistic Justice

Below we present three illustrations of SKILLS students as agents of social change. In each case, young people utilized their linguistic and cultural expertise to identify and respond to an inequity that deeply and personally affected them. And in each case, although the students were accompanied and supported by instructional team members, the social changes they enacted—from changing minds to changing policy—were due to their own efforts as agents and activists of sociolinguistic justice.

Example 1: Elisa and Linguistic Access

Our first example, based on research by graduate student instructor Audrey Lopez (2018), involves social change at a local partner school, Mission City High School (a pseudonym). The student researcher-activist who was the agent of this change, whom we call Elisa, was a senior at the school in 2014 who worked as a volunteer bilingual interpreter between Spanish-speaking adults and English-monolingual institutional representatives, a form of linguistic expertise that has often been overlooked by adults (Valdés 2003).

Because of these experiences, Elisa was acutely aware of the importance of linguistic access for minoritized groups and individuals in institutional contexts. During a SKILL class discussion of youth interpreting, for example, she noted proudly that her interpreting work in local elementary schools enabled Spanish-speaking parents to become more involved in their children's education. Hence, when she herself faced an institutional obstacle to linguistic access at her own high school, she was quick to challenge this exclusionary practice.

Elisa had been selected by school officials as a commencement speaker at Mission City High's graduation ceremony, an honor reserved for the most distinguished seniors. The school required student speakers to submit their speeches in advance for approval. Drawing on her linguistic expertise, Elisa wrote her speech entirely in Spanish. However, when she submitted the speech, she was told that she would have to translate it into English before the ceremony so that the audience could understand what she was saying.

Although she could have easily complied thanks to her bilingual skills, Elisa did not acquiesce to this institutional demand. Instead, she argued that Mission City High School did not have any written policy barring the use of languages other than English in commencement speeches, and she pointed out that because Latinx students were the school's largest ethnoracial group, most audience members would in fact be likely to understand a Spanish-language speech. She also emphasized that she had written her speech in Spanish precisely to ensure that she would be understood by the audience members who were most important to her: her own parents.

Elisa ultimately convinced the school officials, and on graduation day she delivered her speech entirely in Spanish; her English translation appeared in the commencement program. Her language access campaign became the focus of her SKILLS project, and she proudly reported on her success at her final public presentation. Not only was she able to ensure her own family's linguistic inclusion in one of the most important moments in her life, but she also won this right for the families of future student commencement speakers. Elisa's agency and activism are evident in her unflagging work for linguistic access for Spanish speakers, which disrupted in a small but very real way a longstanding pattern of sociolinguistic injustice in the United States.

Example 2: Oaxacan Youth and Linguistic Marginalization

Our second example is taken from the research of SKILLS team members Katie Lateef-Jan, Jessica Love-Nichols, and Anna Bax (2017) at another partner site, a community organization for indigenous Mexicans working in the agricultural industry south of Santa Barbara. The organization primarily serves Mixtec and Zapotec speakers and their families from Oaxaca and adjacent Mexican states, who confront a double burden of inequality due to severe racial, linguistic, and economic discrimination both in Mexico and in the United States (Fox and Rivera-Salgado 2004). Moreover, this highly vulnerable group is often invisible within the larger Mexican immigrant population, and its members are commonly misidentified as Spanish speakers, despite the fact that many indigenous Mexicans are not proficient in Spanish. Along with its many other services, our partner organization hosts a youth group that has undertaken several high-profile activist campaigns to advance linguistic and social justice for indigenous Mexicans in California, including combating the racist bullying of Oaxacan youth in schools and advocating for school-based interpreter services to facilitate greater parental involvement in their children's education.

We began our partnership with the organization in 2016. Most youth group members were bilingual or trilingual in Spanish and/or English and their indigenous home language, although some were losing proficiency in the latter due to pressures from English and Spanish. Because the students were especially interested in maintaining and learning about their languages of heritage— itself a form of activism in the context of U.S. language hierarchies (Leeman, Rabin, and Román-Mendoza 2011)—the instructors' curriculum explored the effects of colonialism on indigenous languages and introduced tools for writing Mixtec and Zapotec, which are mostly unwritten languages. Students used these resources along with their multilingual expertise to create trilingual literacy materials for children and adults in their community (Figure 17.1).

Partway through the SKILLS program, the instructors suggested to the students that they present some of their work at an upcoming local linguistics conference on indigenous languages of the Americas. Eager to raise linguists' awareness of the challenges facing indigenous Mexican communities in the United States, the young people decided to create a documentary film about their experiences of living in multiple languages, from the pain of linguistic racism, linguistic shame, and language shift under conditions of immigration to their strong sense of indigenous identity and their hopes of maintaining or regaining their languages. Two undergraduate film studies students helped the students with the technical aspects of the production. The result was a fifteen-minute multilingual documentary in Mixtec, Zapotec, Spanish, and English, with the Spanish title *Orgullosamente Indígena* ('Proud to be Indigenous').

This deeply affecting film was screened at the linguistics conference as well as at other local venues; portions were also presented at the Linguistic Society of America national conference. However, because of the very real threat to the youth and their families due to federal anti-immigrant policies, the film had to be removed from public circulation. Despite this setback, these youth activists, accompanied by the SKILLS team, were able to reach a wide audience with a powerful message about their ongoing struggle for sociolinguistic justice for themselves and their community.

ORGULLO INDÍGENA

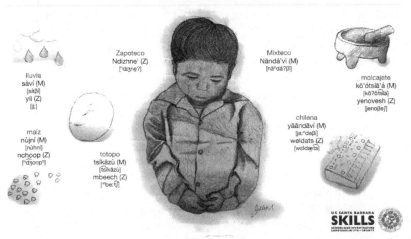

Figure 17.1 Poster Created by Youth of Mixtec and Zapotec Heritage to Foster Trilingual Literacy.

Example 3: Valeria and Linguistic Racism

Our final example focuses on another student at Mission City High School, Valeria (a pseudonym), who participated in SKILLS as a sophomore in 2012 (Ferrada, Bucholtz, and Corella forthcoming). In their curriculum, the graduate instructors developed a strong focus on linguistic discrimination and linguistic racism, issues that spoke powerfully to the largely bilingual Latinx youth they were working with. As the instructors prepared the students to develop their final projects, they shared a set of stark examples of anti-Spanish sentiment in public discourse, such as signs in Mock Spanish (Hill 1999) bearing offensive slogans like "I No Speaka Spanish. I Speak English." One of these examples in particular had a powerful impact on Valeria, a quiet, deep-thinking student.

The example that struck Valeria so profoundly was a video clip of a highly controversial speech by former Republican leader Newt Gingrich in 2007 when he was contemplating running for the U.S. Presidency. In the clip, Gingrich condemns bilingual education, proclaiming, "We should replace bilingual education with . . . immersion in English, so people learn the common language of the country and so they learn the language of prosperity, not the language of living in a ghetto." While all the students responded to this statement with anger and disbelief, Valeria's reaction was particularly strong: She wept quietly throughout the group's discussion of how to challenge such racist discourse through a collaborative public awareness campaign.

Importantly, Valeria's emotions were a source of great strength for her. For the rest of the class period and over the next few weeks, she worked intensively to develop a pair of bilingual posters with the message "Todos los idiomas son creados iguales/All Languages Are Created Equal." Below this slogan, she added more detailed text that concluded as follows (in the English version): "I value Spanish and English equally, just as other multilinguals value their languages equally. My languages make me who I am. I am my language. Respect my voice."

The strength of Valeria's words on her poster was matched by the emotional power of her public presentation. Standing before an audience of a hundred adults and peers, she spoke with quiet dignity through her tears as she described her reaction to Gingrich's hateful words. The poster that she displayed to her hushed and damp-eyed listeners (and that was later posted at her school and elsewhere) features a photo of herself, wearing a solemn expression and an American flag T-shirt (Figure 17.2). As activist interventions, the presentation and poster were decisive rebukes to the un-American values of a national politician. Through her courageous action to confront racist political rhetoric despite the personal pain it caused her to do so, Valeria became an agent for sociolinguistic justice for herself, her family, and her community.

Conclusion

We find it striking, and moving, that members of the post-Proposition 227 generation, who have had little or no access to bilingual resources in their

Figure 17.2 Valeria's Language Awareness Campaign Poster (Spanish Version).

schools, have emerged as powerful activists and advocates for sociolinguistic justice. Such students are facilitating basic human rights for speakers of minoritized languages: to be respected, to communicate—even simply to listen and understand. Abandoned by an educational system that has refused to acknowledge, much less validate, their home languages, these young people nonetheless insist on being recognized as speakers of Spanish, of Mixtec, of Zapotec.

In our work within SKILLS, it is clear to us that young people's positionality as agents, and not merely beneficiaries, of social change, is crucial to the goal of fostering sociolinguistic justice. Youth activism around language takes many forms, from claiming students' right to use their heritage languages to demanding greater public awareness of and accountability for linguistic inequities. Acknowledging, learning from, and accompanying youth in their agentive action has been central to our efforts to make our own teaching and research about language, race, culture, and identity more just, inclusive, humanizing, and culturally sustaining (Bucholtz, Casillas, and Lee 2018; Paris and Alim 2017; Paris and Winn 2014).

Such efforts are more important than ever in the current social and political climate. To be sure, Proposition 58 is a step in the right direction. And in response to Arizona's ethnic studies ban, California educators, students, parents, policymakers, and activists launched the Ethnic Studies Now campaign, leading in September 2016 to the passage of a state law to create an ethnic studies curriculum for California's public schools. Moreover, most of California's public schools, including those in Santa Barbara, have become majority-Latinx, and many school boards are now more representative of the families they serve, in both their demographics and their politics.

But despite these bright spots, the national political climate threatens greater struggles ahead. The openly racist and xenophobic rhetoric inflamed by Republican politicians during and after the 2016 Presidential election has taken a grave toll on young people of color. A sharp increase in incidents of hate speech, harassment, and assault directed at Latinx and immigrant students as well as other vulnerable groups led the Santa Barbara School Board to pass a resolution declaring local public schools safe zones for all students (Hamm 2016). This resolution shows how far Santa Barbara's schools have come in recognizing their responsibility to support and protect young people, but at the same time it also reveals how far we still have to go as a nation to defeat the forces of racism, fear, and hatred. Now more than ever, we are committed to working through the SKILLS program to accompany Latinx youth as agents and activists of social change, as they fight—with passion, with purpose, and with deep wisdom—for greater sociolinguistic justice in an increasingly unjust world.

Acknowledgements

We are extremely grateful to the SKILLS student researcher-activists, the graduate students whose research is discussed here, the rest of the SKILLS team, and the many sponsors of the SKILLS program. Finally, we thank the editors and anonymous reviewers for their suggestions.

Note

1 Proposition 187 was ruled unconstitutional in 1997 but was not removed from the state's legal code until 2014. Proposition 63 remains in effect.

References

Bruni, Frank. 1998. "Bilingual Education Battle Splits Santa Barbara." *New York Times*, May 27. Accessed April 2, 2018 at www.nytimes.com/1998/05/27/us/bilingual-education-battle-splits-santa-barbara.html.

Bucholtz, Mary, Audrey Lopez, Allina Mojarro, Elena Skapoulli, Christopher VanderStouwe, and Shawn Warner-Garcia. 2014. "Sociolinguistic Justice in the Schools: Student Researchers as Linguistic Experts." *Language and Linguistics Compass* 8(4):144–157.

Bucholtz, Mary, Dolores Inés Casillas, and Jin Sook Lee. 2016. "Beyond Empowerment: Accompaniment and Sociolinguistic Justice in a Youth Research Program." In *Sociolinguistic Research: Application and Impact*, edited by Robert Lawson and Dave Sayers, 25–44. London: Routledge.

Bucholtz, Mary, Dolores Inés Casillas, and Jin Sook Lee, eds. 2018. *Feeling It: Language, Race, and Affect in Latinx Youth Learning*. New York: Routledge.

Cabrera, Nolan L., Jeffrey F. Milem, Jaquette Ozan, and Ronald W. Marx. 2014. "Missing the (Student Achievement) Forest for All the (Political) Trees: Empiricism and the Mexican American Studies Controversy in Tucson." *American Educational Research Journal* 51(6): 1084–1118.

Cammarota, Julio, and Michelle Aguilera. 2012. " 'By the Time I Get to Arizona': Race, Language, and Education in America's Racist State." *Race Ethnicity and Education* 15(4): 485–500.

Cammarota, Julio, and Michelle Fine, eds. 2008. *Revolutionizing Education: Youth Participatory Action Research in Motion*. New York: Routledge.

Ferrada, Juan Sebastian, Mary Bucholtz, and Meghan Corella Morales. Forthcoming. "'Respeta mi idioma': Affective Agency and Latinx Youth Activism." *Journal of Language, Identity, and Education*.

Fox, Jonathan, and Gaspar Rivera-Salgado, eds. 2004. *Indigenous Mexican Migrants in the United States*. La Jolla, CA: Center for U.S.–Mexican Studies and Center for Comparative Immigration Studies.

Gutiérrez, Kris D., Patricia Baquedano-López, and Jolynn Asato. 2000. "'English for the Children': The New Literacy of the Old World Order, Language Policy and Educational Reform." *Bilingual Research Journal* 24(1–2): 1–26.

Hamm, Keith. 2016. "Schools Fight Trump Effect: Board of Education, with Three New Trustees, Affirms District as 'Safe Zone.'" *Santa Barbara Independent*, December 15. Accessed April 2, 2018 at www.independent.com/news/2016/dec/15/trump-inspired-hate-seeps-santa-barbara-schools.

Hill, Jane H. 1999. "Language, Race, and White Public Space." *American Anthropologist* 100(3): 680–689.

Lateef-Jan, Katie, Jessica Love-Nichols, and Anna Bax. 2017. "*Orgullosamente Indígena*: Mexican Immigrant Indigenous Youth in Pursuit of Educational and Sociolinguistic Justice." Paper presented at the Linguistic Society of America Annual Meeting, Austin, TX, January.

Leeman, Jennifer, Lisa Rabin, and Esperanza Román-Mendoza. 2011. "Identity and Activism in Heritage Language Education." *Modern Language Journal* 95(4): 481–495.

Lopez, Audrey. 2018 "'Without Me, That Wouldn't Be Possible': Affect in Latinx Youth Discussions of Language Brokering." In *Feeling It: Language, Race, and Affect in Latinx Youth Learning*, edited by Mary Bucholtz, Dolores Inés Casillas, and Jin Sook Lee, 187–211. New York: Routledge.

Paris, Django, and H. Samy Alim, eds. 2017. *Culturally Sustaining Pedagogies: Teaching and Learning for Justice in a Changing World*. New York: Teachers College Press.

Paris, Django, and Maisha T. Winn, eds. 2014. *Humanizing Research: Decolonizing Qualitative Inquiry with Youth and Communities*. Los Angeles, CA: Sage.

Valdés, Guadalupe. 2003. *Expanding Definitions of Giftedness: The Case of Young Interpreters from Immigrant Communities*. Mahwah, NJ: Lawrence Erlbaum Associates.

Wiley, Terrence G., Joy Kreeft Peyton, Donna Christian, Sarah Catherine K. Moore, and Na Liu, eds. 2014. *Handbook of Heritage, Community, and Native American Languages in the United States: Research, Policy, and Educational Practice*. New York: Routledge.

18 Pronouns and Possibilities

Transgender Language Activism and Reform

Lal Zimman

cis – on the side of

trans – across from

Introduction

Over the last decade, there has been enormous growth in the American public's awareness of and interest in transgender people and the social marginalization they face. This change is due not only to the growing number of publicly trans figures such as actress Laverne Cox, athlete and media figure Caitlin Jenner, and filmmakers Lana and Lilly Wachowski, but also crucially to decades of trans activism happening outside the spotlight that made it possible for celebrities to be openly trans today. Language always seems to figure prominently in discussions of trans issues, and for good reason. In a fundamental sense, being transgender isn't just about expressing a gender identity by dressing certain way or modifying one's body; it is also about the crucial role that language plays in creating our identities.

The language used to talk about trans people has become a hot-button issue on many college campuses in particular as some universities are investing in trans-inclusive language practices by, for instance, creating ways for class rosters to indicate whether students should be referred to as *she, he, they*, or some other pronoun, while others affiliated with the academy have expressed resistance to what they see as an imposition of leftist ideology. In fact, transgender activism has often centered around local interventions in language. One recent success has been the introduction of the word *cisgender* or *cis* as a term to refer to people who are not transgender. The promotion of *cisgender* is not just about the need to have a word to talk about non-trans people, but also the need to call attention to *cissexism* or *cisnormativity*, which both refer to the idea that cisgender identities are "normal," "natural," and "factual," while transgender identities are "abnormal," "unnatural," and "fictional."

Beyond the use of overtly hostile language, such as transphobic epithets, there are many subtle ways language enforces cissexism. Among these is the practice of using words like *woman* and *man* to refer interchangeably to a person's physiology (e.g. "women's bodies"), childhood socialization (e.g. "how women are raised"), perceived gender (e.g. "women often experience street harassment"), and gender identity (e.g. "women may be inclined to have other women as friends"). The difficulty of divesting oneself fully of cisnormative language is a common subject of anxiety for aspiring trans allies, but linguistic analysis offers tools for understanding the linguistic strategies trans people themselves have developed for subverting cisnormativity and the gender binary (i.e., the idea that there are only two genders, which exist in opposition to one another). After all, trans people, too, have needed to develop ways of thinking and talking about gender that affirm their own and one another's identities.

This case study focuses on three challenges for trans-inclusive language: how to select gendered labels and pronouns, how to make language more gender-neutral when gender isn't relevant, and how to talk about gender more precisely when it is relevant, such as in discussions of identity, social inequality, physiology, or socialization. Each challenge is accompanied by linguistic strategies promoted in language activism occurring in trans communities across the United States and many other parts of the English-speaking world. Before approaching these challenges, however, some background about the social context of transgender language activism is important.

Why Trans Language Reform Matters

It is worth addressing why language reform is of such central importance to trans people and why cisgender people should take it seriously, particularly at a time when "political correctness" is often framed as a form of censorship or even oppression. Despite growing awareness and acceptance of trans identities, trans people remain enormously vulnerable to verbal harassment, physical, sexual, and state-sanctioned violence, and discrimination in the realms of healthcare, employment, and housing. A major survey of 6,450 transgender Americans (Grant et al. 2012) paints a stark picture of the injustices trans people face in the forms of poverty, harassment, abuse, and suicide. Respondents had nearly universally been mistreated at work, experienced poverty rates almost four times the general public, and reported astronomical rates of attempted suicide (41%, compared with 1.6% of the general population). Trans youth were particularly vulnerable. Respondents who came out as trans during their K–12 education reported being harassed (78%) and assaulted (35%) by other students and even by teachers and staff. Fifteen percent dropped out of school as a result. Suicide attempt rates were even higher among respondents who reported being verbally harassed (51%) and higher still for those who had been assaulted (64%). Students in higher education fared better on these measures, but it is not exactly heartening to learn that 35 percent of trans college students experienced verbal harassment for their gender and that 5 percent had been assaulted on campus for being trans.

Transphobic harassment includes slurs and deliberate rejections of trans people's gender identities, but even subtly cissexist language negatively effects trans people's wellbeing. Recent research indicates that trans people whose communities support them have lower rates of depression, anxiety, and suicidality. What constitutes support for trans people is not merely tolerance of non-normative gender presentations, but the social and linguistic validation of their gender identities. The language used to talk about trans people is not just a matter of political difference, but one of survival.

Transgender Language Reform

The study of language and gender was founded in part on the so-called second-wave feminism of the 1960s and 1970s. The groundbreaking work of feminist linguists like Robin Lakoff, Anne Bodine, and Sally McConnell-Ginet, among others, brought unprecedented attention to linguistic misogyny (i.e., oppression of women) and androcentrism (i.e., treatment of maleness as default). In the 1990s, *queer linguistics* expanded the field's engagement with language activism by addressing homophobic and heteronormative language that assumes heterosexuality and stigmatizes other forms of desire. There is now a sizeable body of literature both on feminist language reform (e.g., Cameron 1998) and gay and lesbian challenges to heteronormative language (e.g., Livia and Hall 1997). However, the linguistic interventions pursued by transgender communities have received relatively little intention from linguists. In what follows, I offer a brief discussion of three major issues in the adoption of trans-inclusive language and some of the strategies trans people use to address them. These reflections are synthesized from over ten years of ethnographic and sociolinguistic research in transgender communities in the United States and English-dominant online spaces and nearly two decades as an activist for trans-affirming language change. The examples provided below, however, are either constructed or modified versions of utterances collected from a range of online sources.

Challenge 1: Gender Labels and Pronouns

The simplest level of trans-inclusive language reform deals with the use of overtly gendered language including words that function as gender labels (*woman, man, trans, non-binary*, etc.), kinship terms (*mother/father/parent, sister/brother/sibling*, etc.), certain professional roles (*waiter/waitress/server, masseuse/masseur/massage therapist*, etc.), and third person pronouns (*she/he/they/*etc.).

The key question here is who gets to determine which gender category someone belongs to. Because of the strength of the standard language ideology, which says there is only one correct way to speak English, it is unsurprising that certain definitions of words related to gender are seen as more correct, true, official, or objective than others. Genital and reproductive anatomy is usually naturalized as the factor that determines whether someone is female or male, but the most fundamental challenge trans activists put forth is that a person's body parts should not determine what kind of person they get to be. Rather than prioritizing physiological traits, trans people see gender as a matter of self-identification in which each individual is the ultimate authority on their own gender identity. At the same time, trans language reform efforts recognize that identity isn't just individual, but *intersubjective*, in that people don't construct their identities alone, but in collaboration with others. From this perspective, when I speak I am not just representing myself, but also constructing a certain image for you that may or may not align with how you see yourself.

Perhaps because they are so frequent and, for many people, so automatic, gendered pronouns like *she, he, they*, and newer options like *ze* and *ey* probably receive more attention than any other aspect of trans-inclusive language. The solution trans people increasingly advocate for is to ask people about their pronouns rather than making assumptions based on someone's appearance or other signifiers of gender. In fact, this promotion of metalinguistic communication—that is, talking about talk—is part of a more general principle underlying trans language activism: it's better to ask than to assume.

Yet this solution brings its own anxieties for those who have been acculturated to the belief that it is deeply offensive to ask someone whether they want to be referred to as *she* or *he*. The prospect of asking someone which pronouns they use may even feel intrusive or like it involves singling out gender ambiguous individuals. These concerns, however, are based on a particular model of gender attribution that must be challenged for trans-affirming language to take hold. The idea that it is offensive to ask people how they should be gendered is grounded in the idea that a person's status as a woman or man must always be easily identifiable and that any suggestion to the contrary indicates they have failed to enact that gender correctly. But all trans people, by definition, have at some point experienced a disconnect between how they see themselves and how they are seen by others. If gender is a matter of internal self-identification, then it may not always be visible from the outside.

There are two common concerns people express when introduced to the practice of "pronoun checks," as they are sometimes called. First, people sometimes worry that asking someone for their pronouns is akin to asking them about their gender identity or body parts—private information that shouldn't be brought up except among intimates. But pronouns are already used publicly and on-record; unless someone goes to great lengths to avoid using a pronoun to refer to someone, they will eventually need to decide which pronouns to use. The question is whether the speaker selects pronouns based on their own perception or whether they allow the person in question to exert some agency over how they are spoken about or addressed.

A second area of worry is whether asking trans people about their pronouns singles them out or calls attention to their gender ambiguity or visibility as a trans person. And, of course, this is exactly what would happen if one only asks people who are obviously trans or gender non-conforming about their pronouns. This is why trans language activists emphasize the importance of making questions about pronouns part of our everyday interactional routines. One way to normalize pronoun checks is to offer your own pronouns when introducing yourself before or instead of asking for someone else's. Treating pronouns more like names—terms of reference that must be asked for rather than assumed—allows us to tap into pre-existing norms that we regularly use to tell people how to refer to us.

Of course, not everyone is familiar with the practice of exchanging pronouns, and in many cases using trans-inclusive language practices requires us to tell people why we ask for or offer our own pronouns. Trans people tend to be prolific metalinguistic commentators, and trans-affirming language reform asks cisgender people to become more conscious of the ways they use language and to be able to discuss their reasoning with others.

Challenge 2: When Gender Isn't Known or Isn't Relevant

The use of language to gender people is so pervasive that it is often done even when a person's gender is arguably irrelevant to the discourse. Speakers often refer to brief encounters with strangers by saying things like, "The guy who made my coffee today did a terrible job," or "A woman who was just hired is teaching statistics." Of course, such details do the work of setting the scene, and at times may be relevant to interpretation of what is said. However, gender attributions like these are built on the assumption that we know how to categorize someone's gender even if they haven't told us how they identify. Furthermore, when identifying an unknown café barista as a man or a statistics instructor as a woman is considered relevant, that relevance often derives from gender stereotypes—perhaps the idea that men are not well-suited to making coffee or that a woman teaching statistics is somehow remarkable. Trans people often employ gender-neutral language when it is not feasible to ask someone what they should be called.

The primary tactic of gender-neutral language use is to seek out epicene, or non-gendered, versions of words that are usually gendered. Some examples of this approach have already been mentioned: *parent* rather than *mother* or *father; person* rather than *woman* or *man; child* rather than *girl* or *boy*; and of course *they* rather than *she* or *he*. At times, the gender-neutral option may feel clunky or unnatural, but the same argument was made against using *he or she*, which is now commonplace, as an alternative to *he* as a generic pronoun. Importantly, the perception of speech as sounding natural, articulate, or aesthetically pleasing derives from a long history of socially informed norms of use. Referring to people's *spouses* rather than their *husbands and wives* may sound less elegant precisely *because* it challenges social and linguistic norms.

Gender neutrality is especially important as a resource for affirming nonbinary gender identities. For instance, groups of people are often addressed as *ladies and gentlemen* when one might call them *honored guests* (or simply *everyone*) while children are frequently called *boys and girls* when they might just as well be called *children*. These phrasings presume that everyone referred to is either female or male. Closely related to the concept of *gender neutrality* is *gender inclusivity*. While gender neutrality avoids marking gender at all, gender-inclusive language recognizes that there are more than two genders. Most conventional attempts at gender inclusivity actually reinforce the binary, as references to "both" genders are common. For example, an utterance like "Both women and men should have access to college-sponsored athletic teams" could be rephrased more inclusively as, "All students should have access to college-sponsored athletic teams." Similarly, "Whether you have a girl or a boy, be sure to show your child lots of love," could become "Regardless of gender, be sure to show your child lots of love." This strategy also problematizes phrasing like "the other sex" (a feminist alternative to "the opposite sex") and offers in its place phrasing like "another sex."

Of course, gender-neutral and gender-inclusive language of this sort only works when the intended meaning is in fact gender neutral or inclusive. Though we might disagree with the sentiment, for someone who believes non-binary individuals should not compete in collegiate sports, "both women and men" is presumably a more accurate wording. This brings us to the final challenge: how to talk about gender when one's intended meaning is *not* gender neutral or gender inclusive.

Challenge 3: When Gender Is Relevant

The final challenge for addressing cissexist language discussed in this essay is more nuanced than the first two. The problem here is the assumption that someone's physiology, gender socialization experiences, perceived gender, and self-identified gender will always align in the expected ways. Words like *woman* and *man* or *female* and *male* are often used to refer to different aspects of sex and gender, which for trans people may not be the same. For example, each of the following sentences uses the word *women* to refer to different aspects of gender or sex.

1   *Women* grow up being taught to accommodate others' needs.
2   *Women* face negative assumptions about their professional capabilities.
3   All *women* need access to cervical cancer screenings.

In example 1, *women* refers to people who were raised in a female gender role. In addition to being an essentializing statement that erases the intersections of gender with race, class, sexuality, age, cultural context, and so on, this example also equates the category of *woman* with people who were assigned to a female gender role at birth. Such an equation implies that trans women are not women because they were not raised as girls and that trans men are women because they were socialized as such. Example 2 uses the word *women* to refer to people who are perceived as women. The cultural logic of misogyny does not care or bother to find out whether the target identifies as a woman, or was raised as such, so a trans man or non-binary person who is perceived as female may be subjected to the same treatment as cisgender and transgender women who are perceived as female. To equate this category with "women" erases women who do not experience this form of misogyny because they are not recognized as women and men and non-binary people who do experience it. Example 3 uses the word *women* in reference to people with a particular body part. The final case is often the most difficult one to absorb as problematic because there is such a tight ideological connection between physiology and gender. But to refer to cervical cancer screening as something that all women need is to define womanhood by the presence or absence of a cervix.

There are two primary strategies for addressing the conflation of different aspects of gender and sex. The simpler strategy is to hedge all generalizations about gender. This would allow us to turn examples 1–3 above into utterances like examples 4–6:

4   Women *often* grow up being taught to accommodate others' needs.
5   *Most* women face negative assumptions about their professional capabilities.
6   Women *typically* need access to cervical cancer screenings.

In addition to being more trans-inclusive, these changes also recognize the variability in cisgender people's bodies and experiences. After all, not all cisgender women are raised to be accommodating, not all cisgender women are assumed to be incompetent in every professional context, and not all cisgender women have cervixes.

The other strategy for making utterances like examples 1–3 trans-inclusive involves being more specific about which aspects of gender or sex are relevant. This approach requires deeper thought than simply hedging a generalization, but this may be required if one wants to be precise about exactly which genders are being referred to. Because the normative gender system does not provide the vocabulary to make these distinctions, trans people have developed an expanded lexicon for gender that overlaps with terminology used by some academic researchers. In addition to distinguishing between *sex*, in reference to the body, and *gender identity*, in reference to the categories individuals claim for themselves, many trans people differentiate *gender assignment*, in reference to the category a person is placed in at birth, and *perceived gender*, in reference to how other people see someone's gender. This vocabulary would transform examples 1–3 into the utterances in examples 7–9:

7   *People assigned female at birth* (often) grow up being taught to accommodate others' needs.
8   (Most) *people who are perceived as women* face negative assumptions about their professional capabilities.
9   *Everyone with a cervix* (typically) needs access to cervical cancer screenings.

To the uninitiated, these phrases can seem wordy, complex, or even amusing. Yet each of these statements manages to express normative expectations about gender without delegitimizing or erasing trans individuals. This approach requires a rehauling not only of the lexicon, but of the way one thinks about gender. It requires more reflection about which aspects of gender really are relevant when we talk about the experiences of women, men, and non-binary people. It requires that we become more comfortable talking about body parts rather than using identity-based euphemisms. It requires that we learn to identify when trans people are included in our ideas and when they are not. It requires us to say what we mean, and mean what we say.

Conclusion

The linguistic practices described above are at times complex, often challenging, and always subject to change as trans activists refine their perspectives on cissexism and language. However difficult some of these strategies may seem, they are all possible: a fact made plain by trans people's own success at reformulating the ways they talk about gender. Although transphobia and cissexism may not be eliminated through changes to language alone, identifying cissexist language patterns is a critical step toward dismantling the oppression trans people experience. For those who are motivated to reshape their linguistic usage to enhance trans people's sense of dignity and affirmation, trans-inclusive language reform may require practice, but it requires no special cognitive or linguistic aptitudes. Though the threat of physical violence always looms large, it is language that serves as the most pervasive ground on which trans identities are delegitimized and transphobic violence is perpetuated. By the same token, it is also the ground on which trans identities can be affirmed, reclaimed, and celebrated.

References

Cameron, Deborah, ed. 1998. *The Feminist Critique of Language: A Reader*. New York: Routledge.

Grant, Jaime M., Lisa A. Mottet, Justin Tanis, Jack Harrison & Mara Keisling. 2012. *Injustice at Every Turn: A Report of the National Transgender Discrimination Survey*. Washington, DC: National Center for Transgender Equality and the National Gay and Lesbian Task Force.

Livia, Anna, and Kira Hall, eds. 1997. *Queerly Phrased: Language, Gender, and Sexuality*. New York: Oxford University Press.

19 (De)Occupying Language

H. Samy Alim

Those of us who are concerned with the relationship between language, social justice, and activism must not only study how language is used, but we must also pay attention to how language is *used against us and our communities*. Toni Morrison reminded us in the beginning of her 1993 Nobel Lecture:

> Oppressive language does more than represent violence; it is violence. Does more than represent the limits of knowledge; it limits knowledge ... However moribund, it is not without effect for it actively thwarts the intellect, stalls conscience, suppresses human potential ...
>
> (Morrison 1993)

She continued: "Sexist language, racist language, theistic language—all are typical of the policing languages of mastery, and cannot, do not permit new knowledge or encourage the mutual exchange of ideas" (ibid.).

Beyond asking us to think about how language is used, and how language is used against us, Morrison's ideas nudge us towards an even more important question, one that is central to achieving our "human potential": If language equals the production of new knowledge and the mutual exchange of ideas, how can we begin to *language* in ever more liberatory and transformative ways?

(De)Occupying Language

In 2011, the Occupy movement—the international, anti-capitalist movement for economic, social and political justice—transformed public spaces and institutions around the world. Activists shut down ports in Oakland, and, for nearly a year, occupied the Hong Kong and Shanghai Banking Corporation (HSBC) in China ("Occupy Central"). But the Occupy movement not only transformed public space, it transformed the public discourse as well. It demonstrated both the oppressive and emancipatory potential of language (Alim 2011).

Occupy

Over the last seven years, it has been nearly impossible to hear the word and not think of the Occupy movement. In fact, linguists noted *occupy*'s influence in January 2012 when the American Dialect Society overwhelmingly voted "occupy" as the 2011 Word of the Year in Portland, Oregon. As Ben Zimmer, Chair of the "New Words Committee" of the American Dialect Society, noted: "It's a very old word, but over the course of just a few months it took on another life and moved in new and unexpected directions, thanks to a national and global movement . . . The movement itself was powered by the word" (American Dialect Society 2012).

Occupy succeeded in shifting the terms of the public debate about economic and social injustice, taking phrases like "debt-ceiling" and "budget crisis" out of the limelight and putting terms like "inequality" and "greed" squarely in the center. We now take terms like "the 1%" and "the 99%" completely for granted. This discursive shift made it more difficult for politicians to continue to promote the spurious reasons for the financial meltdown and the unequal outcomes it has exposed and further produced.

However, to most people, the irony of a progressive social movement using the term "occupy" to reshape how Americans think about issues of democracy and equality has been clear. After all, it is generally nations, armies and police who occupy, usually by force. And in this, the United States has been a global leader. The American government has only just recently, after nearly a decade, ended its overt occupation of Iraq, and is still entrenched in Afghanistan while it maintains troops on the ground in dozens of countries worldwide. The United States also continues to be a staunch supporter of what is perhaps the most controversial occupation in contemporary history—the Israeli occupation of Palestine. All this is not to obscure the fact that the United States as we know it came into existence by way of occupation—a gradual and devastatingly violent one that all but extinguished entire Native American populations across thousands of miles of land. The linguistic irony could not be greater.

Yet in a very short time, this movement dramatically changed how we think about occupation. In early September of 2011, the word "occupation" was tightly bound up with military, capitalist meanings and associations. It signaled both on-going military incursions and fit neatly into the capitalist framework, meaning "a job" or "a profession." Now "to occupy" signifies progressive political protest. It's no longer only about force of military power; instead it signifies standing up to injustice, inequality and abuse of power. It's no longer used just to define one's place in the machinery of capitalism; it reinvigorates the language of anti-capitalist movements.

In this sense, the Occupy movement *occupied* language, transformed oppressive "statist language," which Morrison described as "ruthless in its policing duties." The movement made *occupy* its own. And, importantly, people from diverse ethnic, cultural and linguistic backgrounds participated in this linguistic de- and re-occupation. These new meanings of "occupy" are distinct from both the history of forcible occupation and the force of historic capitalism in that they are meant to accommodate all, not just the most violent or powerful. This is Morrison's agentive act of *doing language*.

But what if we transform the meaning of *occupy* yet again? Specifically, what if we think of Occupy Language as more than the language of the Occupy movement, and begin to think about it as a movement in and of itself? What kinds of issues would we address? What would taking language back from its self-appointed "masters" look like?

We might draw inspiration from both the way that the Occupy movement reshaped definitions of "occupy," which teaches us, like Morrison, that *we* give words meaning and that discourses are not immutable, *and* from the way indigenous movements have contested its use, which teaches us to be ever-mindful about how language both empowers and oppresses, unifies and isolates. For starters, we might first take a reflexive look inward and follow artist-activists within the movement who expanded the English-dominant ethos of "Occupy" by centering multiple languages, as in the Arabic and Spanish language protest art by , for example in Dignidad Rebelde's "Somos el 99%" (dignidadrebelde.com), Ernesto Yerena's silkscreen "Decolonize Wall Street" (www.hechocon ganas.com/social-justice), and Kyle Goen and Dread Scott's Arabic language screen print (www.dreadscott.net/works/we-are-the-99). But we need more than that if our goal is to be truly inclusive.

In an interview, Julian Padilla of the People of Color Working Group pushed the Occupy movement to examine its linguistic choices:

> To occupy means to hold space, and I think a group of anti-capitalists holding space on Wall Street is powerful, but I do wish the NYC movement would change its name to "decolonise Wall Street" to take into account history, indigenous critiques, people of colour and imperialism . . . Occupying space is not inherently bad, it's all about who and how and why. When white colonizers occupy land, they don't just sleep there over night, they steal and destroy. When indigenous people occupied Alcatraz Island it was (an act of) protest.
>
> (D'Almeida 2011)

Padilla's proposed linguistic change can remind Americans that a majority of the 99 percent has benefited from the occupation of native territories. Overall, multilingual protest art attempted to decenter the English-dominant ethos of the Occupy movement, to make global connections visible, and to shift the discourse from "occupying" to "decolonizing." As Angela Davis said when she addressed the crowd in Washington Square Park on October 30, 2011, we must continue to "challenge" and "transform" language, and "remain aware of all of the resonances of the language we use."

Transforming Trumped Up Language

For many People of Color in the U.S., transforming the language of American politics—and transforming language, in general—is not merely an academic exercise but a question of life and death, particularly for the most vulnerable in our communities. Even in the era of "marriage equality," the connection between verbal violence and physical violence against queer communities continues to be as under-discussed as it is alarming. Activists on Twitter (#BlackTransLivesMatter), for example, have been the primary drivers of increased awareness about the 19 trans women of Color murdered in 2015 alone (Dalton 2015).

As I described in *Raciolinguistics: How Language Shapes Our Ideas about Race* (Alim et al. 2016), when racist speech is prevalent in mainstream U.S. political arenas—such as the poisonous, fear-mongering racializing discourses of Donald J. Trump and other high profile Republicans (Ted Cruz, Rudy Guliani, and members of the so-called "Alt-Right" White supremacist movements)—the possibility for violence increases. We have seen this in dozens of attacks on U.S. Muslims, Sikhs, South Asians, Latinos, and African Americans since the 2016 election. Republican (trans)misogynistic, homophobic, anti-Black, anti-Latino and anti-Muslim political discourse provides cover and permission for the physical violence we are now witnessing in the era of Trump.

Raciolinguists—those who study the relationships between language, race and racism—have shown that pejorative, discriminatory language can have real life consequences. For example, we have worried about the coincidence of the rise in the use of the term "illegals" and the spike in hate crimes against all Latinos. As difficult as it might be to prove causation here, the National Institute for Latino Policy reports that the FBI's annual Hate Crime Statistics show that Latinos comprised *two thirds* of the victims of ethnically motivated hate crimes in 2010. Most recently, we witnessed President Trump's attempts to thoroughly dehumanize Latino immigrants: "These aren't people; these are animals," he said (Davis 2018). Words were followed by actions, specifically by policy changes that legalized the separation of children from their caregivers.

For Muslims, in late 2015, after the attacks in Paris, and in the same month that then-presidential candidates Donald Trump and Texas politician Ted Cruz and others fomented anti-Muslim sentiments, violence against Muslims (and those mistaken for Muslims, such as Sikhs and Indian women who wear headscarves) *tripled*, according to California State University's Center for the Study of Hate and Extremism.

According to reporting in 2016 by Kristina Rizga in "The Chilling Rise of Islamophobia in Our Schools," in American schools, the number of students reporting bullying based on Islamophobia was *twice* the number of those who reported being bullied based on gender and race nationwide. In fact, even before the attacks in Paris and San Bernardino, Rizga reports that a 2014 survey by the Council on American Islamic Relations found that "52 percent of

Muslim students in California reported being the target of verbal abuse and insults." On a policy level, we have seen multiple bans of immigrants coming from mostly-Muslim countries. As we have seen with the use of the dehumanizing terms, "illegals" and "animals," when some*one* is repeatedly described as some*thing*, language has quietly paved the way for violent action.

In a report issued in April 2016 by the Southern Poverty Law Center (2016), many students had already "been emboldened by the divisive, often juvenile rhetoric" of Donald Trump. In schools across America, the report outlines that White children are abusing their classmates by yelling "Go back to Africa!", "Go back to Asia!" and "Go back to Mexico!" Others are yanking the *hijabs* off of young Muslim girls' heads, while calling them "terrorists" and drawing from Trump's platform by telling them they should be banned from America. White students are also blocking Latino students from entering school and directly adopting Trump's xenophobic discourses with feverish chants of "Build the wall! Build the wall!" Beyond the chants, others are using Trump's campaign slogan, "Make America Great Again (MAGA)!" in discriminatory notes to People of Color and others as reported by Shaun King, Senior Justice Writer for *New York Daily News* on Twitter, @ShaunKing.

The incidents of racist, xenophobic, Islamophobic and homophobic verbal and physical abuse are too many to recount—this is what Morrison referred to as the racist, sexist "policing language of mastery." As if seeing the coming of trumped up language in her mind's eye, Morrison described this oppressive, statist language as having "no desire or purpose other than maintaining the free range of its own narcotic narcissism, its own exclusivity and dominance."

Following Morrison, we should concern ourselves with more than just the words we use; we should also work towards eliminating systemic language-based racism and discrimination. In the legal system, the U.S. Justice Department confirmed that Arizona's infamous Sheriff Joe Arpaio, among other offenses, discriminated against "Latino inmates with limited English by punishing them and denying critical services." In education, as Ana Celia Zentella (2017, for example) notes, hostility towards teachers and students who speak "English with an accent" continues to be a problem. In housing, the National Fair Housing Alliance has long recognized "accents" as playing a significant role in housing discrimination. On the job market, language-based discrimination intersects with issues of race, ethnicity, class and national origin to make it more difficult for well-qualified applicants to receive equal opportunities.

In the face of such widespread language-based discrimination, scholar-activists can engage in critical, progressive linguistic research that exposes how language is used as a means of social, political and economic control. As Valerie Strauss (2016) wrote in *The Washington Post*, schools cannot ban dialogue on controversial issues ("freedom of speech protects us all"), "but as educators, we are fundamentally responsible for denouncing speech that denigrates or threatens people—and for protecting all students' rights to participate in and benefit from school." By (de)occupying language, we can: expose how educational, political, and social institutions use language to further marginalize oppressed groups; resist attempts to define people with terms rooted in negative stereotypes; begin to reshape the public discourse about our communities, and about the central role of language in racism and discrimination; and resist colonizing language practices that elevate certain language varieties—and certain groups of people—over others.

A Brief Case from Cape Town, South Africa

We must do whatever we can to prevent the normalization of linguistic violence and discrimination, yes, and we must also continue to *language* in ever more radical and transformative ways. So, what might (De)Occupying Language as an anti-capitalist, anti-imperial linguistic movement look like? Specifically, how can the movement go beyond resistance and begin to create new linguistic realities?

Perhaps the most powerful case of (de)occupying language that I have seen in recent years is the *Afrikaaps* (not Afrikaans, see below) linguistic movement led by Cape Town Hip Hop artist-activists in South Africa, itself a (formerly) occupied settler colony of the Dutch and the British.

Hip Hop in Cape Town is a vocal and fervent site of the critique of South African democracy, or as Capetonian Hip Hop pioneer Emile YX? refers to it, "demockery." Like the most innovative of Hip Hop linguists, Emile "occupies" and transforms the word "democracy" by pointing out that the current South African regime makes a mockery of the very term as well as the citizens who believe in this flawed democratic system's ability to bring about social, political, and economic equality. "Demockery," to Emile, can only be understood as the continuation of colonial policies in the context of global capitalist, imperialist, White Supremacy.

Hip Hop for Emile and others becomes a critical vehicle for raising consciousness through language, developing anticolonial resistance, and upending the White Supremacist legacies of apartheid through a radical re-education. By returning to one of Hip Hop's five elements, "Knowledge of Self," Emile, and other artists involved in the Hip Hop theatre production, *Afrikaaps*—including Jitsvinger, Blaq Pearl, Bliksemtraal, Monox, Jethro Louw, Shane Cooper and Kyle Shepherd—view language as a site for the disruption of colonial domination and the transformation of "the colonial mentality" in the psyche of communities of color.

These artists' work produces a new reality for South Africans who speak languages that are racialized and marginalized by White South Africans, who still hold 90 percent of the wealth in this "post-apartheid" demockery. In their view, the language variety spoken by most "Coloured" speakers in the Cape is *not* Afrikaans, at least as it is traditionally understood as the language of White Afrikaner nationalism. These artists remix the creole history of Afrikaans and provide a central and pivotal role to the linguistic contributions of indigenous

Khoisan peoples and enslaved Muslims from India, Malaysia, and other parts of Southeast Asia.

As I and Adam Haupt stated (Alim and Haupt 2017), Capetonian Hip Hop artists are explicitly revising hegemonic understandings of Arikaans. They offer a creative re-writing of the language variety they refer to as Afrikaaps (a neologism that combines the term "Afrika" with the term "Kaaps," meaning "from the Cape" or "Capetonian"). This project of historical linguistic revisionism boldly and creatively challenges traditional, static, colonial definitions of Afrikaans as "the language of the Dutch settlers" in Cape Town, for example, as well as traditional resistance narratives of Afrikaans as "the language of the colonizer." Through a clever, politicized, linguistic move, Afrikaans is rendered Afrikaaps, calling upon everyone to re-evaluate their understanding of this language variety, and importantly, the people who speak it.

Quentin Williams (2017) argues that the Cape Town Hip Hop language movement reclaims Afrikaans by extricating it from colonial Whiteness and lays fertile ground for the radical reshaping of the future of multilingualism in South Africa. Artists have also given a generation of "Coloured" Capetonians the necessary knowledge to combat the violent racism about their culture and language, a violence designed to limit their potential, their mobility, and their very humanity. Beyond that, as described in detail in *Neva Again: Hip Hop Art, Activism, and Education in 'Post'-Apartheid South Africa* (Haupt, et al., 2019), these artists, through their music, theatre productions, and educational curricula, offer a vision of the radical, emancipatory potential of occupying and deoccupying language.

Final Thoughts

I end by returning to Toni Morrison's vision. Morrison spoke in blunt yet mesmerizingly literary terms when she described

> the language of surveillance disguised as research; of politics and history calculated to render the suffering of millions mute; language glamorized to thrill the dissatisfied and bereft into assaulting their neighbors; arrogant pseudo-empirical language crafted to lock creative people into cages of inferiority and hopelessness.
>
> (Morrison 1993)

By the end of her lecture, we realize, however, that language's ability to limit human potential is not an immutable state. In fact, by the very same token, language is also the measure of our humanity. In her own words: "We die. That may be the meaning of life. But we do language. That may be the measure of our lives" (ibid.).

Language—this "mutual exchange of ideas," as Morrison wrote—*is* the revolution, *is* liberation, *is* justice. Cape Town's Afrikaaps Hip Hop movement clearly understands this.

Returning to our consideration of the Occupy movement: Can we, through language, advance insurgent solidarities and emancipatory social relations (Sitrin and Azzellini 2012)? (De)Occupying Language, as a movement, should speak to the power of language to transform how we think about the past, how we act in the present, and how we envision the future. In this way, following Morrison, we will "permit new knowledge" and "the mutual exchange of ideas"; we will reach our "human potential"; we will understand anew what Morrison meant when she ended her speech with these famous words:

> I trust you now. I trust you with the bird that is not in your hands because you have truly caught it. Look. How lovely it is, this thing we have done—together.
>
> (Morrison 1993)

We will have a revolution.

References

Alim, H. Samy. 2011. "What If We Occupied Language?" New York Times, The Opinion Pages, Opinionator website, December 11. Accessed October 23, 2017 at https://opinionator.blogs.nytimes.com/2011/12/21/what-if-we-occupied-language.

Alim, H. Samy, and Adam Haupt. 2017. "Reviving Soul(s) with Afrikaaps: Hip Hop As Culturally Sustaining Pedagogy in South Africa." In *Culturally Sustaining Pedagogies*, edited by D. Paris and H. S. Alim, 155–174. New York: Teachers College Press.

Alim, H. Samy, John Rickford, and Arnetha Ball, eds. 2016. *Raciolinguistics: How Language Shapes Our Ideas of Race*. New York: Oxford University Press.

American Dialect Society. 2012. "'Occupy' is the 2011 Word of the Year." January 6. Accessed October 23, 2017 at www.americandialect.org/occupy-is-the-2011-word-of-the-year.

D'Almeida, Kanya. 2011. "U.S.: Who is the 99 Percent? Part 2." Inter Press Service webstite, October 31. Accessed October 23 at www.ipsnews.net/2011/10/us-who-is-the-99-percent-ndash-part-2.

Dalton, Deron. 2015. "The 22 Trans Women Murdered in 2015." *The Daily Dot*, October 15. Accessed at www.dailydot.com/layer8/trans-women-of-color-murdered.

Davis, Julie Hirschfeld. 2018. "Trump Calls Some Unauthorized Immigrants 'Animals' in Rant." *The New York Times*, May 16. Accessed at www.nytimes.com/2018/05/16/us/politics/trump-undocumented-immigrants-animals.html.

Haupt, Adam, Quentin E. Williams, H. Samy Alim & Emile Jansen, Eds. 2019. Neva Again: Hip Hop Art, Activism, and *Education in 'Post'-Apartheid South Africa*. Cape Town, South Africa: HSRC Press.

Morrison, Toni. 1993. "Nobel Lecture." December 7. Accessed October 3, 2017 at www.nobelprize.org/nobel_prizes/literature/laureates/1993/morrison-lecture.html.

Rizga, Kristina. 2016. "The Chilling Rise of Islamophobia in Our Schools." *Mother Jones*, January 26. Accessed October 23, 2017 at http://m.motherjones.com/politics/2016/01/bullying-islamophobia-in-american-schools.

Sitrin, Marina, and Dario Azzellini. 2012. *Occupying Language: The Secret Rendezvous with History and the Present*. New Jersey: Zuccotti Park Press.

Southern Poverty Law Center. 2016. "The Impact of the Presidential Campaign on Our Nation's Schools." Southern Poverty Law Center website, April 13. Accessed October 23, 2017 at www.splcenter.org/20160413/trump-effect-impact-presidential-campaign-our-nations-schools.

Strauss, Valerie. 2016. "The Frightening Effect of Trump Talk on America's Schools." *The Washington Post*, November 6. Accessed October 23, 2017 at www.washing tonpost.com/news/answer-sheet/wp/2016/11/06/the-frightening-effect-of-trump-talk-on-americas-schools.

Williams, Quentin. 2017. *Remix Multilingualism*. New York: Bloomsbury.

Zentella, Ana Celia. 2017. Trumped Up: Combating Alarming Misinformation about LatinUs and our Language(s). Keynote lecture, William Paterson University, Wayne, New Jersey, October 18.

Part V

Language, Law, and Policy

Introduction

The case studies presented in this section interrogate issues of language and social justice in relation to law. The word justice is of course integral to law; but there is no single notion of justice upon which all people agree. For many in democratic societies, justice—and social justice more specifically—is about making sure that all people have access to the same opportunities, rights, and resources. Law is one of the primary institutions set up to help achieve this goal. Unfortunately, legal institutions do not always live up to this task, and issues of language are often central to this failing. Each chapter in this section explores an instance in which social justice ends are not met by laws, policies, or legal and political institutions. The chapters reveal efforts made to ameliorate these imbalances of justice. Topics covered include indigenous people in Brazil who use road signs to increase the visibility of their language in the national public sphere; the drafting of the Universal Declaration of Linguistic Rights, which reveals how certain economic and political systems have negatively impacted language communities; multilingual speakers in the U.S. who are marginalized by their categorization in the Census; speakers of minority languages whose access to North Carolina legal procedures is hindered by a lack of sufficient interpreter services; and the delicate narrative forms required by capital defense attorneys to provide sufficient, just advocacy for their clients. The chapters in this section reveal that addressing social justice in legal contexts requires critiquing not simply specific rules and laws, but also the ideologies underlying them that classify certain people as undeserving of rights and opportunities that should be afforded to all.

Critical Questions

1   How does language use mediate people's interactions with the law and political institutions in each of the chapters?
2   Given the cases presented here, do you think legal institutions and policies effectively achieve social justice goals? Why or why not?
3   What are some ways people use language to try to change how legal systems and institutions operate in these chapters?

20 *A'uwẽ*-Xavante Represent

Rights and Resistance in Native Language Signage on Brazil's Federal Highways

Laura R. Graham

I first traveled along BR-158, the highway that skirts the perimeter of the Xavante (pronounced Shaw-vahn-tee) territories Areões and Pimentel Barbosa, in January, 1982. It was my first trip to the community of Eténhiritipa in the Pimentel Barbosa Indigenous reserve (see Figures 20.1 and 20.2). At the time, this stretch of one of Brazil's longest highways was no more than a rutted, muddy, red-dirt road. Rough-hewn planks—sometimes only two, an axel's width apart—served as precarious bridges straddling numerous streams and rivers that frequently swelled to overflowing during the rainy season, washing out bridges and causing delays of many hours, sometimes even days. Like BR-070, a major east–west federal highway that cuts through reserves belonging to Xavante and Bororo peoples in eastern Mato Grosso state, no placards indicated safety regulations, Indigenous Territories or even speed limits; in fact, there was not much need for the latter since the condition of this pot-holed washboard of a "highway" prevented even the most rugged 4×4 vehicles from traveling very fast. No signs announced the names of the various towns and hamlets along the route.

Over thirty years later, in July 2016, I drove along these now paved and heavily trafficked roads with Hiparidi Top'tiro, a Xavante leader and activist. As we sped along, Hiparidi proudly directed my attention to new, official bilingual highway signs that mark the beginnings and ends of Indigenous Territories and exits to communities. For Hiparidi and other Xavante, bilingual signs—written in Portuguese (the national language) and *A'uwẽ mrémé* (Xavantes' name for their language)—have immense significance even though most Xavante are not literate. While these signs are only a fraction of what leaders demand to make these federal highways safe and bring them into alignment with current federal environmental and safety standards, they represent a major victory in Xavante efforts to assert and defend their civil rights.

A'uwẽ mrémé signs show that Indigenous rights don't just appear "on paper," in the Constitution or international instruments. They exist in practice. They demonstrate that *A'uwẽ mrémé* is *a language* that can be written just like Portuguese, the national language. Also, since Indigenous languages, humanity, and very existence are often overlooked or denied, bilingual signs affirm Xavante language, people, and culture, and advance both linguistic and

Figure 20.1 Location of Xavante Territories.
Courtesy of Laura R. Graham.

existential recognition (see Graham 2005). Social justice implies the implementation, exercise and upholding of rights, as well as the affirmation of
humanity and human dignity. For Hiparidi and other Xavante, *A'uwẽ mrémé*
signs do precisely this. Hiparidi insists, "Our rights are in the signs. Do you
understand?"

Linguistic Landscapes of BR-070 and BR-158

In 2015 Brazil's National Department of Transportation Infrastructure (DNIT)
posted bilingual signs along stretches of the two federal interstate highways
that run through or adjacent to Xavante Indigenous Territories. The DNIT did
not install these signs because it is committed to native language rights or was
following routine protocol. It only installed them under pressure, specifically
pressure exerted by Xavante activists who were asserting their constitutional

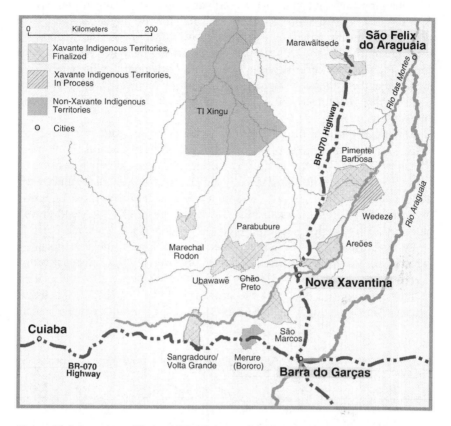

Figure 20.2 Location of Federal BR Highways in Relation to Xavante and Bororo Territories.

Courtesy of Laura R. Graham.

rights as Brazilian citizens. These bilingual signs are the result of years of advocacy efforts by Top'tiro and others standing up for their language and culture, as well as their safety and civil rights.

In socially diverse, multilingual regions or countries, the language that appears on signs in public places can be highly political. This is especially true of official signage. The language or languages used in state-sponsored signs sends messages to those who see them about power, authority and the status of social and ethnic groups, *and* the languages they speak. Which language(s) is/are made visible on official public signs and appear in what linguistic anthropologists and sociolinguists call "linguistic landscapes" ("LL"), creates and shapes attitudes and ideas about languages and their speakers and, at the same time, reveals and reinforces social hierarchies among speakers of different languages. In the U.S. many people, especially members of the dominant social group, tend to think of language primarily in terms of reference or denotation (message content) (see Silverstein 1976; Bauman and Briggs 2003)—what is often called the referential function of language. In the case of signs, this means a focus on what signs "say" rather than on the fact that the language in which signs are written is itself meaningful. When people's ideas about language privilege language's referential function, they may overlook the fact that the language of signage has *pragmatic* (non-referential) meaning. Signs, as Jan Blommaert (2013, 49) observes, transform space into a social and political object.

LL studies consider the visible manifestations of language in diverse settings, from the language(s) of official signs, marquees, placards, impromptu posters and graffiti, to the writing on menus, currencies, clothing (especially t-shirts), even tattoos, and most recently the internet (see Sohohamy and Gorter 2009; Gorter 2013). They provide productive ways to think about linguistic diversity and societal multilingualism, and also means to understand power, authority and resistance (see Rubdy and Ben Said 2015).

Of the LL studies that have proliferated over the last decade, most focus on urban spaces where there is substantial linguistic diversity and "diversity within diversity," or "superdiversity" (see Blommaert 2013). Only a few studies exist in Indigenous regions, which are primarily rural. These demonstrate that native language signage is important as a means of language and culture revitalization.

Figure 20.3 Tall Buffalo Boulevard (*ayani'* "buffalo" *neez* "tall") in Shiprock, NM.
Courtesy Anthony K. Webster, 2014.

Some scholars who analyze native language signage in North American contexts point out that these signs also authenticate indigenous spaces for tourists (Davis forthcoming). If you drive in U.S. "Indian Country" today, you may see traffic and street signs written in, for instance, Cherokee or Navajo (see Figure 20.3) (see Webster 2013; Bender et al. forthcoming). In LL scholarship to date, Latin America is noticeably underrepresented, if not entirely absent (but see Chapter 16, this volume).

Xavante Context

Today over 18,000 *A'uwĕ*, known in Portuguese as "Xavante," live in over 200 autonomous communities located in legally demarcated Indigenous reserves dispersed across eastern Mato Grosso state. Most are monolingual speakers of *A'uwĕ mrémé* (Xavante language). While intergenerational transmission of *A'uwĕ mrémé* is presently robust, Xavante is an endangered language.[1] Bilingualism is increasing rapidly, especially in the younger generation and among males who are the primary mediators of relations with outsiders. The vast majority of the population is not literate in either Xavante, for which there is no is no standardized orthography, or Portuguese.

In 2009, the Xavante Warã Association (*Associação Xavante Warã*, AXW) that works on behalf of communities across Xavante Territories asserted the first demands for official highway signs written in *A'uwĕ mrémé* on the two federal highways that cut through or run near Indigenous lands, BR-070 and BR-158. Led by Hiparidi Top'tiro at the time, the Association made this claim in the context of negotiations with the federal agencies that deal with roads and highways (National Department of Transportation Infrastructure, DNIT, and National Department of Roads and Motorways, DNER) and the National Indian Foundation, FUNAI. Their negotiations concerned improvements necessary to bring these federal highways into alignment with federal environmental and safety standards.

Initially constructed in the 1970s as part of national efforts to support capitalist expansion in the nation's then undeveloped interior, the precarious condition of these highways has grown particularly perilous in the wake of Brazil's turn of the century "soy boom." The region Xavante inhabit lies at the epicenter of the nation's exponentially expanding soy industry and every day convoys of heavily laden big-rig semis race along these two-lane interstates transporting industrially produced agricultural crops, primarily soy, to export hubs. Because laws and international instruments that Brazil has signed, such as the UN Declaration on the Rights of Indigenous Peoples and International Labor Organization Convention 169, require that Indigenous Peoples be consulted and approve of infrastructure projects in or near their territories (a process known as "Free Prior and Informed Consent"), Xavante had the opportunity to assert culturally specific demands into plans for highway improvement.[2] Xavante were not consulted in the 1970s and early 1980s when these roads were first constructed. At that time they were recovering from state-sponsored colonial invasions into their lands and fighting to retain portions of their traditional territories.

Xavante Warã Association's Proposal

In 2009, after meetings in affected communities and consultation with the Center for Indigenous Work (CTI), an urban-based NGO partner that supports Indigenous rights, the Xavante Warã Association took the lead in presenting Xavante and Bororo claims for improvements to federal highways in and near their territories, and negotiating with state authorities. *Warã*'s proposal demanded that "Phase One" of a comprehensive plan, known as the "Emergency Plan," immediately implement specific safety improvements to protect Indigenous people and migratory animals they depend on for their livelihoods. The proposal also demanded that official signage highlight Indigenous Peoples' physical presence and the Xavante language in the Linguistic Landscape. The Bororo of Merure, members of a distinct ethnolinguistic group, declined to press for signs written in the Bororo language despite encouragement from the Xavante Warã Association. At that time Bororo leaders did not appreciate the value of native language signage and its potential benefits for their severely endangered language. Now, after seeing signs written in *A'uwẽ mrémé* in place, they appear to be reconsidering (see Figure 20.4).

Figure 20.4 Bilingual Portuguese/Xavante Sign Marking the Entrance to Xavante
Indigenous Territory.
Courtesy of Laercio Miranda, 2017.

Figure 20.5 Women and Children Collecting Near Highway with Bilingual Sign
   Marking the End of Indigenous Territory.
Courtesy of Laercio Miranda, 2017.

The Xavante Warã Association's proposal to DNIT requested speed limits, velocity monitoring systems and enforcement, paved and widened shoulders without steep edges as required by safety laws, overpasses for foot traffic

Figure 20.6 Cargo Truck Passing Bilingual Sign; Traffic Fatality Memorial to 2016
            Teenage Motorcycle Victim in Foreground.
Courtesy Laercio Miranda, 2017.

and tunnels for migrating animals. It also demanded bilingual *A'uwẽ mrémé*-Portuguese signs marking the beginnings and ends of Indigenous Territories, including their Constitutional demarcation decree numbers, and indicating roads exiting to communities with their written names.

In safety terms, these signs alert motorists to the fact that they are driving in or near Indigenous lands and caution drivers to watch for vehicles exiting and entering the highway from side roads. They also indicate the potential for pedestrians. Xavante, who are traditionally semi-nomadic hunter–gatherers, routinely cross these roads while hunting and collecting, often carrying heavy baskets. Women and children also frequently gather seasonal fruits and nuts along highway margins (see Figure 20.5).

While safety was a paramount concern in the Xavante Warã Association's proposal, especially because the number of traffic accidents and fatalities involving Indigenous people on these roads is rising at alarming rates (see Figure 20.6), for Hiparidi Top'tiro, a main proponent of AXW's plan, there was also a great deal more at stake in Xavante's demand for bilingual signs.

Bilingual Highway Signs Advancing Linguistic Rights and Social Justice

For Hiparidi Top'tiro and other leaders, it was imperative that signs on federal highways in and near Xavante's legally demarcated territories be written in

A'uwẽ mrémé even though most Xavante do not read their native language and those who drive are able to read Portuguese signs. The communication of referential content was not the point of their demand.

To comprehend their insistence, and the legal principle Xavante leaders were defending, it is essential to understand Indigenous Peoples' legal status in Brazil. In 1988, when Brazil passed its new Constitution, for the first time in the nation's history Indigenous Peoples won the right to full citizenship. Previously, Brazil classified Indigenous people as wards of the state, as *legal minors* who had no legal rights. In addition to granting citizenship, Brazil's 1988 Constitution also recognizes Indigenous Peoples' rights to their unique languages and cultures, as well as to their traditional lands. The 1988 Constitution is a tool that Indigenous activists such as Hiparidi Top'tiro use to advance social justice for Brazil's Indigenous People.

Although Brazil's Constitution only explicitly specifies Indigenous Peoples' right to primary education in their languages, Hiparidi Top'tiro and other Xavante leaders understand the right to have signs written in *A'uwẽ mrémé* in Xavante Territories as a Constitutionally guaranteed right. The right to native language signs flows from Constitutional guarantees such as Indigenous rights to land and the right to vote.[3] This is, in fact, their main reason for demanding that signs along federal highways in Xavante Territories be written in *A'uwẽ mrémé.* These signs broadcast, to Xavante and others, that Xavante are citizens and have Constitutional rights. Top'tiro emphasized this when he stated, "*A'uwẽ mrémé* signs underscore our constitutionally guaranteed rights. This is the basic principle that we are defending. It's important to show *waradzu* [non-indigenous people] that we have rights!"

Native language signage is important to Hiparidi Top'tiro for two additional reasons. The first relates to understandings of non-indigenous peoples' perceptions of Xavante. The second has to do with Xavante's understanding of themselves. First, signs written in *A'uwẽ mrémé* proclaim to non-indigenous members of the region, who are newcomers,[4] as well as to others who pass through, that Xavante do, in fact, speak *a language.* Many non-indigenous locals believe that Xavante are mentally inferior and don't speak a real language. They think that Xavante and other Indigenous people are less than fully human and that their "lack of language" is an indicator of their "less-than-human" status. I know this from personal experience. I often have been informed by locals that Xavante don't speak a language; they speak "some dialect" (i.e., inferior code without grammar). Top'tiro explained this attitude stating that many non-indigenous locals "think we are animals. Or, if they think we are human, we speak Guarani." (Guarani is an entirely distinct Indigenous language, spoken hundreds of miles away, that many uninformed Brazilians stereotype as generic "Indian"). He continued, "These signs say to the [non-indigenous] people in our area that we speak our *own language,* we have our *own culture,* our *own political system and social organization.* People in the region don't understand this very well."

Signs written in *A'uwẽ mrémé* highlight not only that Xavante speak "*a language*" but also that their language can be written, just like the national

Figure 20.7 Xavante Transport Ltd. Bus on BR-070 Passing Sign with Village Name
(Marimbu) and Decree Number.

Courtesy Laercio Miranda, 2017.

language, Portuguese. For non-indigenous people, the juxtaposition of written Xavante and written Portuguese validates the native language. The signs
declare that Xavante is a real, legitimate language that can be written and placed
on official signs, like Portuguese. Moreover, the signs underscore the obvious
fact that, as speakers of a legitimate language, Xavante are fully human.

Second, for most Xavante, seeing their language written on official signs is
an important form of endorsement. The signs affirm the language they speak
and, by extension, their culture and themselves. It is irrelevant to Xavante
that Portuguese is positioned above *A'uwẽ mrémé*. In a region where racism
against Indigenous people is rampant, the positive value associated with seeing
Xavante written as a legitimate language extends to Xavante people themselves. The signs affirm Xavantes' humanity and their human dignity. Elders
who do not read at all understand the signs' importance. Top'tiro explained,
"They don't read but they hear others read the signs aloud when they pass by
in cars. This is meaningful for them."

A'uwẽ mrémé signs also must be understood as a significant step forward
in Xavantes' ongoing efforts to communicate their very existence to broad
publics. Prior to the signs' installation in 2015, the linguistic landscape bore
no trace of contemporary Xavante, except for the questionable honor of their
legacy's being recorded as the name of a local frontier town—*Nova Xavantina*

(New Little Xavante Girl), in the diminutive, feminine form—and as the name of a regional bus company (*Viação Xavante*) (see Figure 20.7). Drivers only encountered signs warning against trespass posted by the National Indian Foundation (FUNAI) if they turned *off* the highway onto the dirt roads that enter reserves and lead to Xavante communities. As in the case of minority linguistic groups in many other places, Xavante's presence in the region was erased by the absence of any signage marking Xavante territories or communities. Thus, the bilingual signs on highways BR-070 and BR-158 advance Xavante's "linguistic recognition," as well as their "existential recognition" (Graham 2005). The signs make *A'uwẽ mrémé* visible in the linguistic landscape; they show, as Toptiro stated, "that our language is alive." *A'uwẽ mrémé* signs also proclaim Xavante's very existence.

Finally, it is important to stress that the *A'uwẽ mrémé* signs demonstrate Xavante leaders' command of and ability to negotiate Brazil's Western (i.e., foreign, for them) governing administrative systems. This is no small thing, for Top'tiro and other members of his generation are the first to read and write Portuguese and dominate Western literacy practices. Their ability to draw upon the input from Xavante and Bororo people across numerous communities, enumerate their various demands, meet with NGO consultants and assess their advice, and formulate a written proposal that conforms to bureaucratic guidelines is a significant achievement. The Xavante Warã Association's initial proposal was itself only one small piece of a broader set of ongoing diplomatic negotiations, both on paper and in face-to-face meetings.

The fact that the DNIT has failed to make other infrastructural improvements, such as widening and paving treacherous shoulders, that are essential to improving the safety of these highways in Xavante and Bororo Territories, opens the door to important critiques. For example, are these bilingual signs simply "symbolic window dressing" on the part of a state that represents itself as defending linguistic rights while failing to implement basic safety measures that will undoubtedly have the effect of saving lives? The Xavante Warã Association continues to press the state to meet its other demands and leaders claim they will not consent to other planned roads and infrastructure projects until highway improvements are complete.

Linguistic Rights—Linguistic Resistance

When reflecting on factors that inspired him to press for *A'uwẽ mrémé signs* on federal highways in Xavante lands, Hiparidi observed, "Well, the Bible is translated into *A'uwẽ mrémé*. Why shouldn't road signs be translated as well?" This comment suggests that Hiparidi comprehends Xavante language writing on highway signs in terms of moral equivalence. When Christian missionaries translated the Bible into *A'uwẽ mrémé*, they used language as a means to impose their religion and ways of thinking on Xavante. In Hiparidi's opinion the Bible has functioned (and functions) as a paramount instrument of colonization and cultural oppression (Graham 2014). Forcing the state to post official signs in *A'uwẽ mrémé* resists this kind of colonial domination. Signs written in *A'uwẽ mrémé* push against the continual encroachments of dominant language and society and the constant pressure these exert to diminish Xavante language and culture. Even if some might criticize *A'uwẽ mrémé* road signs as mere symbolic window dressing, Hiparidi and other Xavante leaders understand the language of these signs as important resistance to colonial domination through language. *A'uwẽ mrémé* highway signs are linguistic acts of resistance and affirmation.

Acknowledgements

I am grateful to Hiparidi Top'tiro and all Xavante for friendship, patience and support for my research over the years.

Notes

1 An "endangered language" is one at risk of no longer being spoken (see Woodbury n.d.).
2 For information concerning these international legal instruments, see www.iwgia. org. See also United Nations (2012). For information about Free Prior and Informed Consent, see Cultural Survival (2012).
3 Some Brazilian municipalities have recently passed legislation providing for native language signage. Such legislation does not exist in the region Xavante inhabit.
4 Xavante fiercely resisted encroachment into their territories; by 1963, however, all groups had established peaceful relationships with Brazilian nationals (see, for example, Garfield 2001).

References

Bauman, Richard, and Charles Briggs. 2003. *Voices of Modernity: Language Ideologies and the Politics of Inequality*. Cambridge: Cambridge University Press.
Bender, Margaret, Tom Belt and Hartwell Francis. Forthcoming. "Beyond Indigeneity and Globalization: The Semiotic Reoccupation of Cherokee Country." In *Remediating Cartographies of Erasure: Anthropology, Indigenous Epistemologies, and Global Imaginaries*, edited by Bernard Perley. Lincoln, NE: University of Nebraska Press.
Blommaert, Jan. 2013. *Ethnography, Superdiversity and Linguistic Landscapes: Chronicles of complexity*. Bristol: Multilingual Matters.
Cultural Survival. 2012. "Free, Prior and Informed Consent: Protecting Indigenous Peoples' Rights to Self-Determination, Participation, and Decision-Making." Accessed at www.culturalsurvival.org/publications/cultural-survival-quarterly/free-prior-and-informed-consent-protecting-indigenous.
Davis, Jenny L. Forthcoming. "Language Sits in Places: (Re)claiming the Chickasaw Language Landscape." In *Remediating Cartographies of Erasure: Anthropology, Indigenous Epistemologies, and Global Imaginaries*, edited by Bernard Perley. Lincoln, NE: University of Nebraska Press.

Garfield, Seth. 2001. *Indigenous struggle at the heart of Brazil: State policy, frontier expansion, and the Xavante Indians, 1937–1988*. Durham, NC: Duke University Press.

Gorter, Durk. 2013. "Linguistic Landscape in a Multilingual World." *Annual Review of Applied Linguistics* 33: 190–212.

Graham, Laura R. 2005. "Image and Instrumentality in a Xavante Politics of Existential Recognition: The Public Outreach Work of Eténhiritipa Pimentel Barbosa." *American Ethnologist* 32(4): 622–641.

Graham, Laura R. 2014. "Fluid Subjectivity: Reflections on self and alternative futures in the autobiographical narrative of Hiparidi Top'tiro, a Xavante transcultural leader." In *Fluent Selves: Autobiographical Narratives in Lowland South America*, edited by Suzanne Oakdale and Magnus Course, 235–270. Lincoln: University of Nebraska.

Rubdy, Rani and Selim Ben Said, eds. 2015. *Conflict, Exclusion and Dissent in the Linguistic Landscape*. London: Palgrave Macmillan.

Silverstein, Michael. 1976. "Shifters, Linguistic Categories and Cultural Description." In *Meaning in Anthropology*, edited by K. Basso and H. Selby, 11–55. Albuquerque, NM: University of New Mexico Press.

Sohohamy, Elana and Durk Gorter. 2009. *Linguistic landscape: Expanding the scenery*. New York: Routledge.

United Nations. 2012. "United Nations Declaration on the Rights of Indigenous Peoples." Accessed at www.un.org/esa/socdev/unpfii/documents/DRIPS_en.pdf.

Webster, Anthony K. 2014. "Dif'G'one' and Semiotic Calquing: A Signography of the Linguistic Landscape of the Navajo Nation." *Journal of Anthropological Research* 70: 385–410.

Woodbury, A. n.d. *What is an Endangered Language?* Washington, DC: Linguistic Society of America. Accessed at www.linguisticsociety.org/sites/default/files/Endangered_Languages.pdf.

21 The Universal Declaration of Linguistic Rights

Joyce Milambiling

In 1948, The United Nations drafted the Universal Declaration of Human Rights in a world that was reeling from widespread tyranny and war. This declaration served to set the standard for subsequent decrees in support of the right of every person to live in peace and dignity. In Article 1, the declaration states simply: "All human beings are born free and equal in dignity and rights." Inspired by this human rights pronouncement, the Universal Declaration of Linguistic Rights (UDLR) was signed in 1996 at a conference hosted by the Escarré International Centre for Ethnic Minorities and Nations (CIEMEN) in Barcelona. Attending the event were representatives from a wide variety of organizations, including UNESCO (a branch of the United Nations) and PEN (Poets, Essayists, and Novelists) International. The latter is a worldwide organization of writers "to promote literature and defend freedom of expression around the world" (www.pen-international.org).

Linguistic Rights, Language Policy, and the UDLR

Linguistic rights (also known as language rights or linguistic human rights) are concerned with the right of individuals and groups to preserve, use freely, and pass on their own languages and cultures to future generations. The stated purpose of the UDLR is "to encourage the creation of a political framework for linguistic diversity based upon respect, harmonious coexistence and mutual benefit" (UDLR 1996, Preamble, para. 4). This purpose is compatible with a conception of social justice as an overarching belief that every person and social community deserves equal economic, political, and social rights and opportunities. In this chapter, the UDLR is described and then placed within the context of widespread human migration across the globe, language rights and policies, and the need for inclusive language policy at the local, national, and international levels. The description of the general and specific features of the UDLR found here underscores the connection between this particular declaration and the core belief that widespread social action and political cooperation are essential if the goal of universal social justice is to be attained.

Among the many definitions of language rights, linguistic rights, and linguistic human rights, Spolsky (2004, 132) explains that language rights "can generally be derived from principles established for civil or human rights. They apply to the rights of individuals to use their own language and teach it to their children." Skutnabb-Kangas, a longtime proponent of the preservation of linguistic diversity and an advocate for multilingual education, holds that "universal linguistic human rights should be guaranteed for an *individual* . . ., in relation to an *official language* . . ., in relation to a possible *language shift*, and in *drawing profit from education* as far as the medium of education is concerned" (Skutnabb-Kangas 1998, 22). It is necessary that these guarantees be associated with concrete action, preferably in the form of official language policies that include strategies for enacting them.

Language policies reflect both choice and compromise. Explicit language policies are normally enacted by governments, international organizations, or their representatives. Language planning, a process through which language policies are often produced, can be categorized according to different orientations or assumptions about the value and role of language in any given society. Ruiz's (1984) framework poses three orientations for examining language policies: language-as-problem, language-as-right, and language-as-resource. The UDLR reflects both the language-as-right and language-as-resource orientations. The writers view language as a fundamental right of all peoples, especially for those who are not normally accorded full political or economic rights in a particular society. The UDLR also conveys the belief that language is a valued resource for the preservation of communities, in that it serves as "a natural means of communication and cultural cohesion among its members" (UDLR 1996, Article 1).

Social Justice and the UDLR

In the UDLR, the signatories highlight the link between language and social justice:

> A Universal Declaration of Linguistic Rights is required in order to correct linguistic imbalances with a view to ensuring the respect and full development of all languages and establishing the principles for a just and equitable linguistic peace throughout the world as a key factor in the maintenance of harmonious social relations.
>
> (UDLR 1996, Preliminaries, para. 17)

This linguistic declaration echoes the sentiment of the introduction of the 1948 Universal Declaration of Human Rights, although much less forcefully, in which the members of the United Nations referred to the "disregard and contempt for human rights" that had been recently exhibited in the Second World War. Similarly, the draftees of the UDLR make it clear that their coming together had been prompted by past injustices, many of which were the result of colonization and other forms of social subordination.

The value of the UDLR has been its role as both a reflection of a grassroots movement as well as a call for action on behalf of organizations, governments, and agencies. The wording of and sentiments behind the document reveal a deep dissatisfaction with how political institutions and economic systems have negatively impacted many language communities—in particular, ethnic minorities and other groups that are relatively powerless. The position expressed in the declaration challenges inequities that have resulted from (1) the lack of language policies altogether, and (2) existing national and international language or other policies that fail to promote social justice. In the sphere of language use, unfair practices include restrictions on language use in schools and other institutional settings and preferences (often unstated) for hiring or promoting based on language background.

Language Loss and the UDLR

Some estimates put the number of languages spoken throughout the world today at over 6,000. Despite the wide variety of languages spoken in the world, many individual languages and language groups are losing speakers at an alarming rate to the point that a large number of these languages are endangered or have even become extinct. Many indigenous languages "are in danger of disappearing because they are not being transmitted to the next generation" (Hornberger 1998, 439). Some researchers have compared language endangerment and loss to the endangered status of many plants and animals across the globe. If, indeed, languages and their speakers are similarly imperiled, lack of advocacy and legislation on all levels, including international, will result in an even greater loss of languages. According to information published by the Linguistic Society of America:

> Around a quarter of the world's languages have fewer than a thousand remaining speakers, and linguists generally agree in estimating that the extinction within the next century of at least 3,000 of the 6,909 languages listed by *Ethnologue*, or nearly half, is virtually guaranteed under present circumstances.
>
> (Anderson 2010, 2)

To address the potential loss of many of the world's languages, the UDLR identifies a list of "inalienable rights" that may be exercised in any situation. These include:

- the right to be recognized as a member of a language community; the right to use one's own language both in private and in public; the right to the use of one's own name;
- the right to interrelate and associate with other members of one's language community of origin; and
- the right to maintain and develop one's own culture (UDLR 1996, Article 3.1).

The conferral of the aforementioned rights has the potential to prevent or at least slow language loss within a community as well as to solidify cultural identity. For example, feeling that it is safe to use one's own language in public can engender positive attitudes toward that language rather than lead to shame and eventual abandonment of it altogether.

Education

Education is one area prominently featured in the UDLR. The importance of successful acquisition and use of multiple languages in educational contexts is stated in Article 26:

> All language communities are entitled to an education which will enable their members to acquire a full command of their own language, including the different abilities relating to all the usual spheres of use, as well as the most extensive possible command of any other language they may wish to know.
>
> (UDLR 1996, Article 26)

Advocates of multilingual and bilingual education have called attention to the enduring connections among language, education, and social justice (e.g., García 2008; Skutnabb-Kangas et al. 2009). If social justice is to be understood as economic, political, and social equity, then it stands to reason that children and adults should have the right as well as adequate opportunities to develop their home languages, which are critical social and cultural assets.

A broad statement charging educational systems with assisting language communities in keeping their languages vital explains that "Education must help to maintain and develop the language spoken by the language community of the territory where it is provided" (UDLR 1996, Article 23). Schools can accomplish this in a variety of ways, including providing widespread mother tongue education and bilingual instruction. The heritage language movement in the United States and elsewhere focuses on students whose mother tongue is in danger of being replaced by the majority language either in the society at large or in a family or community (Carreira 2004). This approach to language preservation has resulted in courses, partnerships with public schools and universities, and training programs for teachers in minority and other less commonly spoken languages around the world. However, difficulties can arise in implementing heritage language education, especially in countries in which there are no materials in a particular language and/or a lack of trained teachers.

One of the articles concerning education in Section II of the UDLR draws attention to the importance of language to cultural transmission. It states that "All language communities are entitled to an education which will enable their members to acquire a thorough knowledge of their cultural heritage (history, geography, literature, and other manifestations of their own culture . . .)."

(UDLR 1996, Article 28). Although there is no evidence to suggest that the UDLR has had a direct effect on specific movements and initiatives, a number of programs and educational initiatives are positive indicators that a belief in the important connection between language and the longevity of a culture are alive and well. For instance, there are projects (e.g., Enduring Voices, an initiative of National Geographic) available to indigenous communities who are committed to revitalizing and maintaining their often threatened languages. Furthermore, these language protection initiatives are increasingly being directed by members of the language communities themselves rather than by outside researchers (Alexie, Alexie, and Marlow 2009). This self-determination in researching and preserving their own languages can significantly empower community leaders and other members and thereby result in enduring practices and traditions that promote social justice in that context.

The UDLR, Migration, and the Socioeconomic Sphere

Article 47, included in the section of the UDLR that addresses socioeconomic activities and language, begins by stating, "All language communities have the right to establish the use of their language in all socioeconomic activities within their territory" (UDLR 1996, Article 47.1). This statement refers to the myriad activities that exist in a given area but which are unlikely in many, maybe most, instances to take place in minority languages.

The visibility and everyday utility of minority languages vary widely from place to place. One provision allowed in the UDLR is for "All language communities [to] have the right for their language to occupy a pre-eminent place in advertising, signs, external signposting, and in the image of the country as a whole" (UDLR 1996, Second Title, Section VI, Article 50.1). An example of a place in which this has been successfully instituted is Wales. As of March 2016, new traffic signs must be printed in Welsh and English and the words or phrases in Welsh must appear first (Road Safety GB 2016; see Chapter 20, this volume). This is a positive development, one that other minority language groups may be able to emulate, especially if they are able to obtain sufficient political and financial support.

Migrants are a group especially disadvantaged by lack of access to socio-economic activity conducted in their own languages. Ban Ki-moon, the current Secretary-General of the United Nations, stated that "in our globalized world, it is important to recognize migration as a key enabler for equitable, inclusive, and sustainable social and economic development" and that policies are needed that "recognize the positive contribution of migrants [and] protect their human rights" (United Nations System 2013, 7). Although language is not specifically mentioned in Moon's statement, individuals from minority language communities are disadvantaged if they are not able to use the languages that they know well and are possibly most comfortable in, to go about their daily lives. Although opportunities often exist for immigrants who are, for example, translators, teachers, or health professionals to use their heritage language in order to earn a livelihood, these opportunities are dependent, for the most part, on a high level of proficiency in the majority language. In the meantime, however, it is all too common for immigrants who are not bilingual to be unemployed or underemployed until which time they can function in the language(s) of the wider society.

The extent of worldwide migration since World War II to the present day contributes to the value and urgency of universal protections of the right of all persons to speak their own language(s). According to the United Nations Department of Economic and Social Affairs (2016), there were over 240 million international migrants globally in 2015. Between the years 1990 and 2015, the number of international migrants worldwide rose by 60 percent, an increase of over 91 million people. Many migrants, including refugees seeking security outside of their homelands, have limited, if any, power in their former homelands. Furthermore, these migrants are often not accepted or are only allowed to live temporarily in the receiving countries or territories. The result is that migrants may acquire one or more languages out of necessity and often only at a basic level, depending on whether their stay is permanent. Other factors contribute to migrants' loss of their heritage languages. Children born in countries other than their parents' homeland may not have significant exposure to the parents' home language. It also happens all too often that racist and xenophobic attitudes toward immigrants carry over to the newcomers' languages, and, consequently, speaking any language other than the dominant one in the receiving country is looked upon negatively (see Chapter 22, this volume).

The Migration Policy Institute is an independent, non-partisan, non-profit think tank that provides extensive information on the condition and flows of immigrants in countries and regions throughout the world. Included in the Institute's mission statement is the following:

> Few countries make systematic efforts to integrate immigrants and refugees into their social and political fabric and fewer still can claim success. When such failure coexists with incomplete economic incorporation, immigrants and refugees are marginalized. When marginalization becomes entrenched, it leads the host community to view immigrants as net "consumers" of public assets, rather than contributors to and creators of new assets, and as social and political liabilities, rather than as potential resources.
>
> (Migration Policy Institute n.d., para. 14)

This statement by the Migration Policy Institute is evidence of the organization's position that migrants are legitimate resources with potential to contribute to the society in which they live.

Well-conceived language and education policies that uphold linguistic human rights have the potential to ease the often traumatic transition that refugees face when settling in a new society. Given their centrality to economic and social survival, linguistic resources are akin to food, one bilingual educator states, stressing the value of respecting and making use of refugee students' linguistic abilities and resources (Harvey and Myint 2014, 43). This echoes the UDLR's mandate that "All language communities are entitled to have at their disposal all the human and material resources necessary to ensure that their language is present to the extent they desire at all levels of education" (UDLR 1996, Article 25).

Effects and Limitations of the UDLR

The tone and broad inclusion of topics in the UDLR are idealistic, but this is typical of such documents. The stated goals, albeit lofty, can contribute to measures by which injustices and inequities can be challenged. The earlier 1948 Universal Declaration of Human Rights has had a tremendous impact throughout the world. On the sixtieth anniversary of that groundbreaking document, the members of the United Nations proclaimed, "Since its adoption, it has inspired the world and empowered women and men around the globe to assert their inherent dignity and rights without discrimination on any grounds" (United Nations General Assembly 2009).

The UDLR, unlike the Universal Declaration of Human Rights, has not been officially adopted by the United Nations and thus lacks the kind of prestige and influence that the human rights declaration has had. There have nonetheless been steps taken to facilitate the protection of linguistic rights among international bodies since the signing of the UDLR. One promising development occurred in 1997 when the General Assembly of the United Nations passed a resolution entitled Effective Promotion of the Declaration on the Rights of Persons Belonging to National or Ethnic, Religious, and Linguistic Minorities. This UN report built on the wording and provisions of the Declaration on the Rights of Persons Belonging to National or Ethnic, Religious and Linguistic Minorities, which was adopted by the General Assembly in December 1992. Under the heading of "Protection of Cultural Identity," the author of the 2010 report specifically on the promotion of the 1992 declaration emphasized the part language plays in the transmission of culture and maintained that "the imposition on minority communities of a majority language either through teaching in public schools or formal prohibitions on the use of minority languages, has been a spark that has ignited many violent clashes in every region of the world." Unfortunately, although the 2010 United Nations report identifies problems, it does not focus on potential remedies the way that the UDLR does, nor does the author provide specific recommendations for establishing and sustaining linguistic human rights.

Critics of the UDLR have raised concerns about the tenets and application of the declaration. One of these critics speculates that perhaps linguistic rights are not, in fact universal, and "that such universal claims merely serve to weaken potential rights since many claimed rights patently cannot be enforced in some situations" (Paulston 1997, 82). There may well be situations in which some action called for by one or more of the Articles is unrealistic or difficult to enforce, but that does not necessarily mean that adjustments to the declaration as a whole or in part cannot be made, or that advocacy efforts cannot be intensified.

In the years since 1996, the Universal Declaration of Linguistic Rights has enjoyed extensive visibility in the academic community and within organizations and coalitions such as PEN International. However, declarations, statements, and manifestos are characteristically issued by entities that wish to make known their view on the steps that need to be taken to achieve a given end, but do not have the power to enact laws. Azoz (2007, 8) terms declarations such as the UDLR "soft law" instruments, which can "express standards and international consensus on the need for particular action, when unanimity is lacking in state practice and the will to establish hard law is absent."

Despite the fact that the UDLR does not have the authority of a hard law, it has functioned since its signing as an important catalyst for discussion and analysis at a wide range of international conferences and in print. A critic of the UDLR has nonetheless credited the document with being "the first attempt at formulating language rights at a universal level which has reached a level which enables serious international discussion to start" (Skutnabb-Kangas 1998, 10). The far-reaching dialogue that has taken place in the intervening 21 years engenders hope that the idealism expressed in the UDLR can eventually be transformed into binding instruments such as laws and treaties and thus have an impact on the linguistic rights of both individuals and groups throughout the globe.

References

Alexie, Oscar, Sophie Alexie, and Patrick Marlow. 2009. "Creating Space and Defining Roles: Elders and Adult Yup'ik Immersion." *Journal of American Indian Education* 42(3): 1–18.

Anderson, Stephen. 2010. "How Many Languages are there in the World? Linguistic Society of America Brochure Series: Frequently Asked Questions." *Linguistic Society of America* website. Accessed June 28, 2018 at www.linguisticsociety.org/sites/default/files/how-many-languages.pdf.

Azoz, Xabier. 2007. "The Nature of Language Rights." *Journal on Ethnopolitics and Minority Issues in Europe* 6(2): 1–35.

Carreira, Maria. 2004. "Seeking Explanatory Adequacy: A Dual Approach to Understanding the Term 'Heritage Language Learner.'" *Heritage Language Journal* 2(1): 1–25.

García, Ofelia. 2008. *Bilingual Education in the 21st Century: A Global Perspective.* Hoboken, NJ: Wiley & Sons.

Harvey, Nola, and Htwe Htwe Myint. 2014. "Our Language is Like Food: Can Children Feed on Home Languages to Thrive, Belong and Achieve in Early Childhood Education and Care? *Australasian Journal of Early Childhood* 39(1): 42–50.

Hornberger, Nancy. 1998. "Language Policy, Language Education, Language Rights: Indigenous, Immigrant, and International Perspectives. *Language in Society* 27(4): 439–458.

Migration Policy Institute. n.d. "Mission." Accessed April 3, 2018 at www.migration policy.org/about/mission.

Paulston, Christina Bratt. 1997. "Language Policies and Language Rights. *American Review of Anthropology* 26(1): 73–85.

Road Safety GB. 2016. "Welsh First for New Traffic Signs." Accessed December 15, 2016 at www.roadsafetygb.org.uk/news/4985.html.

Ruiz, Richard. 1984. "Orientations in Language Planning." *NABE Journal* 8(1): 15–34.

Skutnabb-Kangas, Tove. 1998. "Human Rights and Language Wrongs—A Future for Diversity?" *Language Sciences* 20(1): 5–27.

Skutnabb-Kangas, Tove, Robert Philipson, Ajit Mohanty, and Minati Panda, eds. 2009. *Social Justice through Multilingual Education*. Bristol: Multilingual Matters.

Spolsky, Bernard. 2004. *Language Policy*. Cambridge: Cambridge University Press.

UDLR. 1996. "Universal Declaration of Linguistic Rights." Accessed April 2, 2018 at www.egt.ie/udhr/udlr-en.html.

United Nations. 1948. "Universal Declaration of Human Rights." Accessed June 11, 2016 at www.un.org/en/universal-declaration-human-rights.

United Nations Department of Economic and Social Affairs. 2016. *International Migration Report 2015*. New York: United Nations Department of Economic and Social Affairs.

United Nations General Assembly. 1997. Effective Promotion of the Declaration on the Rights of Persons Belonging to National or Ethnic, Religious and Linguistic Minorities. Resolution Adopted by the General Assembly on the report of the Third Committee (A/51/619/Add.2). Fifty-First Session, Agenda item 110 (b), A/RES/51/91, 28 February. Accessed October 12, 2018 at www.un.org/documents/ga/res/51/ares51-91.htm.

United Nations General Assembly. 2009. "Declaration on the Sixtieth Anniversary of the Universal Declaration of Human Rights." Accessed April 2, 2018 at www.un.org/en/ga/search/view_doc.asp?symbol=A/RES/63/25.

United Nations System. 2013. *International Migration and Development: Contributions and Recommendations of the International System*. New York: United Nations.

22 "Linguistically Isolated"

Challenging the U.S. Census Bureau's Harmful Classification

Ana Celia Zentella

Every ten years, the US Census Bureau (CB) collects data to determine the English proficiency levels of US residents. Since 1980, three questions have been asked about language:

1   Does this person speak a language other than English at home?

- Yes
- No

2   What is this language?

3   How well does this person speak English?

- Very well
- Well
- Not well
- Not at all

The Census webpage explains that these data determine "bilingual election requirements under the Voting Rights Act," as well as the "allocation of educational funds to states for helping schools teach students with lower levels of English proficiency" (Census Bureau 2017). If a significant percentage of voters in a district require translations, local governments can provide voting materials and ballots in languages other than English. Also, many educational and other institutions use the data to decide what languages are needed to provide adequate services. Laudable goals, but it is doubtful that the language questions provide accurate data, primarily because the categorization, reporting, and implementation of the results are questionable. Those concerned about the role that language plays in ensuring equality and justice must challenge inadequate government attempts to address these issues and seek effective ways to act on these concerns, while assuring the general public that immigrants are in fact learning English. Unwarranted public fears trigger intolerance. The fear that other languages, especially Spanish, threaten the primacy of English as the nation's dominant language, and the belief that immigrants are unwilling/unable to learn English, led California Senator Hayakawa (R) to propose a constitutional amendment to make English the official language of the U.S. in 1981 (Zentella 1988). The worries that triggered the legislation were unfounded; the 1980 US Census revealed that the majority (59%) of Hispanics who spoke Spanish at home also spoke English "very well." While the 1981 amendment did not pass, national organizations including US English and English First launched successful statewide efforts (in 28 states) promote English as the official language. These groups are increasingly powerful today as anti-immigrant fears are inflamed, despite the fact that 91 percent of the entire US population speaks English "very well" (American Community Survey 2016).

Concerned about reprisals, I was appalled by a report in the *New York Times* (December 7, 1992: B1) which indicated that many who spoke a language other than English at home were officially being labeled "linguistically isolated" by the US government. This label was applied to those who indicated on the census that they lived in households where no adult spoke English "very well." With no explanatory text, this graphic representation of the English skills of children in New York, New Jersey, Connecticut, and the USA, accompanied by dark figures of crouching children, suggested that the children represented were being crushed by an onerous linguistic burden. The bar graph reporting the percent of children who did not speak English at home (approximately 15% in the USA), ignored the fact that those children speak English in their schools and communities. The bar representing "linguistic isolation" was even more troubling. No one in touch with any other human being can be "linguistically isolated." Also, the category suggests that those who speak languages other than English are isolated because they do not speak the "right" language "very well." Moreover, this unscientific category, in use since 1980, lumped together all those who spoke English "well," with those who spoke it "not well" and "not at all," labeling them and every member of their household "linguistically isolated" (Siegel, Martin, and Bruno 2001).

By the year 2000, the CB reported, "there were 11.9 million Americans living in 4.4 million linguistically isolated households in the United States" (Soifer 2009). Damaging labeling aside, the percentage who have difficulty in English is grossly inflated when children who speak only English and adults who speak English "well" are in the same "linguistically isolated" category as those who speak it "not well" and "not at all." As a result, accusations that immigrants are not learning English proliferate. Headlines proclaiming that "linguistic isolation" threatened the unity of the country and the progress of immigrants appeared in media across the nation, promoted by anti-immigrant groups. VDARE.com, "dedicated to preserving our historical unity as Americans into the 21st Century," declared, "The Census has another measure of the failure of the assimilative mechanism: 'linguistic isolation' which 'balkanizes America'" (Rubenstein 2003). NewAmericaMedia.org warned that "Linguistic Isolation Carries a Heavy Cost," and singled out LatinUs:[1] "Comprising 2/3 of all linguistically isolated households, Latinos, more than any other group, are held back educationally and financially" (Soifer 2009). In fact, the Census data for that year indicated that 78 percent of Hispanics spoke only English (24%) or spoke it "very well" (40%) or "well" (14%); only 8 percent of Hispanics did not speak English at all (Dockterman 2009). But because those who speak it "well" (14%) are classified as "linguistically isolated" together with those who do not speak English at all (8%) and those who do not speak it well (14%), the resulting 36 percent feeds unwarranted fears that LatinUs are not assimilating. Between 2005 and 2010, "anti-Latino hate crimes rose disproportionally to other hate crimes" (Costantini 2011).

Frantic media reports and misconceptions about the extent of English proficiency are based on 5-year estimates by the American Community Survey (ACS). For 2005–2009, the ACS reported that less than 5% of all US households were "linguistically isolated," but more than one quarter of the Spanish speaking households and those that spoke Asian and Pacific Island languages were so categorized. In response, I called for an "anthro-political linguistics" perspective (Zentella 1995), because whether we choose to discuss it or not, there is no language without politics. Anthro-political linguistics unmasks the ways in which damaging language ideologies—including the insistence on only one language for the unity of a nation—contribute to the reproduction of inequality. I was encouraged by the creation of the Society for Linguistic Anthropology's Task Group on Language and Social Justice (LSJ) in collaboration with the Committee for Human Rights, both part of the American Anthropology Association (AAA). The LSJ advocated including questions about proficiency in other languages besides English in the US Census, and for replacing "linguistically isolated" with a more accurate and less damaging label. Our LSJ experience underscores the power of collaborative efforts by scholars, professional organizations, and community leaders. The ultimately successful four-pronged attack involved convincing:

1   the inner circle (AAA membership);
2   other national organizations;
3   the broader LatinU community; and
4   the CB.

The Inner Circle (AAA Membership)

From 2005–2010, the LSJ organized panels, presented papers, wrote articles, and proposed resolutions that challenged the CB's questions and categories. Several of us wrote an article in which we pointed out that the CB's language questions could not provide reliable data for decisions about the allocation of resources because the self-assessment of language ability and the four proficiency categories ignore the difficulty of defining "very well," "well," "not well," or "not at all" and the importance of context—where, about what, and to whom we are speaking—in assessing verbal skills (Zentella et al. 2007). In our view, the problematic questions, the failure to inquire about abilities in languages other than English, and the harmful "linguistically isolated" category incited hostility against immigrants, especially LatinUs. We decried the

troubling double standard, since people who speak only English are not classified as "linguistically isolated." We urged the AAA to propose that the CB
ask about proficiency in languages other than English and end its use of "linguistically isolated." In 2007, AAA members voted in favor of the Statement
on Language Questions in the US Census, including the following resolution
(adopted February 6, 2008):

> BE IT RESOLVED THAT
>
> The American Anthropological Association urges the CB to include a
> question about proficiency in languages other than English, and to stop
> classifying those who speak English less than "Very well"–and all mem-
> bers of their households–as "linguistically isolated" because the term is
> inaccurate and discriminatory, and the classification promotes an ideology
> of linguistic superiority that foments linguistic intolerance and conflict.
>
> (American Anthropology Association 2008)

The entire resolution was forwarded to the CB by then AAA President Setha
Low, and the AAA Committee on Human Rights followed up with the
House Subcommittee on Information Policy, Census, and National Archives
(Sanford 2008).

Other National Organizations to Support the Effort

Major academic associations endorsed the AAA resolution. In 2007, before
the November AAA vote, the Conference on College Composition and
Communication/National Council of Teachers of English supported it, encouraged by its Language Policy Committee (CCCC 2007), as did the American
Association for Applied Linguistics (AAAL undated). These well-respected
organizations represent more than 20,000 professionals in language related
fields; their advocacy strengthened the case we made to community organizations and the CB.

The Broader LatinU Community

All speakers of a language other than English were adversely affected by the
inadequacy of the Census questions. But some community representatives
worried that reducing the number of "linguistically isolated" persons would
have a negative impact on services for English language learners, especially
Spanish speakers. It was imperative to seek LatinUs' support and to insist on
the protection and expansion of programs for all English learners.

Angelo Falcón, founder and President of the National Institute for Latino
Policy (NILP), a member of the Advisory Committee on the Hispanic
Population and part of the CB's Race and Ethnicity Advisory Committees
(REAC), wrote a scathing editorial for his widely read *Latino Policy* newsletter

(May 12, 2008), entitled *"Linguistically Isolated?*: I don't need no stinkin Linguistically Isolated!" He also submitted a formal proposal to the REAC, recommending that:

> the U.S. CB conducts a written review of Latino community concerns about the language questions in the American Community Survey (ACS) and their operationalization. This review would respond to the following concerns by some: The view of the term "linguistic isolation" is pejorative and the need for a more neutral term; the need to measure the use of languages other than English . . . This review should also provide a definition and origins of the term "linguistically isolated" and the uses of this measure.
>
> (Falcón, personal communication, May 3, 2008)

Falcón also brought the issue to the attention of the National Hispanic Leadership for its Latino Public Policy Agenda and he spread the word through the NILP's extensive Latino Census Network. Additionally, my editorials in Spanish and English reached out to the broader public (Zentella 2009, 2011a, 2011b). Community support generated by these efforts was essential to our eventual success.

Convincing the CB

From 2008 to 2011, the LSJ/AAA parried with the CB and the overseers of the language questions in the House of Representatives, challenging the limits of the questions, the categorization of proficiency levels, and the labels applied to households and individuals. The Division Chief of Housing and Household Economic Statistics, David S. Johnson, responded (Johnson, letter to AAA, May 7, 2008): "[W]e are unaware of any federal legislative need requiring the assessment of proficiency in languages other than English." He asserted that changing/adding questions to the U.S. Census could only be accomplished by legislative mandate. Regarding "linguistically isolated," he insisted the category was

> an analytic construction which attempts to identify households where there is no single person of adult or near-adult age who is reasonably facile in English . . . The fact that the categorization (irrespective of its label) is used routinely by researchers, policy makers and practitioners tells us that it does have utility.

But the letter ended on a conciliatory note: "Nevertheless, we note and recognize the concern that a label may bring with it, especially in the context of a dynamically-changing cultural environment. We intend to review this terminology." The "dynamically-changing cultural environment" referred to the fact that LatinUs had become the largest minority in the USA as of 2003 (Clemetson 2003).

Given the need for a legislative mandate to change CB questions, we sought the support of Rep. John Dingell of the House Committee on Energy and Commerce—the body in charge of Census legislation—requesting the issue be put on the committee's docket. We also consulted educators and other specialists to help us challenge the CB's separation of those who speak English "very well" from those who speak "well" and the "linguistically isolated" category that combined those who speak "well," "not well," and "not at all." We knew respondents who spoke English "very well" might choose "well" to describe their level of English if they compared it to their native language proficiency. Others who struggled with English might consider their ability to make themselves understood evidence that they spoke it "well." In a letter to Johnson, AAA's then President Virginia Dominguez (2010) urged eliminating "linguistically isolated" and proposed our three alternatives for re-organizing the four proficiency levels:

1   A three-way classification that joins the top two categories ["very well" and "well"] in one group, Proficient/Bi-Multilingual.
2   A three-way classification that joins the bottom two categories ["not well" and "not at all"] in one group, Beginning English Learners.
3   A two-way classification that merges the top two groups ("very well" and "well"/Proficient) and the bottom two ("not well" and "not at all"/ Beginners).

After receiving no response for six months, we arranged a conference call (November 2, 2010), the contentious nature of which was summarized in a December 22 letter from Johnson. The CB rejected "Proficient" and "Fluent" for those who speak "very well" because they were individual labels and inadequate for households, which they maintained was the focus. We pointed out their definition stipulated that "all the members of a 'linguistically isolated' household are tabulated as 'linguistically isolated,'" and that ACS reports and media announcements routinely mentioned "persons" and the "% of the population," not households. They also rejected "Beginning English Learners," claiming there was no evidence that everyone who did not speak English at home was in the process of learning English.

Regarding combining those who spoke English "well" with those who spoke it "not well" and "not at all," we were informed that research conducted in the 1980s concluded that while people at all levels (including native English-only speakers) sometimes failed their English reading tests—the difference between passing and failing was associated with the "very well"/"well" break (cf. Siegel et al. 2001). Clearly, new research based on more reliable tests is needed, and Johnson admitted as much, but he warned that "dropping the cut-point would make many people now classified as 'in need' as being 'proficient.'" His suggestion regarding the "linguistically isolated" label was also disheartening. He issued A Federal Register Notice inviting open comment" was required before any change was made. But he mentioned two possible alternatives:

"English-limited households" or "Households in which no one age 14 years or above speaks English Only or English 'Very well.'" Because the results of the 2010 Census would soon be released, immediate action was necessary.

Fortunately, in December 2010, the new CB Director Groves seemed willing to give up "linguistic isolation" after hearing the concerns we had been raising for three years. Heartened by his attitude, Falcón and I reached out to LatinUs in Johnson's office; we urged forgoing the issuance of a Federal Reserve Notice and in the interest of "the fairest and most accurate reporting," adopting "Households in which no one age 14 years or above speaks English only or English 'very well'" (Zentella, personal correspondence, January 3, 2011). Within a month, Johnson's office acknowledged the stigma attached to the category employed for 30 years:

> In response to concerns expressed by data user groups, the CB decided to eliminate the term "linguistic isolation" . . . starting in 2011. We have changed the terminology to one that we feel is more descriptive and less stigmatizing "Households in which no one 14 and over speaks English only or speaks a language other than English at home and speaks English 'Very well'."
>
> (Email from David S. Johnson, April 18, 2011)

The press release by the AAA recognized the elimination of "linguistically isolated" would allow for "results that are more accurately stated, more in keeping with contemporary scientific research, and more useful in guiding policy at national, state, and local levels," but cautioned that

> all four levels of speakers require financial and programmatic support in order to strengthen their reading and writing skills . . . AAA continues to urge the U.S. CB to expand its language questions, and to acknowledge that those who speak English "Well" should not be grouped with those who speak it "Not well" or "Not at all".
>
> (American Anthropology Association 2011)

Our struggle is clearly not over. The cumbersome phrase in place of "linguistically isolated" has been replaced by "limited English proficient" (LEP), a holdover from the early days of bilingual education when children were sometimes referred to as LEPers. Besides the unfortunate connotation of disease, LEP is inaccurate and limited because it continues to include adults who speak English well along with monolingual English children. It also ignores the bilingual strengths of English learners, defining them in terms of the English they may not know, instead of recognizing the language(s) they speak. Other more appropriate descriptors, like DSEALs (Developing Speakers of English as an Additional Language) have been rejected, and media and national organizations continue to refer to "linguistically isolated" populations (Drake 2014; Turner et al. 2016).

Although English is currently the only language of 79 percent of all US households, and the majority (75%) of the 21 percent that speak another language at home also speak English "well" or "very well" (American Community Survey 2016), recent financial crises, terrorist concerns, and an anti-immigrant administration have triggered widespread fears. Furthermore, efforts to make English the only official language in the U.S. have intensified. English is now the sole official language in 28 states, and a constitutional amendment (HR 997, The English Language Unity Act) was referred to the House Judiciary Committee in February 2017. Because greater acceptance of multilingualism benefits the nation and social justice demands it, we continue to press for more inclusive questions, more accurate labels, and a more equitable categorization of the results.

Note

1 Instead of the traditional Spanish binary gender markers (o/a), or the x which does not distinguish singular from plural and is difficult to pronounce, I advocate the universal U/Us.

References

AAAL. Undated. Position Statements. Accessed October 12, 2018 at www.aaal.org/position-statements.

American Anthropology Association. 2008. "Statement on Language Questions in the US Census." February 6. Accessed July 17, 2017 at www.americananthro.org/ConnectWithAAA/Content.aspx?ItemNumber=2596.

American Anthropology Association. 2011. "American Anthropological Association Spurs Elimination of 'Linguistically Isolated' as Classification by the U.S. CB." May 2. Accessed July 17, 2017 at http://linguisticanthropology.org/wp-content/uploads/2015/02/U-S-Census-Bureau.pdf.

American Community Survey. 2016. "Selected Social Characteristics in the United States. 2012–2016." Accessed January 20, 2018 at https://factfinder.census.gov/faces/tableservices/jsf/pages/productview.xhtml?pid=ACS_16_5YR_DP02&src=pt.

CCCC. 2007. "Resolutions & Sense of the House Motions." Accessed at www.ncte.org/cccc/resolutions/2007.

Census Bureau. 2017. "Language Use." Accessed July 17, 2017 at www.census.gov/topics/population/language-use/about.html

Clemetson, Lynetter. 2003. "Hispanics Now Largest Minority, Census Shows." *New York Times*, January 22. Accessed July 17, 2016 at www.nytimes.com/2003/01/22/us/hispanics-now-largest-minority-census-shows.html.

Costantini, Cristina. 2011. "Anti-Latino Hate Crimes Rise As Immigration Debate Intensifies." *Huffington Post*, October 17. Accessed March 10, 2016 at www.huffingtonpost.com/2011/10/17/anti-latino-hate-crimes-rise-immigration_n_1015668.html.

Dockterman, Daniel. 2009. "Statistical Portrait of Hispanics in the United States, 2009." February 17. Accessed July 17, 2017 at www.pewhispanic.org/2011/02/17/statistical-portrait-of-hispanics-in-the-united-states-2009.

Dominguez, Virginia. 2010. "Letter to CB." May 27. Accessed July 17, 2017 at www. americananthro.org/ParticipateAndAdvocate/AdvocacyDetail.aspx?ItemNumber= 12861&RDtoken=50153&userID=6944.

Drake, Timothy Arthur. 2014. "The Effect of Community Linguistic Isolation on Language-Minority Student Achievement in High School." *Educational Researcher* 43(7): 327–340.

Rubenstein, Edwin S. 2003. "National Data/Linguistic Isolation Balkanizes America." July 16. Accessed July 17, 2017 at www.vdare.com/articles/national-data-by-edwin-s-rubenstein-282.

Sanford, Victoria. 2008. "Letter to Rep. William Lacy Clay, Jr." Accessed January 21, 2018 at http://s3.amazonaws.com/rdcms-aa/files/production/public/FileDownloads/ pdfs/cmtes/cfhr/upload/Census-letter-lacy-clay.pdf.

Siegel, Paul, Elizabeth Martin, and Rosalind Bruno. 2001. "Language Use and Linguistic Isolation: Historical Data and Methodological Issues." February 12. Accessed July 17, 2017 at https://census.gov/content/dam/Census/library/working-papers/2001/demo/2001-Siegel-Martin-Bruno.pdf.

Soifer, Don. 2009. "Linguistic Isolation Carries a Heavy Cost." Accessed July 17, 2017 at http://lexingtoninstitute.org/linguistic-isolation-carries-a-heavy-cost.

Turner, Kimberly, Elizabeth Wildsmith, Lina Guzman, and Marta Alvira-Hammond. 2016. "The Changing Geography of Hispanic Children and Families." January. Accessed July 17, 2017 at www.childtrends.org/wp-content/uploads/2016/01/ Emerging-Communities.pdf.

Zentella, Ana C. 1988. "Language Politics in the USA: The English-Only Movement." In *Literature, Language, and Politics*, edited by B. J. Craige, 39–53. Athens, GA: University of Georgia Press.

Zentella, Ana C. 1995. The "Chiquitafication" of US Latinos and their Languages, or Why We Need an Anthropolitical Linguistics. *SALSA III: Proceedings of a Symposium of Language and Society*, April 7–9, pp. 1–18. Austin, TX: Texas Linguistic Forum.

Zentella, Ana C. 2009. "An Effective Census 2010/ Un censo eficaz en el 2010." *El Diario-La Prensa*, February 23, p. 23.

Zentella, Ana C. 2011a. "Gota a gota, el mar se agota: Combating Linguistic Intolerance." *National Institute for Latino Policy Newsletter*, April 22. Accessed October 12, 2018 at www.nilpnetwork.org/NiLP_-_Zentella_on_Census__2011_.pdf

Zentella, Ana C. 2011b. "Gota a gota, el mar se agota: The Census and Combating Linguistic Intolerance." April 29. Accessed July 17, 2017 at http://laprensa-sandiego. org/stories/gota-a-gota-el-mar-se-agota-the-census-and-combatting-linguistic-intolerance.

Zentella, Ana C., Bonnie Urciuoli, and Laura R. Graham. 2007. Problematic language assessment in the US Census. *Anthropology News* 48(5): 10–11.

23 Immigrants Facing Linguistic Barriers in the U.S. Justice System

Case Studies from North Carolina

Dominika Baran and Quinn Holmquist

The fundamental assumption underlying the operation of the U.S. justice system is that everyone is equal in the eyes of the law. This basic fairness is established by the Fifth Amendment's guarantee of due process and the Sixth Amendment's protection of the right to a fair trial, and further supported by the Fourteenth Amendment and the Civil Rights Act of 1964 (cf. Kahaner 2009). In practice, however, equal treatment under the law is often compromised by socioeconomic disparities (e.g., access to resources such as private attorneys) or ideologies of race and gender that naturalize oppressive power structures (e.g., Ehrlich 2001; Mendoza-Denton 1995). Fair treatment and protection by the law regardless of one's socioeconomic status, gender, ethnicity, or other factors—and, indeed, the ability to enlist the courts to counteract discrimination and inequality based on such factors—are essential aspects of social justice. For immigrants, a crucial factor complicating access to fair treatment is language. Immigrants facing linguistic barriers who become involved with American courts must negotiate linguistic and cultural barriers within a justice system that is often ill-prepared to cope with their needs. This situation results in the marginalization and mishandling of these immigrants' cases, perpetuating or exacerbating their socially disadvantaged positions.

The concept of "meaningful access," which is at the heart of language access policies, is meant to address this problem. The American Bar Association (ABA), in its 2012 *Standards for Language Access in Courts*, defines meaningful access as:

> the provision of services in a manner which allows a meaningful opportunity to participate in the service or program free from intentional and unintentional discriminatory practices ... including, but not limited to, in-person interpreting services, telephonic and video remote interpreting services, translation of written materials, and the use of bilingual staff.
>
> (American Bar Association 2012)

This concept is succinctly stated in a 2007 policy document adopted by the Conference of State Court Administrators (COSCA): "to have equal justice, every litigant, every victim, every witness must understand what is happening in the courtroom" (cited in Hidalgo 2013, 46).

In this chapter, we examine cases where meaningful access for litigants facing linguistic barriers is compromised in the North Carolina justice system, both inside and outside the courtroom. Since 1990, North Carolina has seen an unprecedented growth in its immigrant population, especially among Latinos (Gill 2012). According to the Migration Policy Institute, foreign-born North Carolinians comprised 7.7 percent of the state's population in 2014, up from 1.4 percent in 1990 (MPI 2016). North Carolina had the second highest growth in the number of speakers of languages other than English in the U.S. between 1990 and 2010 (LEP 2011). In 2015, linguistically diverse individuals comprised 4.7 percent of North Carolina's population, and three-quarters of these were Spanish speakers (MPI 2011, n.d.). Other languages spoken by immigrants and refugees in North Carolina include Vietnamese, Chinese, Korean, Karen, Arabic, Haitian Kreyòl, and various African languages. Despite recent efforts to improve language access in North Carolina courts, for many immigrants this access is impeded by a combination of factors: lack of interpreters, limitations on the court interpreter's role, English-only documents, and shortage of funding.

Terminology

In this chapter, we consciously avoid the term "limited-English proficient" (LEP) to refer to speakers of other languages who may not be fluent in English because, as researchers in bilingual education have argued, it emphasizes the speakers' deficiency rather than ability (García and Kleifgen 2010). Instead, we refer to "immigrants/litigants facing linguistic barriers" or "speakers of languages other than English." The term "LEP" will appear only in direct quotations from federal and state legislation.

Data and methods

The cases discussed in this chapter come from 75 hours of observation inside and outside the courtroom in the Durham County courthouse and the smaller, rural Mount Olive courthouse. Data collection from outside the courtroom includes observation at the clerk's office, in the courthouse building, and during lawyer-client conferences, as well as interviews with 25 interpreters, attorneys at Legal Aid of North Carolina, immigrant advocates at the Durham Crisis Response Center, legal scholars, and 13 immigrant clients. The field research was conducted over fifteen months in 2015–2016 by Quinn Holmquist, who is fluent in Spanish and Haitian Kreyòl. While shadowing attorneys and immigrant advocates, Quinn took extensive ethnographic notes and became acquainted with clients. He also interpreted for one Legal Aid attorney during her client meetings and assisted in other meetings when the bilingual immigrant advocate was absent. Our examples illustrate seemingly minor incidents of confusion or misunderstanding that in fact result in serious consequences for defendants and plaintiffs. These data provide a much-needed perspective of these individuals' personal experience with the courts, in contrast to existing research that typically focuses on quantitative analyses of survey data gathered from providers of language access, namely judges, lawyers, and court officials (e.g., Hertog and Van Gucht 2008; Weissman et al. 2010). Other studies focus on trial data (e.g., Berk-Seligson 2002; Hale 2002, 2010; Mikkelson 1995), although fewer than five percent of cases filed in the United States ever make it to trial (Refo 2004). Our chapter offers insight into language-related obstacles faced by immigrants outside the courtroom.

Legal Provisions for Litigants Facing Linguistic Barriers in the U.S. and in North Carolina

Since the passage of the Civil Rights Act in 1964, U.S. courts, judges, and the federal government have recognized the importance of language access for non-English speakers interacting with government institutions (Berk-Seligson 2002). In 1970, the Second Circuit in *United States ex rel. Negron v. New York* determined that in order to exercise their Sixth Amendment rights to confront witnesses, consult with attorneys, and be present at their own trials, non-English speakers must be provided with interpreters (Bowles 2008, 621; Rahel 2014, 2304). In the 1974 landmark case of *Lau v. Nichols* (414 U.S. 563), the Supreme Court ruled that excluding non-English speakers from meaningful access to government services constituted national origin discrimination as defined in Title VI of the Civil Rights Act (Holmquist 2016). The Federal Court Interpreters Act of 1978 required federal courts to provide interpreters for defendants and witnesses facing linguistic barriers (Bowles 2008; Rahel 2014). In 2000, President Bill Clinton's Executive Order 13166, *Improving Access to Services for Persons with Limited English Proficiency*, required federally-funded agencies to "develop and implement a system by which limited English proficient persons can meaningfully access" their services (GPO 2000). In both *Lau v. Nichols* and Executive Order 13166, "federal agencies" include the courts.

The federal provisions outlined above and those detailed in the 2002 guidelines published by the Department of Justice (DOJ) prompted an examination of meaningful access in state courts (GPO 2002). In 2010, Deborah Weissman's team at the UNC School of Law published a report assessing language interpretation in North Carolina courts (Weissman et al. 2010), which concluded that interpreter services in state courts were insufficient and out of compliance with Title VI of the Civil Rights Act. In particular, Weissman et al. found irregular interpreter provisions for speakers of languages other than Spanish, a lack of interpreters at first appearances or notice of their availability, confusion over who is entitled to court interpreters and who bears the cost, and the use of "volunteer" interpreters instead of court-certified interpreters. The North Carolina Justice Center then lodged a complaint with the DOJ against NC courts, requesting an investigation, which confirmed the report's findings. In response, in 2015 the North Carolina Administrative Office of the Courts (NCAOC) published *Standards of Language Access* aimed at regulating language access in state courts. The *Standards* guarantee free, court-certified interpreters in all criminal and most civil cases to speakers of languages other than English. However, the *Standards* are difficult to implement with limited funding, as admitted in the document itself by then-director of NCAOC, Judge John Smith. Outside the courtroom, the *Standards* guarantee interpreters for communication with the district attorney (DA) or public defender, but not with privately-retained counsel and not in civil cases.

Language Access in the Courtroom

Despite the provisions established in federal policy and in the NCAOC *Standards*, meaningful access in the courtroom in North Carolina continues to be compromised. Out of Quinn's 13 litigant interviewees, only two had received interpreters. Furthermore, individuals cannot be designated as requiring an interpreter until they appear before the judge and their English proficiency is assessed through a series of questions. This is problematic because pre-courtroom interactions can have serious consequences for the litigant (Rahel 2014).

Quinn met "Pierre"[1] by chance outside the Mount Olive courthouse and they began talking in Haitian Kreyòl. Pierre had been in North Carolina since the 2010 earthquake that devastated Haiti. In 2015, he was pulled over in Mount Olive and given a citation for driving without a license. Pierre had been studying and practicing English since his arrival, but his factory work does not require much communication and his family and friends speak Kreyòl. With his minimal English, he did not know what had transpired when he had been stopped and given his citation.

At Pierre's first appearance, the DA determined the need for an interpreter. However, the only court-certified Kreyòl interpreter in the state, "Yolande," was not available until Pierre's third court date. At Pierre's third appearance, the DA asked Yolande, "Can you ask him how he pleads, guilty or not guilty?" This question, translated into Kreyòl, was the first time that Pierre had received "meaningful access" to the judicial process. Up until this point, he had not understood the meaning of his citation nor had he obtained legal counsel. Court records indicate that Pierre had waived his right to a public defender at his first court appearance, but since he did not have an interpreter at that time, it is unlikely that he had known about this right or been able to waive it. More likely, an assumption or a clerical error had been made. Now, when Yolande translated the DA's question, Pierre hesitatingly answered in Kreyòl, "kulpab" (*guilty*). Lacking requisite language access, Pierre had been deprived of his Sixth Amendment rights, resulting in his guilty plea, a $210 fine, and an infraction on his driving record—consequences that an attorney may have helped him avoid. Meanwhile, Yolande could not intervene to clarify the situation and help Pierre because, as a court interpreter, she is legally required to translate literally only what each party says, as specified in the NCAOC *Standards*.

Although intended to preserve the integrity of the judicial process by ensuring interpreter impartiality and accuracy, the requirement that court interpreters must limit their role to a "conduit of words," engaging purely in verbatim translation, often places litigants facing linguistic barriers at a disadvantage (Fowler et al. 2013). Most informal interpretation involves some degree of culture brokering (Baran 2017; Orellana 2009). Verbatim translation in the courtroom ignores implicature (Grice 1975; Fowler et al. 2013), differing cultural norms (Morris 1995), and culturally-specific legal concepts (Mikkelson 1995), and it prevents interpreters from answering litigants' requests for clarification. The proscription of cultural mediation in legal interpreting incorrectly assumes that translation can be an objective, mechanistic process (Morris 1995) of word-matching, revealing a tension between the linguistic and legal professions. Morris (ibid., 28) points out legal professionals' frequent hostility towards interpreters and their suspicion of "the alien element, that is the non-English-speaking individual." She argues that requiring verbatim translation "enables the court to function effectively as a monolingual setting" (ibid., 30), which contradicts the central premise of meaningful access for speakers of languages other than English.

A related case is that of "Marcelo," a monolingual Spanish speaker who found himself in a Durham County courtroom for failing to pay a fine. Marcelo's lawyer was absent, but the judge refused to wait because the only interpreter for the courthouse happened to be available. The judge asked why the fine remained unpaid after six months, despite a bill having been mailed first-class to Marcelo's address. Marcelo began to say that he had not known the amount of the fine or where to pay it. The judge interrupted, "I'm not interested in excuses," suggesting that her question, which Marcelo understood literally, had been rhetorical. Marcelo tried to ask for the amount of the fine so that he could go home and retrieve cash, but the judge ordered the bailiff to arrest him. The interpreter could do nothing to offer clarification. At this point, a sympathetic attorney intervened, found out the fine amount, and secured Marcelo's release. Marcelo's right to meaningful access was compromised by a shortage of interpreters whose time is consequently extremely precious, by the interpreter's rigid role as a conduit of words, and by his inability to read English-only bills sent to him. This last point brings us to our next topic.

Outside the Courtroom: Barriers in the In-Between Spaces

Language access policy such as that outlined in the NCAOC *Standards* addresses deficiencies in access during trial, but more than 95 percent of cases never make it that far. Instead, they are handled in what we call "in-between spaces" of judicial procedure: in the courthouse conference rooms and hallways, at the clerk's office, in forms and mailed correspondence, in civil negotiations, and on the streets through law enforcement (Holmquist 2016; cf. Bancroft et al. 2013). Immigrant litigants have the greatest disadvantage in these spaces because they lack regulation and consequently provide little in the way of language access.

The first barrier that non-English speakers encounter is in the paperwork. In criminal cases, defendants receive a citation detailing the charges and the hearing date, which is always in English only. In civil cases, forms are also received or submitted in English. For example, to request a Domestic Violence Protective Order (DVPO), the plaintiff must follow specific procedural steps, including filing appropriate forms. Although the NCAOC website states that there are over fifty bilingual forms available in print (North Carolina Judicial Center n.d.), only a few, including the request for a DVPO form, are available in Spanish/English and Vietnamese/English versions at the clerk's office and online. They are not available anywhere in other languages.

Crucially, moreover, the bilingual forms are intended "for information purposes only," as stated at the top of the form, followed by a further instruction: "Do not complete this form for filing. Use the English version of the AOC-CV-303 instead." In other words, the official version of the form that must be submitted to the court is in English and must be filled out in English, presenting an obvious obstacle to non-English speaking victims of domestic abuse. Bilingual immigrant advocates at the Durham Crisis Response Center help victims navigate the complex form filing process, but they cannot reach every potential plaintiff, and their bilingual services are limited to Spanish.

The second barrier is in the interpersonal encounters in and outside the courthouse. Virtually everyone who enters the courthouse must interact with at least one English-speaking court official before ever walking into the courtroom, which, as we saw in the previous section, has extensive repercussions. In cases of domestic violence, even when victims succeed in filing the requisite forms, protective orders cannot be enforced until the defendant is served with a copy of the order (WomensLaw.org. n.d.). Police officers who serve orders enter Spanish-speaking communities without interpreters and frequently fail to locate defendants because of communication barriers. As a result, cases stall. "Elisa" was one of the victims who dismissed her case after four court dates had passed and "Juan," her alleged abuser, still had not been served with the DVPO. A year later, Juan sexually and physically assaulted her. At this point, she successfully had him arrested, and Juan was charged by the DA with a criminal offense, as well as served with the protective order. When Quinn and the Legal Aid attorney representing Elisa encountered Juan in the courthouse for the DVPO hearing, his criminal case had not begun so he had no legal representation. Elisa's attorney proceeded to speak directly with Juan, with Quinn interpreting. Without a lawyer to negotiate on his behalf, Juan not only agreed to Elisa's terms, but also signed the protective order that included the details of the assault as recounted by Elisa. In other words, Juan admitted to the criminal charges against him without legal counsel, before his criminal case hearing, and this admission would be entered into his criminal case. If Juan had had a public defender, he would have also had an interpreter, but defendants are not entitled to public defenders in civil cases. Indigent non-English speaking defendants with both civil and criminal charges, such as Juan, are forced to rely on the plaintiff's attorney and interpreter. In cases such as Elisa and Juan's, both parties suffer because of inadequate language access in the judicial process. Elisa was assaulted because Juan could not be located and served with the protective order by the English-speaking officer. Juan's Sixth Amendment rights to legal counsel and a fair trial were compromised because he had no lawyer or interpreter to assist him. This case demonstrates that when two individuals facing linguistic barriers compete in an inaccessible judicial system, neither of them wins.

Conclusion

Meaningful access to the judicial process is a right that has been established by federal and state regulations and by case law, and that derives from the U.S. Constitution and legislation such as the Civil Rights Act. Crucially, meaningful access requires adequate language access for non-English speakers, including not just non-English-language monolinguals, but those with survival or conversational English skills that are insufficient to handle legal documents and judicial proceedings (Bowles 2008; Rahel 2014). As we have shown in this chapter, meaningful access can be compromised at numerous stages of the judicial process, in ways for which existing regulations and resources often fail to account. The North Carolina case studies presented above illuminate specific areas where immigrants' encounters with the justice system could be improved and the scope of "meaningful access" extended.

Note

1 All participants' names have been changed.

References

American Bar Association. 2012. "Standards for Language Access in Courts." Accessed March 7 at www.americanbar.org/content/dam/aba/administrative/legal_ aid_indigent_defendants/ls_sclaid_standards_for_language_access_proposal. authcheckdam.pdf.

Bancroft, Marjory A., Lola Bendada, Jean Bruggeman, and Lois Feuerle. 2013. "Interpreting in the Gray Zone: Where Community and Legal Interpreting Intersect." *The International Journal of Translation and Interpreting Research* 5(1): 94–113.

Baran, Dominika. 2017. *Language in Immigrant America.* Cambridge: Cambridge University Press.

Berk-Seligson, Susan. 2002. *The Bilingual Courtroom: Court Interpreters in the Judicial Process.* Chicago, IL: University of Chicago Press.

Bowles, John R. 2008. "Court Interpreters in Alabama State Courts: Present Perils, Practices, and Possibilities." *American Journal of Trial Advocacy* 31: 619–649.

Ehrlich, Susan. 2001. *Representing Rape: Language and Sexual Consent.* New York: Routledge.

Fowler, Yvonne, Eva Ng, and Malcolm Coulthard. 2013. "Legal Interpreting." In *The Routledge Handbook of Translation Studies*, edited by Carmen Millán and Francesca Bartrina, 402–414. Abingdon: Routledge.

Gill, Hannah. 2012. "Latinos in North Carolina: A Growing Part of the State's Economic and Social Landscape." Special Report, Immigration Policy Center. Accessed December 13, 2016 at www.americanimmigrationcouncil.org/research/latinos-north-carolina-growing-part-states-economic-and-social-landscape.

GPO. 2000. *Federal Register*, August 16. Accessed March 7, 2016 at www.gpo.gov/fdsys/pkg/FR-2000-08-16/pdf/00-20938.pdf.

GPO. 2002. *Federal Register*, June 18. Accessed December 13, 2016 at www.gpo.gov/fdsys/pkg/FR-2002-06-18/pdf/02-15207.pdf.

Grice, H.P. 1975. "Logic and Conversation." In *Syntax and Semantics 9: Pragmatics*, edited by P. Cole, 113–127. New York: Academic Press.

Hale, Sandra. 2002. "'How Faithfully Do Court Interpreters Render the Style of Non-English Speaking Witnesses' Testimonies?' A Data-based Study of Spanish-English Bilingual Proceedings." *Discourse Studies* 4(1): 25.

Hale, Sandra. 2010. "The Need to Raise the Bar: Court Interpreters as Specialized Experts." In *Routledge Handbook of Forensic Linguistics*, edited by M. Coulthard and A. Johnson, 440–454. New York: Routledge.

Hertog, Erik and Jan Van Gucht, eds. 2008. *Status Quaestionis: Questionnaire on the Provision of Legal Interpreting and Translation in the EU*. Portland, OR: Intersentia.

Hidalgo, Rosie. 2013. "Ensuring 'Meaningful Access' to the Courts for Individuals with Limited English Proficiency." *Juvenile and Family Court Journal* 64: 45–49.

Holmquist, Quinn. 2016. "Strange Chains: A Microanthropological Study of Non-English Speakers' Courtroom Experience." Unpublished BA thesis, Duke University, Durham, NC.

Kahaner, Steven. 2009. "The Administration of Justice in a Multilingual Society: Open to Interpretation or Lost in Translation?" *Judicature* 92(4): 224–231.

LEP. 2011. *LEP Data Brief*, December. Accessed December 13, 2016 at www.migrationpolicy.org/sites/default/files/publications/LEPdatabrief.pdf.

Mendoza-Denton, Norma. 1995. "Pregnant Pauses: Silence and Authority in the Anita Hills-Clarence Thomas Hearings." In *Gender Articulated: Language and the Socially Constructed Self*, edited by Kira Hall and Mary Bucholtz, 51–66. New York: Routledge.

Mikkelson, Holly. 1995. "On the Horns of a Dilemma: Accuracy vs. Brevity in the Use of Legal Terms by Court Interpreters." In *Translation and the Law, ATA Monograph Series, Vol. 8*, edited by Marshall Morris, 201–218. Amsterdam: John Benjamins.

Morris, Ruth. 1995. "The Moral Dilemmas of Court Interpreting." *The Translator* 1(1): 25–46.

MPI. 2011. "Limited English Proficient Individuals in the United States: Linguistic Diversity at the County Level." Accessed December 12, 2016 at www.migration policy.org/sites/default/files/datahub/LEPstate-countyData.xlsx.

MPI. 2016. "North Carolina." Accessed December 13, 2016 at www.migrationpolicy.org/data/state-profiles/state/demographics/NC.

MPI. n.d. "U.S. Immigration Trends." Accessed December 12, 2016 at www.migrationpolicy.org/programs/data-hub/us-immigration-trends#lep.

North Carolina Judicial Center. n.d. "Office of Language Access Services." Accessed December 15, 2016 at www.nccourts.org/LanguageAccess.

Orellana, Marjorie Faulstich. 2009. *Translating Childhoods: Immigrant Youth, Language and Culture*. New Brunswick, NJ: Rutgers University Press.

Rahel, Kate O. 2014. "Why the Sixth Amendment Right to Counsel Includes an Out-of-Court Interpreter." *Iowa Law Review* 99: 2299–2333.

Refo, Patricia Lee. 2004. "The Vanishing Trial." *Litigation Online* 30(2): 1–4. Accessed December 11, 2015 at www.americanbar.org/content/dam/aba/publishing/litiga tion_journal/04winter_openingstatement.authcheckdam.pdf.

Weissman, Deborah, Emily Kirby, Sarah Long, and Sonal Raja. 2010. "An Analysis of the Systemic Problems Regarding Foreign Language Interpretation in the North Carolina Court System and Potential Solutions." Accessed March 7, 2016 at www. law.unc.edu/documents/clinicalprograms/foreignlanguageinterpretationproblem snc.pdf.

WomensLaw.org. n.d. "Restraining Orders." Accessed December 15, 2016 at www. womenslaw.org/laws_state_type.php?id=563&state_code=NC.

24 Communicating Humanity

How Defense Attorneys Use Mitigation Narratives to Advocate for Clients

Robin Conley Riner and
Elizabeth S. Vartkessian

Social Justice through Law

Foundational theories of democracy propose that justice entails the fair distribution of opportunities and resources to all people; this is what is often referred to as social justice. Actually realizing such conditions requires institutions, including laws, set up to protect individual freedoms and, at the same time, to assure that the "greatest good" is shared with the greatest number of people (Sandel 2009). Achieving social justice through legal institutions involves ensuring that all people have the same access to and treatment under the law (formal justice) and it is in part up to our laws as written to guarantee that this is achieved (substantive justice). In reality, however, the law rarely works this way. Extensive research has shown, for example, that people of color and low socio-economic classes are significantly disadvantaged in the U.S. legal system (e.g., Cole 1999).

Legal practice is a discursive process that "define[s] and delimit[s]" the events and people it engages (Ehrlich 2001, 1). The unequal treatment of people in legal contexts is therefore partially a result of the language used to construct the law. In criminal trials, legal discourse, including legal rules and the words used by attorneys and judges, often dehumanizes defendants (Conley 2016). This dehumanization is founded on and reproduces (often racist) ideologies of criminality that essentialize the accused and disregard important contextual factors regarding their lives and actions (Haney 2005).

Defense attorneys must use language in strategic ways to try to combat these dehumanizing tendencies and attempt to garner empathy for defendants. Narrative, as language practice, is a vital tool in this respect, as it encourages more individualized, variegated, and humanizing ways of thinking and acting than the legal process typically entails. It fills in the much needed context of a defendant's life ignored by canonical depictions of crime.

Using U.S. death penalty trials as a case study, this chapter analyzes narrative forms that frame what is called mitigating evidence: evidence presented by the defense about the history and background of the accused that is meant to support a sentence less than death. In the context of mitigation, we identify ways in which defense attorneys can begin to undo the essentializing language of criminal trials and help ensure that defendants receive the full and fair consideration they are entitled to in a just legal system.

Empathy and Mitigation

In the case of the ultimate punishment of death, the law requires that jurors take an individual, comprehensive look at each defendant's life. After a jury has convicted a defendant of a death eligible crime, they are often presented with additional evidence meant to aid them in determining whether to sentence the defendant to death or life in prison. In addition to considering information typically presented by the prosecution that focuses on the defendant's criminal history, the harm caused to victims and their loved ones, and why a particular crime might justify execution, jurors must also consider the defense's mitigation evidence, which can include personal and historical information about the defendant and those acquainted with them, testimony and records regarding their emotional and psychological state, the defendant's behavior during and after the offense, potential for a positive adjustment to prison, and any other details related to the moral blame of the defendant. Depending on the statutory requirements, mitigating factors may be listed for the jury or there might simply be an instruction requiring jurors to consider such evidence when determining a sentence.

The presentation of mitigating evidence is an active, discursive process, through which, if it is done well, jurors come to experience and know a defendant (Martinovsky 2006). The presentation of sentencing evidence in death penalty trials is not subject to the same rules of evidence that constrain the presentation of facts when determining guilt. The relative lack of constraints on mitigating evidence makes sentencing decisions potentially more open to bias, as what a juror can consider in their decision is less curtailed. This leads to the potential "double-edged sword of mitigation": evidence about the character of the defendant, such as their psychological state, can either be read as mitigating (in that it may lessen their moral culpability for the crime) or aggravating (in that it may indicate that the defendant is likely to act violently again in the future, even in prison) (Vartkessian 2011, 245). Jurors' consideration of mitigating evidence is thus vulnerable to bias, as the significance of a variety of personal information about a particular defendant is subject to individual interpretation.

Capital jurors, like most of us, enter the trial with beliefs about criminal behavior. In particular, they come to court primed to do harm to defendants, having been exposed to media that dehumanizes the accused (Haney 1997). Violence, whether legally sanctioned or not, always involves dehumanizing its object. For instance, Lt. Col. David Grossman (2009) describes killing in military contexts. The closer (physically or mentally) a soldier is to the enemy, the harder it is to kill, so euphemistic language and a focus on differences are employed to increase soldiers' ability to kill. Capital jurors also display this linguistic distancing; they use specific linguistic constructions to dehumanize defendants, blocking empathy with them, thereby making it easier to sentence them to death (Conley 2016). The capital trial employs various mechanisms of moral disengagement, which are endemic to the structure of the proceedings (Haney 1997). These decrease jurors' tendency to consider an individual defendant's personal circumstances in determining a sentence.

Language used in death penalty trials frequently distances the law-abiding citizen from the criminal who is supposedly infecting their community. Thus, the person facing capital charges is often not referred to by name, but rather as "the defendant" or the more distancing form "that defendant" (Conley 2016), typically when described as having perpetrated evil, inhumane, or animalistic acts. These decontextualized forms essentialize the criminal identity of the human who is on trial by erasing the processes by which he or she came to be called a "defendant." Such forms frame defendants' actions as reflections of individual pathology, rather than as acts embedded in larger social and political structures. In capital trials, it is the job of the defense to overcome these psychological and linguistic forms of dehumanization. Narrative, with its ability to merge temporal and spatial worlds and provide orienting and evaluative frameworks for events (Ochs and Capps 2001), serves as an invaluable device to weave contextualizing elements of defendants' lives back into the discursive fabric of the trial. A successful mitigation narrative places the defendant and their actions back within the broader community of which jurors are a part.

Narrative framing, moreover, is crucial to successful mitigation, as no piece of defense evidence is inherently mitigating; rather, jurors must be provided a context that will make it so. Research has determined that jurors consider certain kinds of information more mitigating than others, such as evidence of abuse, neglect, disadvantaged background, mental health issues, and lesser relative culpability for the crime (Garvey 1998). Even so, what must be present throughout the presentation of mitigation evidence are stories that connect jurors to the experiences of defendants:

> The empathic divide describes jurors' relative inability to perceive capital defendants as enough like themselves to readily feel any of their pains, to appreciate the true nature of the struggles they have faced, or to genuinely understand how and why their lives have taken very different courses from the jurors' own.
>
> (Haney 2004, 1558)

Without such connective narratives, a defendant will appear so damaged as to be unsalvageable or so different as to be non-human, making a death sentence more likely. Mitigation evidence seeks to aid jurors in understanding how someone, who is not unlike themselves, is capable of engaging in harmful behavior, but is still deserving of mercy. It should invoke empathy of jurors so they feel human kinship to the defendant and therefore come to be less likely to advocate for his or her death.

Mitigation Narratives in Texas Capital Trials

Empathy is often described as the ability to experience something from another person's perspective. Narrative is lauded as one of the most effective devices for enabling jurors to empathize with defendants. Narratives provide familiar frameworks through which jurors can process defendants' experiences, helping jurors potentially understand the perspective of a defendant who may be quite different from them. Mitigation narratives aim to wrest jurors from their standard thinking about criminal behavior, hopefully presenting defendants as complex individuals, rather than merely as tokens of a criminal type. By presenting excerpts from interviews with Texas capital jurors[1] and portions of attorneys' sentencing arguments, we detail how particular narrative frameworks can be used to establish empathy with defendants and thereby help jurors fully consider the lives of defendants as required by law.

A commonly held stance regarding empathy is that it is harder to empathize with someone who is not like you. For most capital jurors, a death penalty trial is the first time they will be exposed to the details of a life such as the defendant's. Many capital defendants come from impoverished upbringings and have been involved in or exposed to criminal behavior before. Many are also mentally ill or have cognitive impairments and have suffered extreme abuse and neglect by caretakers.

Perhaps the trickiest line defense attorneys must walk is to present the defendant as unique—as a product of extraordinary circumstances that may help explain the criminal act—while at the same time making the defendant relatable enough so that jurors may empathize with him or her. Narrative structure provides a framework to straddle this line, for one of its properties is that it must be unique enough to be authentic, while remaining familiar enough to be believable (Ochs and Capps 2001). In other words, if a narrative is too far out, people won't believe it, but if it is too mundane, no one will want to listen.

In this first excerpt from a capital juror interview, a white, female juror discusses the jury's reasoning for sentencing the defendant, a white male, to life without parole for the killing of a police officer. She states:

> There was a lot of support there for the death penalty for **an individual**[2] that truly had no conscience—that the discussion this is for the worst of the worst, the serial rapist, **the people** who go out and intentionally target an individual for the purpose of killing that person, and we did not see that in this case whatsoever, although James[3] had been abusive. When he had been in jail it seemed like when he wasn't on drugs he had a conscience—**he was a good person** even—and he held a job—he was a good worker. It seemed like the drugs were the primary, not cause, but led him to be a different person. But **even that person was not so horrible as, like I said, someone with absolutely no conscience**. And again it came down to the fact of the majority of the individuals, including me, thinking that **the death penalty is for the worst of the worst**

and he just didn't quite fit that category. We didn't feel he was that person and again I'll throw out that word stupid, he was just stupid. He got himself backed into a corner and instead of thinking it through he just acted very stupidly.

This juror establishes a familiar character, "someone with absolutely no conscience," that her jury agreed would have been deserving of the death penalty. She uses generalized language to refer to this stock character, including "an individual," "someone," and "the people." She contrasts the defendant in this case to such a character, explaining that her defendant was not so out of the ordinary to qualify as "the worst of the worst" and thus as someone who should be put to death. Instead, the defendant fit into the category of a "good person" and a "good worker," at least when he was not on drugs. Instead of being a bad person, he simply found himself in a relatable situation in which he "just acted very stupidly." This juror's logic for voting for a life sentence thus rests on establishing a canonical narrative framework in which the worst of the worst deserves the death penalty and reasoning that the defendant's story did not fit these circumstances.

Similarly, this next juror, a Hispanic female, establishes a familiar character that she uses to explain the defendant's actions. Her jury voted for a sentence of life without parole; the defendant was a Hispanic man, found guilty of killing a convenience store clerk during a robbery:

[T]he way he grew up he saw his brother got killed, I believe in front of his eyes. If I'm not mistaken, pretty much I think before that time I think he was **a pretty good kid**. It's not an excuse because **there are people that grow up in bad neighborhoods and done okay**. I think sometimes when **you're** lost and **you** need help and there's nobody there **you** do crazy things outside.

The juror explains that this defendant was a "pretty good kid" who was exposed to traumatic experiences. She uses a contrastive framework to explain what the defendant is not. "There are people," she explains, "that grow up in bad neighborhoods and done okay." This defendant's life, however, was more exceptional than these people's. Because of the trauma he experienced and his lack of help getting over it, he was not one of those who was okay. Even though she presents his circumstances as unique, she retains an empathetic stance to describe his plight, using the generalized "you" to relate to his actions (Stirling and Manderson 2011): "sometimes when **you're** lost and **you** need help and there's nobody there **you** do crazy things outside." She thus characterizes this defendant as unique enough to explain his extreme actions, while still presenting him and his circumstances as relatable.

A prosecutor's argument during the sentencing phase of another capital trial reveals an attempt to diminish the uniqueness of the defendant, encouraging jurors to minimize the impact of physical violence on the defendant's development. In this case, she describes abuse that the defendant underwent as a child and argues:

> [We're] talking grabbing the arm, spanking on the bottom with a belt or a hand. Sounds like reasonable discipline to me . . . nothing to suggest he had it harder than anybody growing up in Texas, many people we know including ourselves.

The prosecutor attempts to establish the defendant's circumstances as mundane, as anything anyone growing up in Texas could have experienced. In this case, she uses empathy against the defendant; she presents his circumstances as so relatable that she undermines their role in explaining his violent behavior.

In contrast, the defense attorney's closing sentencing argument in the same case highlights the defendant's uniqueness, but still within a generalized framework, so that the defendant is not depicted as too exceptional so as not to be relatable. The attorney describes the defendant's home life while growing up:

> **Jose Ricardo Gutierrez Silva,** for whatever reason, his whole life has understood to be the one in **the family** who messed up. He's the one that **the father**, **the family** has understood to be a failure. . .Look at his actual deeds. What's this misbehavior that he came home late sometimes. They're not talking about real misbehavior, they are not talking about a **bad kid**.

The attorney refers to the defendant with his full name, thus individualizing him. At the same time, she describes the details of his home life in a generalizable framework. His family, his father, becomes "the family" and "the father," thus establishing a generic family to which the jurors can relate. The defendant is also contrasted to a recognizable category, a "bad kid," which the attorney argues does not fit this defendant. It is not that attorneys and jurors forego categorical thinking altogether when empathizing with defendants, but, rather, work is put into establishing that particular defendants do not fit into the categories we usually associate with criminal behavior.

The same attorney continues this logic later as she describes the circumstances of the murder for which Jose was on trial:

> He was in a panic. It's not a premeditated thing, it's not someone who is out there committing crimes for gain, out there committing crimes for money. This is **a hard-working person**, this is **a family person**, this is **someone who's got problems** and as his friend said, he fell off the edge.

The attorney's narrative opposes two sets of circumstances, two types of characters. One of a patterned, violent criminal, the other of a hard-working person who fell into unfortunate experiences. As in the previous excerpts, the attorney's language generalizes the defendant's experiences, encouraging an empathic perspective. She describes him as "a hard-working person," "a family person," "someone who's got problems." The individual circumstances of this defendant, as told through his family members and friends during the trial, also invoke empathy. Scholars have shown the empathetic effects of emotional testimony from parties and those close to them in criminal trials (Garvey 2000). The intricate combination of relatable narrative frameworks and individual, emotional connections with defendants helps jurors relate to the defendants and their circumstances and connect to their individual humanity. The key to getting jurors to consider fully the lives of defendants rests in striking a balance between their individuality and their relatedness.

Social Justice and Empathy in the Law

Calls for a more just society and a more humane legal system both suggest empathy as a critical building block. But how exactly to achieve empathy and what forms of empathy are most likely to lead to just legal decision-making are not straight-forward questions. The ability of narrative to present the complex, unique characteristics of individual defendants' lives in familiar frameworks is a crucial element to achieving justice within our legal system. It is a task that falls on defense teams in capital trials and so it is critical that defense teams understand the importance that narrative plays in humanizing their clients and the sophistication attorneys must bring to the task of storytelling in a context that is designed to resist empathic expressions.

Moreover, the inclusion of a variety of narratives, and thus a variety of voices, in law is integral to maintaining social justice (Bandes 1996). There is no one type of person upon which we can base our laws and ideas of justice. In order to attain justice, the law needs to incorporate a "reformulation of the self as. . .constituted and fragmented. . .by the intersections of social categories such as race, gender, and sexual orientation" and thus should operate according to a concept of the "multi-self," rather than a unitary self (Powell 2012, 164). Providing thorough mitigating narratives through which jurors can understand the complex experiences of each individual defendant thus reaches beyond saving a single life; it may also be the basis under which we can imagine a more just, humane system of law.

Notes

1 Post-verdict juror interviews were conducted by Vartkessian.
2 Notable portions of transcripts are highlighted by the authors in bold.
3 Names of defendants and other actors have been changed to ensure juror anonymity.

References

Bandes, Susan. 1996. "Empathy, Narrative, and Victim Impact Statements." *University of Chicago Law Review* 63(2): 361–412.
Cole, David. 1999. *No Equal Justice: Race and Class in the American Criminal Justice System*. New York: The New Press.

Conley, Robin. 2016. *Confronting the Death Penalty: How Language Influences Jurors in Capital Cases*. New York: Oxford University Press.

Ehrlich, Susan. 2001. *Representing Rape: Language and Sexual Consent*. New York: Routledge.

Garvey, Stephen P. 1998. "Aggravation and Mitigation in Capital Cases: What do Jurors Think?" *Columbia Law Review* 98: 1538–1576.

Garvey, Stephen P. 2000. "The Emotional Economy of Capital Sentencing." *New York University Law Review* 75(1): 26–73.

Grossman, Lt. Col. Dave. 2009. *On Killing: The Psychological Cost of Learning to Kill in War and Society*. New York: Back Bay Books.

Haney, Craig. 1997. "Violence and the Capital Jury: Mechanisms of Moral Disengagement and the Impulse to Condemn to Death." *Stanford Law Review* 49(6): 1447–1486.

Haney, Craig. 2004. "Condemning the Other in Death Penalty Trials: Biographical Racism, Structural Mitigation, and the Empathic Divide." *DePaul Law Review* 53(4): 1557–1589.

Haney, Craig. 2005. *Death by Design: Capital Punishment as a Social Psychological System*. Oxford: Oxford University Press.

Martinovsky, Bilyana. 2006. "A Framework for Analysis of Mitigation in Courts: Toward a Theory of Mitigation." *Journal of Pragmatics* 38(12): 2065–2086.

Ochs, Elinor, and Lisa Capps. 2001. *Living Narrative: Creating Lives in Everyday Storytelling*. Cambridge, MA: Harvard University Press.

Powell, John A. 2012. *Racing to Justice: Transforming our Conceptions of Self and Other to Build an Inclusive Society*. Bloomington: Indiana University Press.

Sandel, Michael J. 2009. *Justice: What's the Right Thing to Do?* New York: Farrar, Straus, and Giroux.

Stirling, Lesley, and Lenore Manderson. 2011. "About You: Empathy, Objectivity, and Authority." *Journal of Pragmatics* 43: 1581–1602.

Vartkessian, Elizabeth S. 2011. "Dangerously Biased: How the Texas Capital Sentencing Statute Encourages Jurors to be Unreceptive to Mitigation Evidence." *Quinnipiac Law Review* 29: 237–288.

Index